# His Story

# His Story
The Story of Why
We Are Here

Stuart Hacking

RESOURCE *Publications* • Eugene, Oregon

HIS STORY
The Story of Why We Are Here

Copyright © 2014 Stuart Hacking. All rights reserved. Except for brief quotations in critical publications or reviews, no part of this book may be reproduced in any manner without prior written permission from the publisher. Write: Permissions. Wipf and Stock Publishers, 199 W. 8th Ave., Suite 3, Eugene, OR 97401.

Resource Publications
An Imprint of Wipf and Stock Publishers
199 W. 8th Ave., Suite 3
Eugene, OR 97401

www.wipfandstock.com

ISBN 13: 978-1-62564-559-3

Manufactured in the U.S.A.                                         08/12/2014

To my long suffering family who have allowed me to tap away on my laptop on every family holiday for the last few years.

"May God open a door for our message, so that we may tell people the mysterious story of the Messiah."

—Colossians 4:3

# Contents

*Foreward by Revd Hugh Palmer* | xi

PROLOGUE
*The Cosmic Doorway* | xiii

1 Nothing | 1
2 Something | 4
3 Clever Dust | 6
4 One Man and a Boat | 11
5 Bricks | 14
6 One Man Nation | 17
7 D.I.Y. or Destiny? | 19
8 God will Provide | 22
9 Bloodthirsty versus Bloodsucker | 25
10 One Family Nation | 28
11 Twelve Brothers—One King | 32
12 Safe; Well Fed; with a Family | 38
13 Mini Noah | 39
14 A Fish out of Water | 42
15 Creator versus Created | 46
16 Good God | 50
17 Broken | 56
18 Our Story or His Story? | 59
19 Kill or be Killed | 64
20 Follow the Leader? | 68
21 Boy meets Girl | 76

22　The King-Maker | 79

23　One Nation: Two Kings | 84

24　A Proper Nation | 90

25　The Good, the Bad and the Ugly | 94

26　Wisdom and Foolishness | 98

27　The Right Track? | 109

28　Outnumbered? | 114

29　Barking up the Wrong Tree | 119

30　Meanwhile Back at the Branch | 123

31　Almah, Immanu-El and Pele-Joez-El-Gibbor-Abi-Ad-Sar-Shalom | 129

32　Caged Bird? | 135

33　Lost | 140

34　Dead and Alive | 145

35　The Sequel | 154

36　You can take the Boy out of Isra-El but not Isra-El out of the Boy | 158

37　The Real Deal | 165

38　God's Signet Ring | 169

39　Miss Star of Persia | 172

40　Learn the Lesson of His Story! | 177

41　Hammered | 184

42　One Small Stepson for a Man: One Giant Leap for Mankind | 186

43　Tzippori or Nazareth? | 189

44　The Asylum-seeking Peasant King | 192

45　Lost and Found | 199

46　U-Turn | 201

47　Big Splash | 205

48　Kingdom | 208

49　The Clash | 214

50  Groundhog Day? | 218

51  Testing, Testing One, Two, Three | 224

52  Lost the Plot? | 227

53  Long Weekend | 233

54  Black Hole | 240

55  Impossible or Improbable? | 243

56  The Greatest Miracle of Yeh-shua-Jesus—Yeh-shua-Jesus Never Did | 247

57  Soul-mates | 249

58  Hell-ish | 254

59  Harvest | 257

60  Humanity Reborn | 264

61  Never-Ending Story | 268

62  Love Story | 273

63  Size Doesn't Matter | 277

64  Then What? | 282

65  So? | 287

# Foreword

WHAT STORY COULD BE more important than the one which explains the world and reveals both our origins and our destiny? We live in a culture where an increasing minority of us know that story well and cherish it, while it is becoming less and less known to a growing majority.

Stuart Hacking takes it and faithfully retells it in a fresh way to bring it alive again. For those of us who are all too familiar with it, here is a chance to wonder again at God's remarkable grace, but it also engages with those who have had little or no exposure to the story of the God who is our Maker and Redeemer.

Stuart uses his experience of life and of school chaplaincy to write in a way that is simple, clear, engaging and yet isn't afraid of exploring the depths of the Christian story.

Revd Hugh Palmer

Rector of All Souls Church,
Langham Place, London, UK

PROLOGUE

## The Cosmic Doorway

THERE ARE SOME NAGGING questions too big for humans to answer. "What happened the split-second before time began?" "What should I do whilst I am alive?" "What will happen to me when I die?" "What will happen at the end of time?"

All of these eternal human questions can be seen as dependent on our answer to this one massive question, "What is outside of the Universe?" Or to put it another way, "If the whole of the Universe is like a massive balloon still being blown up by the Big Bang at the beginning of time, then what is our Universe expanding into?" The answer isn't what we call Space. Space is the air inside the balloon and not whatever the Universe is continually expanding into.

So what can we know about the unknown area or entity that surrounds our Universe? If nothing else, we can assume that whatever is outside of our Universe balloon is bigger and older than our Universe.

If so, what could be bigger and more ancient than our Universal reality? What could be older than all the stuff, visible and invisible, that makes up our Universe? What in comparison to our Universe makes our Universe seem young? And at the other end of the timescale, what is powerful enough to remain after our Universe balloon goes pop and skitters away into oblivion?

Whatever it is (if anything) is outside of our grasp, mentally or physically. It is the other side of the sealed system of our Universe. To find out its nature we would need a Doorway through the fabric of our existence into the outside the Universe. Then we would need whatever is outside the Universe to come and visit us through the Doorway in a format we could comprehend—in a form that doesn't fry our brains.

Or maybe we could go and visit it? Maybe we could punch a Doorway out of our Universe? But despite the fact that N.A.S.A.'s Voyager One probe has now left our Solar System and is entering interstellar space eleven billion miles away from our Sun, it will still take forty thousand years for it to be nearer another star than our own Sun. Even then it would be nowhere near the edge of our Galaxy, never mind our expanding Universe. So, it is all but impossible for such a probe to pierce the skin of the Universe and discover whatever lies outside.

But even if it were possible, it would be like sticking a pin into a tightly-inflated balloon. Any such Doorway would surely tear open the fabric of reality. Any such Doorway would mix two realities that haven't met since before time began. The Universe began with a Big Bang and probably any messing with the structure of the Universe would end up the same.

But despite this, there have been numerous accounts of such an impossible Doorway existing: accounts not written by the unstable or the simple; accounts woven into the fabric of human history over at least four thousand years; accounts so serious that they have re-written human history.

These accounts describe a Being who exists beyond the Universe. These accounts describe this Being interacting with human history. This Being is traditionally referred to as a male, but he is a Being that transcends our idea of gender. The story of his interaction with the Universe through the cosmic Doorway is His Story. It is also the story of humanity.

Human history and His Story are fundamentally the same story. His Story is the story of his Doorway into the Universe: where it has appeared and how humanity can open his Doorway. His Story tells of how he has entered the Universe through the Doorway and how humans can make the return journey. His Story is an adventure story that has its origins beyond the Universe.

For many on earth today, His Story is hidden. Not hidden in some dusty tome in a far away museum or buried deep in some yet to be excavated tomb. Not hidden in an enigmatic sect's secret rituals or weird beliefs, but hidden in full view. It is hiding in the most published, most translated, most sold book in history that is now little read, little believed and little trusted. It is often thought inaccessible, dry and boring—irrelevant to all but one small devoted group of fans. Even on the rare occasions when the book is read, the true breathtaking vista of the story remains unclear due to it being sliced up into fragmented quotations and sayings.

Even if you have already read this best-selling book (known as the Bible), you may have missed His Story lying in its pages. You may have overlooked the overarching story of the Doorway—the how, where and when we can experience life through the Doorway and beyond our Universe. What follows are the highlights of His Story—a story which spans the whole of history. This story has inspired humanity more than any other story. This story has been shared and heard by countless generations of humans. It is entangled in our human history. It is an indispensable part of the human heritage. Its enduring popularity is explained by one simple strap line.

His Story—the story of why we're here.

# 1

# Nothing

THE FACT THAT YOU are reading these words reveals that there is one overwhelming truth about you that is undeniable: whoever you are, whatever you are, wherever you live—you are alive. You exist.

There is also probably one other overwhelming fact about you that is all but undeniable. You have asked on more than one occasion, "Why?" "Why am I alive?" "Why do I exist?" And while we're at it, let's add, "Why does the world that sustains my life exist?" It's the biggest and best of all questions. It's a question that has been asked by humans ever since humans asked questions.

It's also a question that humans have tried to ignore since humans asked questions. Because the answer to this question must be found in the foundational story of everything and this fundamental story is too frighteningly massive for most humans to deal with routinely.

It's a story that began before anything had begun. It's a story that has its origins outside of the Universe. It's a story that was started by whatever you think or believe existed before time and then made time—created our Universe.

But this is exactly why we humans avoid this story in our everyday life. It doesn't make daily sense. It demands that once there was nothing, then there was everything. But we know that nothing comes out of nothing. Everything has to start from something. Whatever part of the Universe you choose—it has always been something else before. The Universe is a gigantic recycling plant—even you (if you think about it).

But at some point this recycling plant we know as the Universe, had to begin. At the very beginning of the history of the Universe, there must have been a time when nothing turned into something—even if that's impossible (as we know things don't appear out of nothing not even rabbits out of hats). But despite our down to earth skepticism or scientific cleverness, we instinctively know it must have happened—once.

## 2  His Story

Humanity has given a name for the magician who created this cosmic conjuring trick. We call him or her or it—God. God: a power that is more potent than time; a Being that has always been; a force that has no finish. A Being that is in one word—eternal.

But what is the story that lies behind this power we call, "God"? It's a story that has been known for thousands of years. It's a story that has been known by billions of people. But it's a story that nowadays we often don't know, don't value, don't trust, don't use.

It's a story that started with God having an idea. He decided to make and shape the earth. But why did he do it? Maybe he was bored and wanted something to do? Maybe he was lonely and wanted someone like himself to talk to? More likely, he was generous and wanted to share his riches with others. Just one problem—there were no "others." He was alone. He had to make "others". He had to make beings like him who could respond to his generosity. And while he was at it, he had to make a place where these other beings could live and breathe and flourish. And so, the story of human beings and the story of our earth and Universe are inseparable. His Story and history are the same story.

But what did he use to make the earth and human beings when nothing at all existed? By definition—nothing or he wasn't the Creator, just the developer. So how did he do it? His Story does not tell us. It simply tells us that God was there and did it.[1] This may offend our inquisitive human minds, but if we could see how he did the trick, God would no longer be the greatest magician of all time. Even what we do know of the behavior of matter in the first trillionths of a second of the story of the Universe challenges our brainpower. Many scientists believe that all the stuff that makes up not only our own world, but our galaxy and our endless Universe, at one point was squashed so tight it fitted into something that was so tiny it was too small to measure. Not only too small to measure, it was so squashed it inevitably burst out into one great explosion that hurtled outwards at a million billion miles a minute.

This is unbelievable enough, but His Story is more amazing than even all the squashed stuff of the Universe exploding. His Story is even bigger than the nearly fourteen billion years it has taken for that stuff to start to look like the Universe we know today. To the eternal God, billions of years are just like a few days—six to be precise.[2] God's like that. As one famous believer in God's Story was to comment many years later, "With God a day

---

1. Genesis 1:1.
2. Genesis 1:31.

is like a thousand years, and a thousand years are like a day."³ God's Story is much more important than years, days, hours and minutes or even about Big Bangs. His Story is about opening up the Doorway of the Universe in order to answer one simple question.

Why?

---

3. 2 Peter 3:8.

## 2

# Something

TRYING TO FIND OUT why we exist might be interesting, but maybe there isn't a reason why we're here. Maybe it's just luck or coincidence. Maybe the eternal force outside of the Universe accidentally propelled the Universe into existence and then couldn't put it back how it had been. Maybe the Universe is simply a fantastic by-product of an almighty accident.

But what are the chances of a massive explosion creating something that works so well like the Universe? It's a well known fact that if the Universe had at any point come together just a tiny bit differently, we wouldn't be having this discussion. In fact, there wouldn't be anyone anywhere having any sort of discussion. There would be no life at all, as we know it.

Life, as we know it, is a one in infinity chance. You wouldn't have put a bet on things ending up so well even if you were the Solar System's most daredevil gambler. It would be like betting on an explosion in a car scrapyard resulting in all the right car parts being blown together in the right order to produce a car bolted up, fuelled up, and ready to go. Chaos creating order doesn't happen. Look at your house—does it get tidy on its own if you leave it long enough? How about if you toss a few hand grenades in?

So, is it luck that the Universe is so well ordered? Or is it chance? Or is it coincidence? Or plan? His Story starts by telling us that the Universe is no lucky chance—no flukey coincidence. God's power hovered like a mighty bird over the new formless, sloshing, primeval, liquid molten earth and squeezed it into shape on which humans could live.[1] A form that was user-friendly and the users were humans.

It might be that there are other forms of life on many of the other planets that circle the one hundred thousand million stars in our galaxy or orbit the stars in the other million upon millions of other galaxies. It may be that this is more than probable, maybe it's even without a doubt. But His Story isn't about little green men in far away galaxies. It's just about our

---

1. Genesis 1:1–2.

little planet in the outer suburbs of this small galaxy. It's about one unique and amazing form of life—humans—us. Maybe aliens on other planets have their own version of His Story. But until "first contact" we will have to be content with our earth version of His Story.

The story of us.

# 3

## Clever Dust

THE UNIVERSE MAY HAVE come out of nothing, just for us, but where did we come from? His Story is not very flattering. It says—from the dust of the earth.

It's not a great beginning, but if we're honest it's how we all end up when our life is over. It is also how we end up every minute of every day. Funny thing about common house dust is that it's made up mainly of bits of us—bits of skin and human debris that has dropped off us. It's dead life.

His Story says that God brought earth-dust to life when he gave the first human the kiss of life.[1] This first human became known as "Adam" which means "earth-man". But what was this pre-human "earth-dust" made up of? What was this "dust" before it was transformed into earth-man? It was obviously stuff that God had made already, but stuff that wasn't alive in the way God wanted humans to be alive. God couldn't have a particularly exciting, creative relationship with this pre-human stuff. Dust even to dust experts is not that good company. What specifically this stuff was before God gave it life we will probably never know for certain, but whatever it was didn't meet God's strict criteria for a friend. We might not know what it was, but we know what it became—us.

It was just like us but also this new humanity was just like God. God modelled humans on himself.[2] Earth-dust humanity modelled on the creator of star-dust! Able to think, love, choose, create, and worship; able to respond to his generosity. In many ways Adam was just like God. But at the same time still just like us—a typical human able to achieve and appreciate great goodness as well as descend back to the dirt from which he came.

And in typical human style, Adam, the first human, grumbled. Yes, he had a special heavenly earth to himself—an unpolluted, unspoilt paradise, a vast playground garden totally open to beyond the Universe which even

---

1. Genesis 2:7.
2. Genesis 1:27.

God enjoyed but he was lonely.[3] Soon Adam wasn't satisfied. He wanted a friend. Even though God allowed him to have power over all the animals, it just wasn't quite what he was looking for.[4] He was dissatisfied. It was all just a bit disappointing. So much for God's great human project!

So, God made Adam a friend called Eve, this time not out of earth-dust but out of Adam.[5] But she wasn't a clone. She was she and he was he and so the history of the sexes began. This story didn't get off to a glorious beginning, because they were just like us. They were now together in Eden (which meant "paradise") discovering each other: enjoying each other. But after a while, it again wasn't paradise. It wasn't enough. They wanted more—just like us. God let them try out and test everything in his world, but they wanted more. The more they wanted was the one thing that God had said wasn't good for them—being bad—knowing and doing bad things; rebelling against God, and going against God the Maker's instructions. This was a rebellion that God couldn't allow to happen in an area still joined by an open Doorway to his home outside of the Universe. Going against God was like a dangerous virus which could attack the very stability of the source of life. It was an infection that couldn't be allowed to pass through the Doorway to disease God's perfect domain outside of the Universe itself.

So like any good parent, God tried to protect them by warning them that no good would come out of doing bad. But like all normal children, they wouldn't listen. In the end, the fall-out between God and humanity was over very little—like it always is—over God saying they couldn't eat the fruit of one very special tree and Adam and Eve having a strop and eating it anyway.

Instead of listening to God who had made them, they were influenced by another part of God's creation. By a created snake who played the "devil's advocate."[6] The snake seemed to do whatever it liked—its independence challenged God. It spoke of rebellion against God. It excited the new humans' desire for their own independence. The snake's existence tempted them to believe that God was overbearing and simply trying to frighten them into doing what he wanted. God obviously wanted to control them! He wanted to spoil their lives! And for some reason Adam and Eve were swayed by a pathetic created snake rather than the one who had created them and given them the Universe.[7] And when God challenged them about

3. Genesis 3:8.
4. Genesis 2:19.
5. Genesis 2:20b-23.
6. Genesis 3:1–5.
7. Genesis 3:6.

their suicidal choice, they realized their mistake and what they had to lose. So they both blamed each other and the snake—both desperately trying to hide their own stupidity.[8]

So why did they do it? Because, they didn't want to stay like children—they wanted to grow up and explore evil as well as love and beauty. They wanted to choose whether they did good things or bad things. They wanted to choose whether they would do as God told them.

And in eating the forbidden fruit of the special tree, they discovered the deep meaning of the special tree. It was the tree of knowledge—knowledge of good and bad. And as they munched on the fruit, they also discovered that they were exercising their power to choose. This choosing was part of God's special kiss of life given to them to make them unique—a gift given them by God but a gift they used against him. They chose freedom. They chose power. They chose independence. They chose to make their own way in the world and not be told what to do! They chose to be just like God—just like us.

And God let them, as God lets us. God couldn't treat them as just another part of his creation. They had to be allowed to make mistakes—to fail. But now on they would be on their own. They had chosen to leave God's protective care in paradise linked to his eternal dimension beyond the Universe. And so he let them go. With a heavy heart he closed the Door linking paradise with the earth. With a sonorous crash of shooting bolts God withdrew from his creation leaving humanity out in the cold not linked to the heart of the Universe any longer. The Door between earth and beyond the Universe was closed—locked and unable to be opened by humans from earth. The link passage between earth and God's perfect home was shut, locked and guarded.[9]

Even the snake lost the protection of God. In fact, God promised that in the future as punishment for his role in the expulsion, the children of human women would crush him under their heel as the snake tried to bite them. One child in particular would be the greatest snake crusher.[10] That human child is the Super-star of His Story. But for now, the history of evil began. Up to then, evil was just a possibility. Now it was reality. And nothing could or would be the same ever again. Now humans had brought badness into the world. The cut-off earth was infected by the germs of selfishness.

Their once perfect paradise was safely isolated behind the infection control Doorway—air locked and safe. But as a result of this rebellious

---

8. Genesis 3:8–13.
9. Genesis 3:23–24.
10. Genesis 3:15.

infection, earth and humanity wouldn't be the same again. For a start, nothing on earth would ever again last for ever. Humans were trapped inside a bubble of time, disconnected from outside of the Universe where life was and is timeless. Only God can live for ever. Only God is bigger than time. And now Adam and Eve had chosen to go it alone, without God. They were fatally infected and with no cure.

Their new independent lifestyle didn't start well. The family brought to life by God suddenly knew death—not just natural death but violent death. The second generation of God's humans inherited the worst of their parents' character. Adam and Eve's son, Cain, viciously attacked and killed his brother, Abel, for no other reason except that he was jealous of him.[11]

But in other ways in this brave new world of independence, things seemed to be so good. These new clever grown-up humans had few predators or enemies. They ruled God's world. As the new special family of humans grew in numbers they also grew in age. Maybe there were so few pollutants or toxins, or so little time for harmful genetic mutations or maybe it was the healthy food or the lack of germs, but everyone who lived, lived and lived. True, they had lost their perfect link with God but they still had the secret of eternal youth—almost. One man, Methuselah, lived for nine hundred and sixty nine years.[12] Maybe they counted personal age differently in those pre-history days, who knows? Whatever the reason, they all lived to a good old age. One man even went further—Methuselah's mysterious father, Enoch. He never died at all. He disappeared off the face of the earth. It was said that he was taken back by God at the age of three hundred and sixty-five.[13] He just disappeared through the invisible Door of the Universe back to God. So, the Doorway must have still been there but with no handle on the earth side. Maybe in those early days of humans, God was like a protective Father allowing his children to play outside the garden on the street but still watching through the window. Maybe God loved Enoch so much God opened the Door and spirited him away back into the heavenly dimension to keep him safe from some imminent danger. He unlocked the Door for just a brief moment. God was still very close, giving his children a bit of independence and distance but desperate to keep them safe. Maybe, outside of the Universe was still closer to the inside than we might think it is now.

At one point, His Story says that even the strange alien beings who lived with God outside of the Universe, were able to sneak through the Door onto earth for day trips to see what an amazingly realistic human theme

11. Genesis 4:1–16.
12. Genesis 5:27.
13. Genesis 5:23–24.

park God had made.[14] No harm done, you would think, but instead of just watching, they wanted to take part. They rather fancied being human—or more like they rather fancied human beings. And some of the humans thought they were just angels! God soon put an end to these relationships and made sure that there was a clear divide between human life and out-of-this-world life. God shut the Door on the outside and inside of the Universe. No way through either way.

And as time went on, the Doorway was forgotten—overgrown by the forgetfulness of humanity. People just got on with life. The gap between heaven-life and earth-life grew larger as things on earth went from bad to worse. Humans had lost Paradise. Humans could never have a perfect endless life ever again. The two dimensions—outside and inside of the Universe—drifted further apart.

His Story records that things got so bad that God started to question his own sanity in making such a beautiful world for it just to be trashed by his own children.[15] He contemplated pulling the plug on the whole experiment: cutting his losses and getting out of the creation business; going back to being alone—just with his strange alien helpers.

But then he noticed one man.

---

14. Genesis 6:1–5.
15. Genesis 6:5–7.

# 4

## One Man and a Boat

NINE MASSIVE EPIC GENERATIONS after Adam came one special human—Noah—the many times great grandson of Adam. But what was also great about him was the way he changed God's mind about finishing off his whole earth and Universe project. After meeting Noah, God re-wrote the end of His Story. It became a happy ending—a happy-ever-after ending (which is good news for you and me). Without Noah, humanity wouldn't exist. We would be another extinct species like the dinosaurs.

But fortunately, Noah restored God's faith in his special creation—human beings. But still the rest of the world of Noah was a cess pit of violence and evil. Humans were out of control.[1] Like children left by their parents "home alone" in their luxury house for weeks on end with money, opportunity, alcohol, cars, and nobody close to keep an eye on them, they went wild. Things were exciting but seriously and scarily out of control. What had begun with the first humans doing just what they wanted with a piece of fruit had ended up with humans doing just what they wanted with each other.

It wasn't a pretty sight: no rules; no law; no order; no peace. The good people were frightened to stand up for what was right. It was savagery. The humans were worse than the animals. God needed to start afresh. And so he chose one man to restart the new version of the human race—Noah.

Why Noah? Because he was the only one who remembered that God had given humans the kiss of life; that humans owed their existence to him. Why Noah? Because he remembered that God had given humans the special ability to choose. And Noah used his choice to choose to listen to God. Why Noah? Because he was the only one listening to God shouting through the locked Door of the Universe.

And what did Noah hear? "Build a boat." Not a little rowing boat. But an Ark.[2] A big boat—longer than the biggest full size soccer pitch but half

1. Genesis 6:5–8.
2. Genesis 6:11–14.

the width. Not that Noah was going to have a game of soccer. He was told to herd together a male and female of all the animals and birds and reptiles in the inhabited part of the world. For humans at that time, this was the same as the whole world. God wanted the animal kingdom to survive, after all, the mess on the earth wasn't their fault.

All this in the one boat. Bit tight you might think. But we are in the early days of humanity. The world of Noah was a very much smaller place. Migration and travel hadn't really happened. Noah's world was limited with far fewer living species local to Noah than we now know about. But though a smaller place, still a place with very special inhabitants: humanity.

Noah was told only to take his family on the boat. So, a small group of humans trooped onto the boat—a small family who would have to become the new beginning of the post-flood human race. All of these in one boat. But all of these in one boat—on dry land. Stupid? Must have certainly looked it, but they didn't look so stupid when after a week the rain started and underground rivers burst through onto the surface. Water fell from the sky above. Water bubbled up from the underground streams below—floods for forty days non-stop. God was going to turn the earth back into formless liquid—back to the beginning again like a potter crushing his spoilt clay pot and starting to form it again into a new perfect creation.

The flood was so bad, it has seeped its way into the stories of ancient cultures throughout the world. Some people say that there are over five hundred flood legends worldwide. From China to Scandinavia, all have their own versions of a giant flood.

The flood was so bad that soon Noah's boat started bobbing past the top of mountains. As far as the eye could see there was water. As far as the eye could see there was no one left alive, except for Noah, his family and his rescued animals, birds and reptiles.

His Story looked all but washed out. But then slowly, but surely, the water started to drain away and the rain stopped. Like hair caught in a plughole, Noah's boat was grounded on a mountain, possibly Turkish. Then Noah sent out one of his doves to search for dry land only to have it return to the safety of the boat. Then he sent it again and it came back with a leaf from an olive tree. The dove had found somewhere to perch. The water was draining away below the rocks and trees.[3] The earth was returning to normal. Then Noah sent the dove out again and it didn't return at all as it had found a safe place to nest. So Noah took this as a sign that the earth was now a safe place for him to live as well.

---

3. Genesis 8:6–12.

What was the first thing Noah did when back on dry land? He killed and burnt some of the animals he had just saved.[4] Was this sensible? The animals were some of the extra special ones he had brought on board but still this was risky. He needed as many animals as possible. He needed the animals to breed and populate the newly cleaned world. These animals were his hope of food in the future, especially until the plants grew again. It was a great sacrifice. The animals were vital and valuable.

But the sacrifice was vital and valuable too. It was Noah's way of saying thank you to God for giving him prior-warning of the destruction. It was Noah's way of showing how much he meant his thank you. It was Noah's way of showing that he still trusted God for his future. And so sacrifice started to become the way that humans thanked God. God had used his ultimate weapon of mass destruction. He had taken the life away he had given. He had swept away humanity in a torrent. But Noah's sacrifice softened God's anger. In return, God promised never again to use the ultimate solution. And to remind humanity of his promise, he gave an ethereal heavenly guarantee. When it rains, sometimes the sun shines in such a way that it brings beauty out of the rain instead of destruction. God makes a bow in the sky—not a crossbow, but a rainbow as a reminder of his peaceful and beautiful intentions for the world.[5] The rain now was not God's weapon but a shimmering heavenly sign ending with the pot of gold of God's promise.

"Never again."

---

4. Genesis 8:20–21.
5. Genesis 9:12–16.

# 5

## Bricks

"Never again" may have been a promise that God might have wished he hadn't made. Over generations the human race grew and spread again. Noah's genes spread and re-populated this part of the earth which was the whole world to these humans. But Noah's ability to listen to God didn't spread. The humans went back to what human always go back to—thinking they are God.

It seemed to all be going so well for the humans. They were starting even to stick together and work together. They discovered that if you stop fighting and attacking each other, you could achieve so much more.

Another great discovery they made was the brick. Not the most exciting discovery you might think but for the first time you could build amazing structures not limited by stone or mud. These clever humans started to stick their bricks together with tar and found they could build higher and stronger than ever before. They began by reaching for the sky by building a Tower.[1] His Story doesn't say actually how high it was or how high it was aiming to be, but there are lots of stories saying it was anything from just a bit smaller than the Eiffel tower to something three and half miles high and eighty miles around the bottom. But this is fantasy time. It has been calculated by some optimistic boffins that by using bricks you might build to almost a mile and a quarter into the sky before the bricks at the bottom crushed. If you tapered your building to a point you might have even get to the height that humans would need oxygen to put the last bricks on the top!

But why do it? To impress, of course! Even now, humans haven't changed. We're still building up into the sky to impress our neighbors. But so far, the tallest we've managed is half a mile straight up. But before air travel and satellites, the sky was seen as God's territory—out of reach to humans. They thought he lived up there—that it was the Doorway back into paradise. So if you got there, you would be super-human and live in a super-human world. So going back thousands of years, this craze of pre-historic

1. Genesis 11:3–4.

skyscrapers wasn't just about outdoing their neighbors but was also about a desire to outdo God. These humans wanted to show God how clever they were. God was going to be within reach. They were going to beat God at his own game. God had sent rain down from the heavens onto the earth and washed humans away. Now humans were going to storm the heavens and wipe God off the face of the earth! By their own efforts humanity was going to force God to do what they wanted. After all there were lots of humans and only one God! It hadn't dawned on them that the Door to God's home was invisible and locked shut. And it certainly wasn't up in the sky.

But how was God going to react to this stupid, childish, futile attempt to get rid of him—another flood? No—he'd promised never again. Something much simpler, but just as effective was all he needed—get them to fall out. Just when the humans had learnt to work together and understand each other, God encouraged local language: local words; phrases; dialects. And before you knew it, within a very few years, each group, each tribe of humans had their own language. As humans populated wider areas, they became more cut off from each other. Individual separate language and cultures grew up. And of course every human group's language was the best.

Language is one of those defining things. It gives raw feelings shape. It makes grunts into meaningful ideas. It can build things: friendships; love; emotions; even towers. It is one of those things that makes us special as humans. And it's one of those things that humans fall out over through prejudice and misunderstanding. Language shows up our differences as well as our similarities as humans.

And after God's intervention the intelligible grunts of the humans went back to just being grunts to everyone apart from someone from your own tribe. No one could understand anyone else.[2] Misunderstanding—everywhere. No delicate diplomacy or disarming discussion possible. Everyone fell out and fell back into their tribal groups: all suspicious of each other; scared of each other; all at each other's throats. Cohesion collapsed into chaos. Building work stopped. Constructive partnership dissolved. The only thing that was built was distrust. The tower was left half-finished as a memorial to unrealized human hopes—a folly reminding humanity of its folly.

The human race would never be united on its own in this way again. Humanity now was about lots of groups of humans doing their own thing: splitting up; dividing; moving out over the face of the earth. Humanity was now living in isolation with each ethnic group trying to be better than God—each trying to be better than each other.

---

2. Genesis 11:5–7.

This messing up of language took place in an area which became known as Babble—the name mimicking the unintelligible grunting sound that the stranger next to you made when he asked you to pass him a brick. This may have been the very early beginnings of a place called Babylon—a place that would feature more than once in His Story.[3]

His Story was falling apart with all the humans falling out with each other. God had stopped the human's insane attempt to manipulate him. But for His Story to have a happy ending, he needed another human to star in His Story. It was fitting that it should be a descendant of Noah. In fact, Noah's son, Shem's several times great grandson.

His name was Terah.

---

3. Genesis 11:8–9.

# 6

## One Man Nation

BUT TERAH MESSED UP. Like many of us, he only did half a job. God had called to Terah through the Doorway to leave his hometown, Ur, in the surrounding area of the Babble-onians. And Terah did hear and obey. He set off West for his new clean start with all his extended family. His destination was the land of Canaan—the home of His Story.

But Terah had a stopover in Haran and that was it. He couldn't be bothered to go any further.[1] In fact Haran was where he spent the rest of his life. Terah had followed the weird feeling that had prompted him to move West but he didn't seem to recognize the inner compulsion as being God himself calling him to star in the next stage of His Story. Terah only half listened—certainly only half-obeyed. He lived to two hundred and five, but never lived to complete the life God had planned for him in His Story.

But Abram, his Son, was more in tune with God. Abram was another one like Noah who remembered that even though the Doorway to outside of the Universe was closed, God was still the big Father involved in the life of his children. Abram became God's next special agent on earth—God's star in His Story. The call came to him to finish off what his father had failed to do—go west.[2] No definite destination, just a general call from God, but it did come with a promise—"Follow my directions and I will make your descendants great." This promise was for Abram and his extended family. This promise was that his extended family would be the people that God would use to save humanity—a promise that turned out to be for thousands and thousands and now millions and millions of other people. Abram was a one man nation. His family was going to be God's family. One of his special family was destined to be the Super-star of His Story. God promised it. This promise to Abram was the second big promise from God in His Story.

Why did God make this promise? God had changed his strategy. Instead of trying to get all humans to do the right thing, he was going to

1. Genesis 11:31–32.
2. Genesis 12:1–4.

concentrate his efforts on one family. This family would become his agents for change on earth. And so began the exciting story of the Abram family. This story took place in what we now call, "history" and not pre-history. We can definitely plot and measure where Abram and his tribe fits into the whole list of years that stretch before our time. Abram lived around four thousand years ago. This is a long time ago, but not that long ago as far as human history goes. It's an era that is well recorded in our museums. You can go and see the things people in those days and in Abram's part of the world drew, sculpted, wrote and used. These people weren't primitive savages. The people were very much like us. And Abram was no exception. He worried. What about? Well, logically to start to be a one man nation you do need to have one thing—children.

Or let's set our sights a little lower—a child.

# 7

# D.I.Y. or Destiny?

ONE LITTLE CHILD IS all you need to start a nation. But Abram didn't have even that. Hard to start a family without one, never mind a nation! Time yet, you might think even though Abram was seventy-five —the age lengthening effect was still present (even if it was beginning to weaken). At least, Abram did have a wife—Sarai. She wasn't exactly young but she was beautiful—beautiful enough for Pharaoh to fancy her. Yes, a Pharaoh of pyramid building fame.[1] Abram's journey west had ended up in Egypt. He had overshot Canaan due to a famine there. And with a little bit of self-help and God-help, Pharaoh decided it was not in his interest to take Sarai into his harem.

So still time for a baby. But the years go by and still no baby. No panic. God promises again that he would work through Abram's children.[2] But Abram still worries. He can't see how God is going to be able to make his promise come true. And of course when the God who gave birth to the Universe seems to be in difficulty giving birth, what do you do? Do something to help him—obviously. God all-mighty sometimes needs human help! As if.

But unaware of the irony, Abram decides to help God. He tries for a baby with a younger woman—in fact his wife's servant.[3] This doesn't sound good and it isn't good, but at least it was his wife's idea as well as his and it wasn't illegal in those days or even seen as abusive.

But it was wrong. Why? Because there's always two sides to a promise—there's one who promises and one who trusts. God had promised; Abram had to trust. But he didn't. Instead, he decided to go it alone. Sound familiar? Abram was just like Adam and Eve—just like us. He wanted to be independent and like Adam and Eve he did his own thing.

And it worked (sort of). The servant girl became pregnant. But as her bump grew, the insecurity and jealousy and bitterness grew in the Abram

1. Genesis 12:10–20.
2. Genesis 13:14–17; Genesis 15:1–6.
3. Genesis 16:1–4.

family as well. God had to intervene to protect the unborn child from the insanely jealous Sarai.[4] And when the servant girl's baby was born, God had to promise that he too would become the father of a great people.[5] Many people now believe that this boy, called Ishmael, is the father of the tribes of Arabia—tribes that would produce two and a half thousand years later again, one man called Mohammed—the greatest prophet of Allah and Islam, according to Muslims.

Here is one of those massive "what ifs" of His Story: a branch in the road; an alternative storyline; another possible ending. Why couldn't Ishmael be the next starring character in His Story? Abram certainly thought this was a good idea, and told God so.[6] But God had different plans. His Story's plot controversially wasn't to go with Ishmael, even though he was the all-important firstborn son of Abram.

His Story is God's story—God's plan, not a human plan. To reinforce (painfully) this message, God gave circumcision as a sign to Abram and his family. This ritual cutting was to be a personal reminder to all Abram family men that sex was God's gift to humans—a great gift, but not one to be used without reference to God. God wanted to have a say in the most fundamentally human and intimate of human matters—sex. God the Creator wanted sex not to be used indiscriminately, but in a way which fitted with his plan for humanity.[7] Ishmael was born simply as a result of human sex, not God's plan. It's not that God was against humans enjoying sex—after all it was part of his plan for humanity, but God wanted sex to be enjoyed in the way that God had designed—as part of His Story. God knew that sex could easily become a god in its own right—worshipped by humans, rather than encouraging humans to worship God. Abram thought he could use sex to sort out his problems. But sex can't solve problems. It can cause a lot though. By having sex with his wife's servant, Abram thought he could write his own version of God's Story. But God doesn't need co-authors. The child God was going to work through was still to be born. And even though Abram was now a hundred years old and his wife ninety, it would happen. And as another reminder of the promise, Abram would have a new name—Abraham. Yes, not a big change, but an important one. Abraham meant "Father of many" not just "Father."[8] This yet-to-be father was to become not only the father of

---

4. Genesis 16:4b–10.
5. Genesis 16:11–12.
6. Genesis 17:18.
7. Genesis 17:9–14.
8. Genesis 17:1–8.

a special nation in His Story, but arguably the father of three great World religions: Judaism; Christianity; and Islam.

Not bad for an old man.

# 8

## God will Provide

ABRAHAM—THE "FATHER OF MANY." But first he had to be the father of one! Surely it was going to happen now. But no—still no baby. So God decided to encourage Abraham. He did something he hadn't done since the days of the first humans—enter the earth. He went through the dimensional Doorway and visited his creation.

What would God look like if you bumped into him? Would you notice if he sat next to you on the bus or the train? Would you avoid eye contact or surreptitiously move away? Would you be able to cope with the sight of him? It is a thought but how on earth could God appear on earth in a form we could understand, cope with, and relate to?

Bearing this in mind and to help the humans he was about to meet, God stepped through the Doorway disguised as three human beings: three human strangers; travelers; visitors.[1] But not human—just appearing human. One day he would do more, but that's much further on in His Story. And so God appeared in one very specific point in time and space in the whole of the Universe namely, right next to Abraham's nomadic tent. Abraham immediately spotted them and in good eastern style invited them for a meal. And in good universal male style ran off to tell his wife to make tea.

It was only after the other-worldly visitors asked to meet Abraham's wife using her new secret name given by her by God earlier (Sarah)[2] that Abraham realized he was sharing his food with the greatest Being inside or outside of the Universe. This knowledge must have shocked Abraham (to put it mildly). Two thousand years later, a follower of God thinking about this event warned, "Don't forget to feed strangers, because you never know—they might be an angel."[3]

The strangers had given away their real identity. Why? Because the point of God's visit was to reassure Abraham again that he would be a father

---

1. Genesis 18:1–15.
2. Genesis 17:15–16.
3. Hebrews 13:2.

*god will provide* 23

in a year's time. Sarah listening at the tent's door laughed. She'd heard it all before, and nothing had happened. But God told her off for her understandable cynicism. She would never be allowed to forget her telling off as God made sure the promised child was going to be called "Isaac", which means "laughter." And so the joke was on Sarah when the long awaited baby eventually came. God was true to his word. Sarah did give birth eventually to God's promised child—Isaac.[4] But this meant a resurgence of the tensions in the home with Ishmael and his mother, Hagar. For their own safety the mother and child left Family Abraham, protected by God's special messenger who had been sent through the Doorway. Their story veers off away from His Story.[5] The way was clear for the promised special child—the first special child in His Story—the first of many in His Story.

So what do you do when you've waited over a hundred years for your first miraculous baby boy: protect him; nourish him; keep him wrapped up in cotton wool? Yes, but first you kill him. At least, sacrifice him (which amounts to much the same for Isaac). Not only sacrifice him but do it whilst he's still a young man—too young to have had a family; too young to have produced a grandchild for Father of Many, Abraham; too young to make God's promise of a massive extended family for Abraham coming true.

Was Abraham mad? But remember. What did you do in those days to show how much you thank God? You made a sacrifice like Noah did. God had given Abraham the gift of a son in his old age, against all the odds. As a thank you, God said the sacrifice he wanted was Isaac.[6] It was certainly one unbelievable sacrifice on Abraham's behalf. Abraham showed he still remembered that God was boss by following God's instructions, even when God was telling him to do something that seemed so pointless and self-defeating. And frankly, morally wrong.

Abraham had to tell his young innocent promised child that he was about to kill him. Understandably, he couldn't bring himself directly to tell him. Instead, he told a half-truth, as he placed the sacrificial firewood on his son's shoulders. But then young Isaac asked him directly which animal were they going to sacrifice. Abraham's answer to Isaac's question was simple but shows why Abraham is the great Father of His Story. His answer is the model answer for any human trying to trust God when everything happening all around seems to scream that God doesn't know what he's doing—"God

---

4. Genesis 21:1–7.
5. Genesis 21:8–12.
6. Genesis 22:1–2.

will provide."[7] God promised so Abraham trusted his promise. That's trust. That's contract.

But God pushed Abraham's faith in him to the point of complete destruction. He did provide but only in the nick of time—in fact only after Abraham had tied Isaac onto the bonfire and had lifted his knife above his head ready to bring it crashing down with as much force as he could to make his only son's death quick and painless as possible.

"Abraham! Abraham! Stop!" A special messenger from outside of the Universe suddenly appeared shouting through the Doorway as if he were just waiting for the most dramatic entry ever. Maybe he was. One second more and two world religions would have been wiped off the face of the earth. One second more and human sacrifice would have become part of the expected worship of God. It was that close.

Abraham stopped with the pressure of the blade tip blanching his son's young flesh. Out the corner of his eye, he saw a sacrificial lamb caught in the bushes. This lamb took Isaac's place as the sacrifice.

Where did all this happen? A place called, Mount Moriah—a very special place. Some people in the past have called it, "the navel of the world." These same people believed that the navel was the center of the body. So Moriah was the center of the whole world. Some go further and say that Moriah is the Doorway to heaven. Some say that it holds the foundation stone—the first part of the world to be made.

What is definite is that Moriah later became the foundation stone of a future Temple—a building to mark the Doorway to the beyond. The actual Doorway was meant to be in a small room at the center of the Temple building—the Holy of Holies. The Holy of Holies has now gone—destroyed by the Romans around forty years after a man who was nicknamed "The Lamb of God" died close by whilst claiming he was saving humanity.[8] This ground zero is now under the famous international city of Jeru-Salem—in fact under the ruins of the Temple which used to stand at the heart of Jeru-Salem two thousand years ago. It is now under a holy Islamic building—the Dome of the Rock. This Dome is said to be built on the Foundation Stone and is now a place holy to Muslims as well as to the family of Abraham.

But we are rushing ahead. Four thousand years ago, it was the place where Isaac lived to see another day. It was the place where His Story continued and didn't end in a bloody mess. So what was so special about this first miracle baby? What sort of life did this miracle baby grow up to have?

A lonely life.

7. Genesis 22:8.
8. John 1:29–30.

# 9

## Bloodthirsty versus Bloodsucker

FINDING SOMEONE WHO WILL go out with you isn't simple. Choosing the right partner for life is even more difficult—for anyone. But when God needs you to find a wife who will become the mother of a nation destined to save the world, then it's enough to scare any young woman off. Talk about marriages needing to be made in heaven!

On top of this, Isaac's mother had now died. Isaac missed her. He wanted someone to comfort him in his grief. So he also wanted a substitute mother. It's no wonder that Isaac was still single at forty years old. The pressure of expectations must have been unbearable for any suitable partner.

In the end, his old man, Abraham, had to help him out. Abraham sent his servant to find his son a wife—not any old wife—but a special young wife from back in his old home country. How? Hold auditions? No, he would use the same secret technique that Abraham had in mind when he had set off to sacrifice Isaac—"God will provide."

His plan was simple. The servant would ask the first young woman he met to bring him a drink of water for himself and then all of his ten camels. If she agreed, she was the one God was providing.[1] And "Bobs your Uncle" or at least your wife.

The first woman he met did exactly that. Rebekah was her name. Amazingly it turned out that she just so happened to be a close relative of Abraham. Even more amazingly, she agreed to go with Abraham's old servant by return camel and marry her relative she had never seen. The rest, as they say, is His Story.

For God to continue to make sure his earth became the place he had created it to be, he needed another generation of humans to follow him. His Story needed another child star—another special child chosen by God. But as usual it wasn't easy. It took twenty years and a lot of Isaac begging God, for Rebekah to become pregnant. And then when she did become pregnant, the choice for God wasn't easy—twins.

---

1. Genesis 24:1–67.

Which one was going to be the next star of His Story? Which one was going to be the one to keep God's promise to Abraham alive? At least they weren't identical—anything but. They were opposites. But instead of opposites attracting, they fought, even when they were still inside their mother.

The first to be born, Esau, had wild red hair and became a wild bloodthirsty out-in-the-wilds hunter. The second to be born, Jacob, was smooth and became a smooth, slick stay-at-home shepherd.[2] With Esau—what you saw was what you got. He acted first; thought second. With Jacob—what you saw was just the tip of the iceberg. He thought first and acted second. Esau was his dad's favorite; Jacob was his mum's favorite. It was destined to end in an almighty bust-up. And it did.[3]

Esau had been on a long hunting trip slaughtering wild animals. He got back home starving. His younger twin "happened" to be cooking at home. "Give me some of that red stew NOW," he ordered. Jacob knew his brother's weak spot and refused to cook for him and feed him unless of course, he exchanged his status as the firstborn eldest twin in return for the meat. Being firstborn, even if by only a few minutes, was a great advantage in those days. The firstborn inherited the lion's share of his father's wealth. But did Esau remember this in his hunger? No. Well, yes, if you count shouting, "I'm going to die of hunger soon—what good are rights when you're starving!" Not exactly Einstein our Esau. There again Jacob was no Saint. He took advantage of his brother's thick brain to value thick soup above inheritance. Esau lost his inheritance to his brother over an empty stomach and a full bowl of broth. And so His Story changed from working through the firstborn dim but honest hunter to working through a younger slick, scheming conniving mummy's boy.

When it was time to receive the inheritance near to their father's death, mummy helped Jacob to trick the now old and blind, Isaac, to give his blessing of inheritance to Jacob instead of his brother Esau. Mummy dressed him up in smelly animal skins so that when dim-sighted father, Isaac, put his hand out to bless what he thought was his dim-witted smelly son Esau, he blessed sharp, sly Jacob instead.[4] The child of promise should have been thick-but-honest Esau but through a bowl of meat stew and the smell and feel of meaty animal skins, Jacob became God's next unlikely star of His Story. Had meat changed His Story? No. God's not like Esau or Isaac—fooled by a bit of meat. God knew exactly what he was doing. Unlikely though it

---

2. Genesis 25:21–28.
3. Genesis 25:29–34.
4. Genesis 27:1–40.

sounds, God wanted the scheming mummy's boy as his next special agent on earth.

Jacob was the next star in God's plans for saving humanity.

## 10

## One Family Nation

It was important Jacob knew how central he was in God's plans—that he had the next starring role in His Story. But first God needed to do a lot of hands-on work with the unlovable grandson of Abraham.

So God broke into earth—again. For a moment God re-opened the long sealed up Doorway between heaven and earth at a place called Luz. Jacob was running away from his hunter brother who was now hunting him down for "stealing" his birthright after slowly working out that he had been tricked.[1] Jacob was running for his life by escaping to his Uncle, but had run out of energy and had laid down to sleep.

How did God appear this time? Not disguised as a human but as a vision that was more real than reality. God broke into earth through Jacob's sleep and using his subconscious eyes let him see a stairway going up through a Doorway into the dimension outside of the Universe. Otherworldly creatures from beyond the Doorway, were again allowed a brief moment to come through into earth.[2] At the top of the stairs, God himself stood and told Jacob that he was the God of his father and grandfather and that through Jacob his promise to Father of many, Abraham, would come true. Through Jacob God was going to grow Family Abraham into a nation with more members than dust on earth. (Even if you are very house-proud and obsessively anti-dust, this is still a big number. You are meant to be impressed. Jacob was.)

When Jacob woke up he renamed the place "Beth-El" which in the language of Family Abraham meant "House of El." The common name for the divine God-being who lived outside of the Universe in those days was "El." And Jacob promised to follow El's instructions for the rest of his life if . . . (yes there was a condition, because don't forget, this was Jacob the hustler who was always looking to do a good deal to his own advantage) . . . if . . . God kept him safe. Jacob may have got God, but he hadn't lost his wheeling

---

1. Genesis 27:41.
2. Genesis 28:10–22.

and dealing, It was a way of life, Jacob would need as he was about to meet his match in his Uncle Laban who knew a trick or two himself. Uncle Laban had made a nice little farming business for himself up in Haran. Haran was where Jacob's great grandfather had stopped half way to Canaan and adopted it as his home.

Jacob used his skills as a shepherd to pay his way living at Uncle Laban's. But after a while, Laban told him he wasn't happy with the arrangement, he wanted to pay his nephew a proper wage. He asked Jacob to name his price.[3] Dangerous where Jacob was concerned, except Laban was even more dangerous. But unaware of the dangers, Jacob saw a chance to trade to his advantage. He fancied his cousin Rachel. She was shapely, young and beautiful. Laban equally saw a chance to trade to his own advantage. He had another daughter called, Leah. She was cross-eyed, old and left on the shelf. Jacob said he would work for his Uncle for free for seven years if he could marry Rachel. Laban agreed. And the seven years seemed like seven days to the love-struck Jacob (apparently).[4]

And so the wedding day eventually came. The tradition was that on your wedding night your bride wore the full veil with even the eyes obscured—an important detail as it turned out. It was only in the morning after the wedding night that the light of day revealed his Uncle's trick. Jacob realized he had married the wrong sister. He'd married Leah.

One-nil to Laban. Seven years free work and one difficult-to-shift daughter off his hands. Not bad for Laban. Jacob protested but Jacob's complaints came to nothing. Laban defended himself saying that, "didn't Jacob know the local tradition that the eldest daughter was always to be married first?" Knowing Uncle Laban this was probably the first time this tradition had ever been heard of anywhere. But at least in those days you could marry more than one wife and so after a week, Laban let him marry Rachel as well. One-all. But this was only after Jacob promised yet another seven years of free work. (I bet they didn't feel like seven days this time.) Two-one to Laban.

Later, Jacob threatened to leave and go back to his home and take his chances with Esau. Laban panicked, he didn't want to lose his free shepherd. So he offered Jacob wages again—Jacob just had to say how much he wanted.[5] Jacob said he would have a few sheep and goats—nothing special—just the odd ones—in fact the ones with the speckled or black coats would be fine. Laban saw a good deal and took it. But this was the time for Jacob to

---

3. Genesis 29:1–30.
4. Genesis 29:20.
5. Genesis 30:25–43.

find his skills again. As a shepherd he knew how to mate the sheep and goats in such a way that more and more young lambs and goats were born with speckled coats. In fact they began to take over the flock.

A hustler knows when he's been hustled. And Laban knew he had been tricked. Things were going to get nasty. And so Jacob for the second time in his life had to escape—this time from his uncle not his brother—not on his own, but with his two wives and also the very significant children born to them and their maidservants.[6]

Two-all. But on his way back to an uncertain reunion with his hunter brother, Esau, El-God stepped through the Doorway yet again; hunted down Jacob and forced Jacob to deal with him.[7] This time, El-God appeared as just one man. El-God wanted to get hold of Jacob and make sure he didn't run away from his destiny. He needed to remind Jacob why he had chosen him.

So what would you do if you met God face to face, man to man and he tries to get hold of you and force you to obey him? Wrestle, of course. Well, not "of course," but Jacob is not your average man. He engaged in a bizarre human-divine struggle with God—a struggle that in many ways prefigures the struggle that happens between God and every human since. This was the fight all humans have when they have to decide between giving into God or being their own god.

In this first seemingly unfair, unequal fight Jacob nearly won. El-God's human body was no match to Jacob's until El-God at the last minute used his divine power to cheat by dislocating Jacob's hip to stop him running away. Jacob the cheat had met his match. But even though incapacitated, Jacob wanted to trade. He held onto the man who was El and wouldn't let him go until he had given him something for his injury. He wanted a blessing—a special gift from El. And El gave him a gift like he had given Abraham—a new name—a better name than Abraham's. Not just two new letters, but a whole new name. A name that meant "wrestles with El." This was a name that began to hint at the future identity of the special Family Abraham. The name was "Isra-El."[8]

Abraham had been a potential one-man nation. Now Jacob, as Isra-El, was a one-family nation. His children were to become the pillars of the nation of Isra-El. In the last one thousand seven hundred plus years, Isra-El's twelve sons have turned into well over twelve million people alive today.

As his family grew up, Jacob-Isra-El went back to Beth-El and there El reassured him again that his promises to his grandfather, Abraham, now

---

6. Genesis 31:1–21.
7. Genesis 32:22–32.
8. Genesis 32:28.

applied to him. But there was a condition—he had to get rid of his gods—the foreign pagan images that the humans around him worshipped instead of the god who was God—the one who had made everything. He had to follow exclusively the God known as El.

And for once Jacob agreed: no negotiation; no dealing; no tricks.

## 11

## Twelve Brothers—One King

From the beginning, the family of Isra-El faced threats. In fact, down the centuries, Family Abraham known also as Isra-El has faced many threats throughout the world and throughout time. But for now the threats were close at home, namely, Esau—Jacob-Isra-El's hunter brother.

But fortunately, time had taken the edge off Esau's temper and he let Jacob-Isra-El and his family back into their special homeland of Canaan to settle. They lived alongside each other but sensibly far enough away to avoid misunderstandings.[1] This allowed both families to prosper. Esau's extended family became the nation of Edom which means "Red" in honor of their originator's red hair and love of red meat. Many hundreds of years later one of Esau's family would be the controversial King who would threaten to kill a special Isra-El baby-King born in Beth-Lehem—a little baby who is crucial to His Story.[2]

But for now, the threat to the family of Isra-El wasn't from another family, but from within the family—from internal fighting amongst Jacob-Isra-El's own family. Abraham had learnt by bitter experience that having children through different wives and their maidservants didn't make for a peaceful family. But his grandson hadn't learnt the same lesson. Soon, Isra-El had twelve sons born to him by four different women.[3] But his favorite partner was still his beloved beautiful Rachel. She had given him his favorite boys—Joseph first and then later, his youngest child, Benjamin. But Rachel died as she gave birth to Benjamin and as a result Benjamin understandably became incredibly precious to Jacob-Isra-El. He was a special living memorial to his beloved wife.

But which of the twelve sons would be God's special one—the next star of His Story? Would it be Reuben, Jacob-Isra-El's first born son—the

---

1. Genesis 33.
2. Matthew 2:16.
3. Genesis 35:23–26.

first born to Leah whom he had married by mistake, or would it be Joseph, Jacob-Isra-El's favorite son—the first born to Rachel whom he had married out of love?

Joseph thought it would be him. He was clearly his father's favorite. He wore his dad's favor on his sleeve all the time. To be exact, he wore his dad's favorite colorful coat with flamboyant sleeves all the time. He told tales on his brothers and told his brothers tales about himself. Like the one about his dreams.[4] He dreamt that he and his brothers were bundles of wheat and all his brotherly bundles suddenly jumped up and bowed down to his. If this weren't enough, he also dreamt that the sun and the moon and eleven stars bowed down to him. It didn't take a genius to work out who were the eleven stars. Or what Joseph thought about himself.

This cosmic dream was even too rich for Jacob-Isra-El to stomach. He questioned whether Joseph included his parents in the bowing down. But at the same time, Joseph's dad wondered whether these dreams were signs that God had chosen Joseph to star in the next part of His Story. After all, Jacob knew from his vision at Beth-El that God sometimes opens the Door between heaven and earth through sub-conscious dreams.

No such pondering and wondering for Joseph's brothers. They hated Joseph. Forget understandable sibling rivalry—think vicious domestic violence. The brothers' opportunity came when Joseph was sent to find his brothers who were miles from home looking after the sheep. When the brothers saw him coming, they planned that they would make the dream hero zero. The plan? Kill him and stick his body down a pit and pretend to dad that poor old Joseph had been eaten by a wild animal.[5]

Oldest brother, Reuben though, planned to protect Joseph by suggesting they should cut out the killing—just chuck him down the pit. He had secretly planned to rescue him later. Maybe he was showing oldest brother maturity that would persuade God to choose him to inherit the title, star of His Story? But as it turned out a camel caravan turned up too soon for Reuben to complete his plan. These traders were descendants of great grandfather's first son, Ishmael. They were now exporters, with a bit of slave trading on the side. They traded with Egypt. So what do you do if you are obnoxious Joseph's brothers—kill your detested brother and make no money or trade your horrible brother off and make some money in the process? It was a no-brainer. These boys weren't Jacob's sons for nothing. They sold Joseph to the slave traders. Were the Ishmaelites—the descendants of the one rejected by God in a previous generation—going to rob the present generation of God's

4. Genesis 37:1–11.
5. Genesis 37:12–36.

chosen one? Certainly looked that way. Through the help of the Ishmaelites, Joseph ended up in Egypt as a slave. And Jacob-Isra-El ended up grieving for his dead son killed by a wild animal. The brothers carry on as if nothing had happened. They simply try to forget Joseph. After all, life goes on.

It did for Joseph, but it wasn't a normal life. Whilst in slavery in Egypt, he worked for an important solider. He did well. He was trusted. He was handsome, athletic, and good at his work. But sometimes success brings its own dangers. He was noticed by his master's wife. She tried several times to seduce the young slave. But each time, Joseph rejected her. He countered her increasingly desperate harassment by explaining that he would never cheat on his master, Potiphar. Things came to a head when Joseph had to escape Potiphar's obsessive wife by running out of the house leaving part of his clothing in her insatiable grip. And all that Joseph got in reward for his loyalty to his master was prison—accused by his master of the attempted rape of his wife.[6]

Hundreds of miles away back home in Canaan, one of Joseph's brothers, Judah, was having his own problems.[7] One of his daughters-in-law, Tamar, was a widow with no children. But she was desperate for a child. So she dressed as a prostitute and sat by the kerb when she knew her Father-in-law, Judah, was passing by. Judah didn't recognize her, but had sex with her and paid for it by giving her his unique signet ring and special walking stick. Not a bright idea as it turned out. Several months later, Judah found out that his widow daughter-in-law was pregnant and had behaved like a prostitute. He was angry and called for her to be burned to death. But it was only when she was being dragged off to the bonfire, that she produced Judah's unique signet ring and walking stick. Judah had to admit that they were his and that the child must be his as well. Tamar was understandably saved. The resulting child turned out to be twins. Judah never went near his daughter in law, Tamar, ever again. Again he had learnt that using sex in a way that breaks God's purpose and rules always ends in tears.

So which of these two would God choose to be his next star of His Story—Judah or Joseph? Which would you choose? If you're in any doubt, let's fast forward Joseph's life. In prison in Egypt Joseph was so able and trustworthy that he was put in charge of the day to day running of the prison office. But his skills didn't end at being good at admin. His dream-skills were put to good use again, correctly interpreting the dreams of Pharaoh's personal servant and chef who had both been thrown into prison.[8] He

---

6. Genesis 39:1–23.
7. Genesis 38:1–30.
8. Genesis 40–41.

predicted that the personal servant's dream meant he would be saved by Pharaoh. And he was. He predicted that Pharaoh's chef would come to a sticky end. And he did.

Two years later, the now reinstated personal servant remembered Joseph's dream-skill when Pharaoh had a disturbing dream which baffled all his advisors. The dream was of seven fat cows eaten by seven skinny ones; and seven ripe grains of corn eaten by seven blighted ones. Joseph was called out of prison to solve the dream. To Joseph the great dream-man, it was simple. Joseph predicted seven years of great harvests followed by seven years of famine. His advice? Save food in the seven good years and then use the reserves to survive the seven years of famine. Pharaoh believed him. Not only that, he put Joseph in charge of food plans. And right on time, seven years of famine followed seven years of bumper harvests. But because of Joseph's dreams; because of Joseph's forward planning; Egypt was the only place in the world that food was available and people weren't dying.

A great story made greater in the eyes of the Egyptians because it may have reminded them of the great and mysterious, Imhotep, who was credited for saving them from famine using dreams hundreds of years earlier. A great story made greater also, because after a while Joseph's own brothers, driven by hunger, arrived in Egypt looking to beg for food from Pharaoh.[9] They begged Pharaoh's right hand man in charge of food to sell them some supplies. But this right hand man was no other than the brother they had sold into slavery.[10] Ironic? Yes and not only that it broke Joseph's youthful dreams about his position in the family. Joseph's dreams about them bowing down to him came true.

This great story was made even more dramatic by the way Joseph recognized his brothers, but the brothers didn't recognize Joseph (disguised as he was in his new rich Egyptian finery and bearing his new resplendently powerful Egyptian name of Zaphenath-Paneah). How was Joseph to react to his anonymity? Joseph decided to use his unwitting disguise to test them. He resolved to test his brothers' honesty by making them promise to bring their youngest brother, Benjamin—their dad's other favorite son—to Egypt, "that's if you want food."[11] This honesty test was not surprising, bearing in mind the last time Joseph had seen his brothers they had attacked him and traded him in to the Ishmaelites.

The brothers reluctantly returned to their father with the offer of food but with Joseph's strings attached. When Jacob-Isra-El heard this condition,

---

9. Genesis 42:1–2.
10. Genesis 42:8.
11. Genesis 42:14–17.

he was worried. He knew his sons weren't to be trusted where Rachel's sons were concerned. They'd lost one already. Now history was in danger of repeating itself. But in desperation, he let Benjamin go. It broke Jacob-Isra-El's heart. It broke Joseph's heart as well—he could hardly keep up the disguise once his full brother, Benjamin, arrived in Egypt.[12] But he had to be sure that his brothers had learnt their lesson—that they had changed. He secretly planted one of his expensive golden goblets on Benjamin and when the brothers left to go home with their food supplies, he ordered a routine security search at the border. This of course revealed the stolen item in Benjamin's suitcase. The brothers were detained and brought back to Joseph. Joseph arrested Benjamin and ordered his brothers to go back home without their youngest brother. Benjamin was to be held captive.[13] Like Joseph was years before, but Judah (yes Judah, the kerb-crawling, flesh-crawling Judah), begged Joseph to swap Benjamin for himself. He would stay and rot in an Egyptian prison instead of his brother. He did this out of love for his little step-brother and for the sake of his old man, Jacob-Isra-El. Judah offered to sacrifice himself.[14]

What a change! The past is broken. And Joseph is broken. He couldn't keep up the pretense any longer and revealed himself to his brothers.[15] Cue hugs and kisses and tears and probably a lot of awkward moments. The result was that the whole of the Isra-El family come to Egypt to live and see out the famine. This special family of Father Abraham was saved from extinction by starvation—and all because the brothers sold Joseph into slavery. Strange how good comes out of bad. This is a recurring theme of His Story. Just when you think it can't get any worse, it doesn't—it gets better.

His Story is saved from a dead end, not for the first time and certainly not for the last or greatest time. The future greatest star of His Story was also going to be saved from a dead end, many years later. He would also be saved from an act of treachery. Evil again was going to be turned to good. But for now what started with a vicious attack by a group of brothers on one lone brother, was twisted by God into that same lone brother saving the group of brothers. Joseph later explained it to his brothers, "You intended to harm me, but God intended it for good."[16]

Surely a man who could forgive like this, must be God's next star in His Story? Surely a man who could have insight like this, must be God's

---

12. Genesis 43:29–30.
13. Genesis 44:12–17.
14. Genesis 44:18–34.
15. Genesis 45:1–9.
16. Genesis 50:19–20.

next star in His Story? Joseph—Zaphenath-Paneah of Egypt—Imhotep resurrected—Pharaoh's right hand man—Savior of the Isra-El family—this Joseph must be the key man for God! His children must become God's children. His direct family must be the ones to continue His Story by fulfilling God's promise to Abraham to become a special family of humans. Surely!

No. Not through Joseph's children, but through Judah. Judah had redeemed himself by offering to be a hostage so that his baby brother Benjamin could go free. But still he must have seemed to be a poor choice for God to work through. Joseph had all the credentials. But Judah it was though—and his children—the twins born to the play-acting prostitute Tamar; the twins whose father, Judah, was at the same time their grandfather. One of the twins was called Perez. He was the firstborn . . . just. His brother nearly beat him to it but at the last minute decided to spend a little longer inside mum.[17] This little confused boy was God's next chosen child—the next link in His Story.

Joseph tried his best to fix it so that his chosen son and heir gained his father Jacob-Isra-El's premier blessing.[18] But Jacob knew all about making sure a father's blessing went to the right child now and made sure that the unlikely Judah got the richest blessing instead. He did call Joseph, "a prince among his brothers."[19] But over Judah he said, "The mark of royalty will not leave you, Judah, or your children, until the coming of the special King, the one whom all nations will honor."[20] Out of an incestuous, immoral, sad liaison would eventually come a King of Kings who would be celebrated by all nations.

His Story was headed towards a very special unique King of Judah.

17. Genesis 38:27–30.
18. Genesis 48:1–22.
19. Genesis 49:26.
20. Genesis 49:10.

# 12

## Safe; Well Fed; with a Family

Judah's son, Perez, grew up in Egypt: safe; well fed; with a family.[1] One of his sons was called Hezron.[2] He grew up in Egypt: safe; well fed; with a family. One of his great, great grandsons built the most famous, most mysterious, most sought after magical boxes that has ever existed in the whole of time and space—the Ark of the Covenant.[3]

This gold box would contain God's dictated words. This box that would a few hundred years later, disappear, never to be found again despite every archaeologist who has ever lived, dreaming of digging it up—but more of that later.

Backtracking a little, Hezron had a son called Ram.[4] Ram grew up in Egypt: safe; well fed; with a family. One of his sons was called Amminadab.[5] Amminadab grew up in Egypt: safe; well fed; with a family. In particular he had a daughter called, El-isheba.[6] She married a man called Aaron. This in itself doesn't sound very exciting. But Aaron was the Father of the elite priests or Go-Betweens between God and Family Abraham—the men who helped people try to persuade God to open up the locked Doorway just a tiny crack so they could get the very end of their toe in the jamb. Aaron's descendants would later run all the religious ritual of Family Abraham for generations and generations ahead. But even that's boring unless you're one of an exclusive club who are into religious ritual.

But Aaron had one other claim to fame—he was the brother of Moses.[7]

1. Genesis 46:12.
2. Genesis 46:12.
3. 1 Chronicles 2:5, 9; 18–20; Exodus 31:1–11; Exodus 37:1.
4. 1 Chronicles 2:5, 9–10.
5. 1 Chronicles 2:10.
6. Exodus 6:23.
7. Exodus 6:20.

# 13

## Mini Noah

MOSES WAS ANYTHING BUT just another name in the list of Abraham's growing family of children. God gave him a unique and crucial role to play in His Story. In the same way that Joseph saved the Isra-El family from starvation, Moses saved the chosen family from genocide. Without him, the whole Family Abraham project would have been obliterated as each family member was annihilated—murdered simply because of their ethnicity. His Story would have ended in Egypt over three thousand years ago. But Moses was not just a savior, he was himself a victim of ethnic cleansing that swept Egypt when he was just a few days old. Family Abraham was still in Egypt, but now not safe; not well fed but still having families. And this fact angered the new Pharaoh of Egypt. Family Abraham was growing too strong, too big.

The new Pharaoh of Egypt blamed the immigrant descendants of Isra-El for all his country's problems. He felt no need to support Joseph's extended and extending family.[1] Like dictators and bad politicians down the ages, blaming the immigrants was a quick fix to his complex national problems. In short, the new Pharaoh was a racist politician. And what is the quickest most effective way to stop an immigrant population becoming too dominant if you are a racist tyrant?—birth control—but not what we usually mean by this.[2] Pharaoh decided to kill all the Family Abraham's babies—specifically the male babies. Babies like the newly born Moses.

Baby Moses had endured the most risky journey any human can make when he journeyed from conception to birth only to find an even riskier one waiting for him—a journey with a death sentence as its destination. His only crime was being born of parents from the extended family promised to Abraham. This would not be the first or last time that a special baby of Family Abraham would be born with a death sentence hanging over them.

1. Exodus 1:8–14.
2. Exodus 1:15–22.

But the next famous time, Egypt would be the baby's safe haven not its place of threat.[3]

Moses' mother knew she had to distance her son from herself and her ethnicity to keep him safe. In a mini re-run of Noah's story, she made a little boat.[4] This time only big enough for one newly born baby—not a family and a whole menagerie—this time, not to rescue from a flood of water, but from a flood of racist bigotry. Moses' mother was hoping for a miracle like Noah's—a rescue by water. But not just any water—River Nile water.

She launched the mini Noah's ark into the most holy and magical river of the Egyptians. It was believed to be the divine life blood of great Egypt. Its ebb and flow was believed to be the heartbeat of Egypt. All sorts of religious ritual and superstition were associated with its waters. Egypt believed it was almost god-like. Its waters gave birth to life of all kinds: animal; plant and in this instance—human.

Moses' mother's prayer was answered by a rich young Egyptian woman who came down to the Nile to find a new life through her religious washing in its special waters.[5] She found a surprising answer in the Nile that particular day. She discovered a newly born baby floating past her. But His Story shows that the Nile wasn't the giver. It was God—the God who put the Nile there in the first place—the God who oversaw its cycle—the God who persuaded Moses' mother to trust him like Noah did.

The young Egyptian woman who fished him out was very important, and rich. By her intervention, God had rescued the one who was going to be his special family's rescuer. But God hadn't just rescued him, he had assured him of a secure future—no ordinary secure future—a royal future. A future assured by the young Egyptian woman who fished him out. She was Pharaoh's daughter—coincidence or His Story? Ironic—Moses saved by the daughter of the man who wanted him dead.

Not only that, but when the daughter of Pharaoh wanted help in caring for the boy, she was directed by the onlooking sister of Moses to Moses' actual mother—coincidence or His Story? Unbelievable? Maybe not so unbelievably coincidental when you know that one Pharaoh of the time is recorded has having over one hundred children. Many must have been daughters. But this one particular child of Pharaoh is one of the great heroines of His Story. She had the fascinating name of Bith-Yah.[6] Names are important, especially this one. It isn't Egyptian but means in the Isra-El language "Daughter of

---

3. Matthew 2:13–15.
4. Exodus 2:1–4.
5. Exodus 2:5–10.
6. 1 Chronicles 4:18.

Yah-weh." But why is this strange name so important? Because it used God's secret personal name.

"God" is a name like "human." It's impersonal. It is used by many religions and people to mean lots of different things. It is like—"El"—the widely used ancient name of God.

But "Yah-weh" was El-God's personal name—his own name. A name not known on earth until God revealed it to one special man a few years after the Nile incident. That man was Moses.

Moses' surrogate mother may well have later changed her birth-name to use the special personal name of God revealed for the very first time on earth to her adopted son. If she did, it probably reveals that not only did she adopt her adopted son's faith, she also married one of his extended family. The great Pharaoh of Egypt was now related to the people he despised.

Coincidence or His Story?

# 14

## A Fish out of Water

Yah-weh—the secret personal name of God—revealed to Moses. The great intimate revelation of God's personal name was given to Moses the man. But for now Moses the baby needed to grow up into a young man.

This he did in two different worlds. He was an Egyptian prince and he was a son of Family Abraham. His adopted Egyptian princess mother named him, Moses. His name is mysterious in both his worlds. In Egyptian it could mean "draw out of the water." In the Abraham family language it meant "get out" in the sense of escape. Moses had meaning in Egyptian and Family Abraham language (Hebrew). Moses had a life in Egyptian culture and Isra-Elite culture. What is true is that Moses was like a "fish out of water" in Egypt and that he would grow up to organize the "escape" of Family Abraham out of hot water in Egypt.

Moses was part of the Egyptian royal "divine" dynasty and part of the oppressed victimized people of Family Abraham. Family Abraham members were now second class citizens in Egypt; good enough only to be Pharaoh's slaves—slaves who were only good enough to make bricks.[1]

Bricks—again! This great building material invention was again being used against God. Pharaoh forced all of Family Abraham to make bricks and more bricks—thousands and thousands. With these bricks he built his dynasty. Each day Moses would have been conflicted. Dressed as a rich powerful Egyptian prince, he would enjoy the best of all that Egypt could offer. But brought up by his mother in the Egyptian palace, he would have heard of all his people's pain. Despite his exciting, sumptuous rich Egyptian lifestyle, the truth was that his heart beat in time with the beatings given to his enslaved family.

Something had to give—and it did. One day, he witnessed an Egyptian overseer striking one of his own people—one of his "brothers" from Family Abraham. Suddenly his heart took over from his head. He murdered the

---

1. Exodus 1:11; Exodus 5:6–9.

Egyptian and hid his body. But the man Moses had saved told everyone and soon Moses knew he was going to be found out and tried as a murderer.[2]

At this turning point in His Story, Moses showed his true nature. He wasn't Egyptian. He was part of God's family. So he ran. He left all the luxury of the royal Palace and ran into the desert—royalty roughing it. Was this a right royal mess? But His Story can't be a mess because God is the author. It's a well crafted story. In choosing to leave his palatial idyll and identify himself with the poor and oppressed, Moses set a precedent that would be followed even by the Super-star of His Story.[3]

Moses ends up in the part of the desert where the nomadic Midianites wandered. The Midianites were the children of Ishmael, Abraham's first child—the D.I.Y. child. Not God's first choice child. But still special—still part of this plan. We've met these descendants of Ishmael before. They took Joseph into Egypt in the first place and in so doing had an indirect hand in the process that saved Family Abraham. Here again, they have a hand in saving the one who would rescue Family Abraham.

One of the Midianites was called Jethro.[4] He was a shepherd and a religious man. He was known as "the priest of Midian." He had seven daughters who were shepherds—women alone out in the desert—women vulnerable to men. And when they were one day abused by some men, Moses came to their rescue—Moses standing up for the victim again. But this time he won the approval of the bystanders. Jethro adopted him as his son and later his son-in-law after Moses married one of his daughters, Zipporah. And so, Moses lived as a shepherd in Midian. As he grew famous, he brought respect to the shepherd's role. Two to three hundred years later a shepherd would even become King of Isra-El.[5]

But for now, God made Moses special by breaking through the Doorway from heaven to meet with the ex-Prince, now shepherd. How did God do it? Not as a human; not as a stairway between earth and heaven this time but as a common type of bramble.[6] An ordinary thorny shrub but one caught in the gap between the inside and outside of the Universe. The blackberry bush sparked and burst into flames as it was trapped between the two opposite dimensions—two realities rubbing up against each other in the threshold between heaven and earth creating unbelievable power and heat. Moses noticed—even though tinder-dry plants burning in the searing

2. Exodus 2:11–15.
3. Hebrews 11:24–26; Philippians 2:5–8.
4. Exodus 2:16–22.
5. 1 Samuel 16:10–13.
6. Exodus 3:1–10.

sun of the desert must have happened often. But this time the shrub wasn't burning. It wasn't going black. It wasn't turning to ash. It was on fire. It was full of flames but not being destroyed. It was a like a flashing neon sign to Moses who now knew the desert like the back of his hand.

Out of the bush Doorway God called Moses using the voice of an out-of-this-world messenger who stood in the flames. Moses heard God's instructions—not to build a boat this time, but to keep his distance from the bush for his own good. He was on the Doorstep of heaven—the Doorstep of the Universe. Sensible advice—human physical bodies can't cross through the Door into the eternal non-time dimension of heaven. Just as humans can't survive under water or in space without air, human bodies can't live outside the Universe without time. Human bodies work using time. From our brains to all our systems in our body, they all work on one thing following another—cause and effect. They work using time. In a non-time environment our physical bodies would implode. This can't be proved as no one has ever been able to try it. But we struggle to get our heads around science fiction stories that have the main characters time-travelling, never mind trying it ourselves. Only one human body has ever bridged the two dimensions but that comes later in His Story. For now, Moses was teetering on the edge of a very other-worldly place. There is a simple word in His Story for such a threshold bridging the inside and outside of the Universe—holy. This was holy ground and Moses was told to remove his shoes. The dirt of earth couldn't enter into this other-worldly place. Moses obeyed. He took off his sandals and hid his face from the mind blowing gap into the beyond.

But where was this gap in earthly time and space? Where had God opened a gateway through from heaven to earth? Where was this bush that had been partially dragged into non-time? It was on a mountain called "Horeb"—a mountain which has another more famous name—Sinai. This was a mountain to which Moses would return, but next time not alone—next time with the whole people of Isra-El. Next time, God would open the Door again and fire would shoot out as before. Next time, El-God wouldn't just call to Moses at this place. Next time God would call the whole of the descendants of Abraham to follow his instructions—instructions that would become fundamental to the whole of humanity.

But for now, God had a special message just for Moses. God told him to go and rescue his extended family from slavery in Egypt. He promised that through Moses he would bring his family back home to the promised land of Abraham—to a land "overflowing with milk and honey"—sweet and delicious.

Amazingly, despite Moses' fear and awe, he had enough about him to ask who it was who was speaking to him.[7] It was a sensible question for a person in Moses' predicament—a fugitive murderer on the run being asked to return to the scene of his crime. And it produced an answer that would never be forgotten. "I am the God of your ancestor Abraham." Moses would have known the stories about how God called Abraham to be the Father of nations—the Father of a new humanity. And then after him, how God called Isaac and Jacob-Isra-El. And now he was telling Moses that he was key to this secret plan to save humanity coming true.

But God did more than remind him of the past. He gave him something new. So new that no one before on earth had heard it. A cosmic secret—God's secret personal name—a name that had never been revealed before in all of time and space. The name was Yah-weh. It doesn't sound much to us but in the language of Isra-El it meant "I am."[8]

How do you describe God? How do you put into words who or what God is? He is bigger than words. He is bigger than human language. He is bigger than humans. He is bigger than the world. He is bigger than the Universe. He is bigger than all of our scales to measure or quantify—we can't even begin to weigh him up. He is—or as God would say, "I am"—Yah-weh.

And so, Moses' surrogate mother became known as Bith-Yah—"Daughter of Yah-weh (Yah)."[9] Just as she adopted a child of God's, Yah-weh adopted her as his child. Maybe she had discovered that it makes sense not to worship the Nile itself but Yah-weh who created the Nile. Maybe she discovered the truth made famous by a Yah-weh believer well over a thousand years later, that it is foolish to worship "created things" rather than the "Creator."[10] Maybe the name Bith-Yah was given to her by later generations of Family Abraham in honor of the crucial role she played in saving the savior of Isra-El. She didn't simply save the savior, Moses, but through saving him she saved the ancestors of the ultimate Savior of God's people—the Super-star of His Story.

But he wasn't to be born for over a thousand years.

---

7. Exodus 3:11–13.
8. Exodus 3:14.
9. 1 Chronicles 4:18.
10. Romans 1:25.

# 15

## Creator versus Created

MOSES OBEYED YAH-WEH'S CALL through the Doorway to be the Savior of Isra-El. He dutifully returned to Egypt to persuade Pharaoh to release the people of Isra-El to return to their promised land.

But Moses was not over confident. In fact he was scared witless. He knew about the power of his step-father, Pharaoh. But before he set off back to Egypt, Yah-weh gave him a memento of the time he had stood in the Doorway to the outside of the Universe—a stick.[1] The stick wasn't the gift, after all, it was only Moses' stick for guiding the sheep. It was the new powers the stick contained—that was the gift. This stick had been magnetized by Yah-weh's power. It was a portable piece of heaven—made into a piece of heaven by the Doorway hiding in the burning bush.

Just as the ordinary stick was now extra-ordinary, so Moses was going to be an extra-ordinary shepherd. Moses was now going to shepherd Yah-weh's family out of danger in Egypt. After a thousand years, another man would claim to be, "The Good Shepherd"[2] and become the most famous man born into Family Abraham and even the whole of humanity—a man who would shepherd the whole of humanity out of danger.

But back to the stick—what super-natural powers did the stick now have? Moses only found out when ordered by Yah-weh to throw it on the floor. Immediately it transformed into a snake so real that Moses jumped out of his skin. Yah-weh ordered him to catch the snake by the tail. When he did, it jumped out of its skin and changed back into a stick. Moses took the stick into Pharaoh's palace and turned it into a snake to prove to his evil stepfather his seriousness. But despite this and the moral support of his brother, Aaron, Pharaoh wouldn't budge.[3] It took a crescendo of cataclysmic natural disasters to persuade Pharaoh to part with his free labor. These so called "plagues" may all have had natural causes, but from the first of them

---

1. Exodus 4:1–5.
2. John 10:11, 14.
3. Exodus 7:8–13.

## creator versus created

to the last, it was clear that Yah-weh was the unnatural cause. All of them started by Moses waving his holy stick—the symbol of Yah-weh having power on his earth.[4]

The first disaster showed what the great "I am," thought about the self appointed god, Pharaoh, and his magical River Nile. Yah-weh proved the lifeblood of Egypt had no life without him. He polluted the River Nile. The lifeblood of Egypt poisoned red like blood—the divine spirit of Egypt shown to be less powerful than Yah-weh.

The fish in the Nile died. But the amphibians that could get out did, resulting in frogs plaguing the land.[5] Pharaoh begged Moses to make them go away and die. And they did right on cue—rotting dead frogs underfoot everywhere. But Pharaoh still didn't give in.

Next there were a series of disasters caused by the death and decay caused by the Nile. Clouds of mosquitoes and flies spread disease from the rotting remains of the fish and frogs.[6] The cattle died leaving rotting carcasses.[7] Humans contracted skin disease.[8] Everyone had weeping sores. Everyone had septic lesions. Even Pharaoh's advisors couldn't advise because they couldn't stand up because of them—never mind stand up in front of Pharaoh. Everyone was ill. That is, apart from Family Abraham—coincidence or His Story?

But still Pharaoh wouldn't release his slaves. And so, next came another wave of painful natural disasters to hit the already weakened country. Heavy hail destroyed the crops before harvest.[9] Then locusts ate any vegetation left.[10] The weakened Egyptians now had no food. And then they had no Sun—for three days, caused possibly by an epic dust storm.[11] No wonder the result of this series of disasters was death, but not widespread death—specific death—only the eldest son or male animal.[12] But not one of the eldest offspring of Family Abraham died but only Egyptians. Even Pharaoh's eldest son died—coincidence or His Story?

Before this final disaster, Yah-weh had instructed Moses to tell Family Abraham to put the blood of a sacrificed lamb on the doors of their houses.

---

4. Exodus 7:14–24.
5. Exodus 7:25—8:15.
6. Exodus 8:16–32.
7. Exodus 9:1–7.
8. Exodus 9:8–12.
9. Exodus 9:13–35.
10. Exodus 10:1–20.
11. Exodus 10:21–29.
12. Exodus 11:1—12:30.

This was a sign to tell the angel of death sent through the Doorway to pass-over their house without attacking their eldest son.

Why a lamb? Why the eldest male? It was a message going back hundreds of years—right back to Father Abraham. Right back to the moment when Father Abraham was called to kill his God-given eldest Son, Isaac.[13] His willingness to give the most valuable thing in his life to God—his long awaited son—was rewarded by a lamb being given by God as a substitute. The first ever eldest son of Abraham was saved by the blood of a lamb. Now the eldest sons of Family Abraham were to be saved again by the blood of a lamb. There would come a time when the most famous son of Abraham would not be saved by the blood of the lamb, but would be the lamb itself. This "lamb" wouldn't just save Family Abraham but the family of all nations.[14] But over a thousand years of His Story has yet to come before this storyline.

For now, as Egypt mourned, Family Abraham got ready to run as death had passed-over their houses without landing. The grief-stricken Pharaoh had had enough. Pharaoh had ordered them out. And they ran for their lives.[15] This great escape would be celebrated every year at what has become known simply by one word: Pass-Over.

But the story of the great escape had one more twist. Family Abraham as they ran for their lives, became trapped by the body of water called "Yam Sup"—the Reed Sea.[16] It stood between them and freedom in the desert beyond Egyptian control. Behind them, the Egyptian forces' shock at the widespread death had turned to anger and they were hard on the heels of the scuttling slaves. Egypt was out for revenge. Family Abraham was trapped on the sea's bank. But Moses took his stick that had been infused by Yah-weh's out-of-this-world "holy" power and waved it at the water. A timely gale-force wind suddenly blew and the waters opened up for Family Abraham to cross on the drying sea-bed, only to crash back down on the Egyptian army as they pursued—coincidence or His Story?

It was a great victory for Yah-weh and a great vindication for Moses. But also a great moment for one young twenty year old man—Nahshon—the son of a man we've met already—Amminadab.[17] As Amminadab's son, Nahshon was the brother of Moses' sister-in-law and the next one in the special

---

13. Genesis 22:1–19.
14. John 1:36.
15. Exodus 12:31–51.
16. Exodus 13:17—14:31.
17. 1 Chronicles 2:10.

line of Yah-weh's children.[18] Nahshon had grown up in Egypt—a slave. But ancient folk stories say he was the first to step into freedom through the sea. Impatient to get the escape underway, he waded in before Moses stretched out his hand. With great faith in Moses, he kept walking until the waters lapped up his nose. At the last moment, they parted into two walls of water on each side. Nahshon's step of faith was the first of many steps of faith he took as a leader of Judah.[19] His step of faith was the first of many steps for Family Abraham as they journeyed towards the Promised Land.

Faith is a journey of discovery about Yah-weh and a journey of discovery about ourselves. For Family Abraham, their journey back to their homeland of Canaan could have taken even the slowest, oldest or youngest of their group less than a year, but in the end it took them nearly forty years. Why? Because again people thought they knew a better route than Yah-weh. And as usual, they were wrong. They got lost. They had forgotten again who was boss. They had forgotten they were only like sheep. They had forgotten who their real shepherd was on their journey.

The return leg of Family Abraham's journey that had begun with an extended family of eleven men plus wives and children arriving in Egypt to find food was now continuing with six hundred thousand men plus families leaving Egypt. This new journey would turn Family Abraham into what became known as the nation of Isra-El.

Family Abraham was now Nation Isra-El

---

18. Exodus 6:23.
19. Numbers 2:3; Numbers 10:14.

## 16

# Good God

On this epic journey before Sat. Nav., compasses, maps and road signs, how did Moses navigate the way from Egypt to the Promised Land? He was led by Yah-weh—by Yah-weh's cloud in the day and by Yah-weh's fire at night.[1] These were special signposts sent through the Doorway.

But also Moses knew the desert. He possibly guessed where the signposts were leading—back to Horeb; back to Sinai; back to Yah-weh's Doorway to the outside of the Universe. This time, not back to a single burning bramble bush but to a whole burning mountain: this time not just a message for him, but for the whole of Family Abraham and the fledgling proto-type nation of Isra-El.

What he didn't know was that at Sinai he would be given a message for the whole of humanity. Yah-weh had planned this to be also a new beginning for humans, starting with Abraham's extended family tribe.

Humans had messed it up in Paradise—Yah-weh had mended it through Noah. Humans had messed it up in Babel—Yah-weh had mended it through Abraham. The repair for humanity would be offered first to the extended family of Abraham. But then this fix would be offered to the whole family of humanity.

The repair kit took the form of direct instructions on how humans should live in Yah-weh's creation—the world: Yah-weh's "Maker's Instructions"; Yah-weh's "Handbook for Life"; Yah-weh's "How to be successful at being Human." Up to now, Yah-weh had left humans to try their best to hear his safety instructions transmitted through the Doorway into the Universe. But now they would be in no doubt. Yah-weh would step through the Doorway and write them down himself—carve them into stone with no chance of human editing or deleting. This time, Moses would not just hear Yah-weh calling through the Doorway, but meet Yah-weh himself. Yah-weh was going to enter earth through the Doorway again—direct contact face to face.

1. Exodus 13:21–22.

*good god* 51

And when it came to the epoch-making moment, no one else in Family Abraham was allowed within the non-time exclusion zone around Mount Sinai. The whole mountain was transformed into a Doorway into the heavenly dimension: a Gateway between the created and the Creator; a wormhole between time and non-time. The whole mountain strained under the clashing realities—not just causing a few sparks and flames this time, but fiery volcanic eruptions on the surface and lightning and thunder in the sky above.[2]

To stop anyone seeing what it looked like outside of time and space and suffering the tragic consequences, the whole mountain was shrouded in thick smoke. But right in the center, Moses was chosen to enter the maelstrom—one human facing Yah-weh God alone.

And after this risky unique encounter with Yah-weh, Moses returned down from the mountain holding the two stones carved by Yah-weh with his instructions. But he didn't just have the stones to show for his meeting with Yah-weh. His face glowed.[3] He had been at the limits of human viability looking into eternity, facing timelessness. His body was reflecting eternity—irradiated by the charged atmosphere that exists outside of the Universe.

Despite the opening titles of "The Simpsons," radiation doesn't give you a green glow. It just kills you. But Moses wasn't dead. He was very much alive because he wasn't irradiated by earthly nuclear fission. Instead, he was temporarily showing signs of becoming super-human—of being the sort of human who could live in an area open to the outside of the Universe—the sort of human we could have been if we hadn't blown it as a human race and had the Door to beyond the Universe slammed in our faces in Eden.[4] Many years later, one man would show the same super-human irradiation again for a brief time, but this time this man would open up a permanent way for humanity to have a chance to be super-human—to be the people God designed them to be. But well over a thousand years of His Story would have to elapse before this human was on earth.[5]

Moses' strange glow was linked to the two stones he carried down the mountain—two stones written on by Yah-weh-God himself.[6] These two stones would eventually be stored in the strange magical mysterious

2. Exodus 19:1–25.
3. Exodus 34:29–35.
4. Genesis 3:22–24.
5. Mark 9:2–3.
6. Exodus 31:18.

box[7] called "the Ark of Covenant," which itself was stored in a special tent. This tent became known as the "Tent of Meeting"—the portable Doorway between the human beings' representative, Moses and the Divine Being's representative, Yah-weh. The Tent of Meeting was carried whenever God ordered Family Abraham to move. It became a mobile Mount Sinai—a mysterious transportable Doorway to beyond the Universe.

But the instructions on the stones weren't magical or mysterious. They weren't strange or secretive. They were very down to earth. Ten instructions: ten ways to live successfully as a human.[8] They were quite simple and could be divided into two distinct sections.

The first dealt with the central issue of His Story so far—how humans were always to remember that they had been created and that they had a Creator. This was important. Noah had remembered this. Abraham had remembered this. Now as Family Abraham were beginning their epic journey to become Nation Isra-El, they needed to remember this.

So, "No two-timing Yah-weh—there is no other Creator God." God had no rivals in his Kingdom outside the Universe—he wasn't just Family Abraham's deity, he was God of everything.

Also, "No pretending that anyone or anything else in the Universe is equal to Creator God." This was to include treating yourself as your own god.

And again, "No disrespecting Yah-weh the Creator," especially after he had shown great respect to Family Abraham by revealing to them his personal name that up to then had remained hidden.

The second section dealt with how respect for Yah-weh should make Family Abraham behave. The people were to be told that there was to be "No disrespecting Yah-weh by leaving him out of the weekly routine." Family Abraham were to show that they hadn't forgotten that Yah-weh was their Creator by stopping their usual business and their work one day a week. It probably cost them financially, but regardless of this they were to stop. Instead of rushing around "24/7" pretending they could build themselves a successful life by their own non-stop puny efforts, they were to stop and let Creator Yah-weh re-create them. At the end of his work of Creation, Yah-weh stopped, rested and reflected.[9] Yah-weh's instructions were clear—what was good enough for him was good enough for his greatest creation—humanity.

In addition there was to be "No disrespecting the people Yah-weh put in charge of his fundamental unit of creation, namely parents." Yah-weh had decided to save his Universe starting with one family. Family to Yah-weh

---

7. Exodus 25:16.
8. Exodus 20:1–17; Deuteronomy 5:6–21.
9. Genesis 2:2–3.

was crucial. Disrespect of the heads of the family unit unzipped Yah-weh's basic building block of creation. Respecting the family unit would bring success for generation after generation and would keep peace in the land that would become known as Isra-El.

Leading on from this there was to be "No disrespecting the exclusivity of the creative gift Yah-weh had given the heads of the family unit." Sex was Yah-weh's gift to humanity designed to serve the fundamental unit of the family and not for any other use. Yah-weh had made a contract with the family of humanity and he expected that each human family would respect their contract to each other and not break the exclusive bond of family loyalty.

Then followed rules for the wider family of humanity. At heart was the fundamental rule of "No disrespecting Yah-weh's greatest act of creation by hurting and destroying humanity." No human was to think that their right to life was greater than others—that some other humans in the family of humanity were a waste of space that could be got rid of on their personal whim—murdered. All humans were Yah-weh's creation. All humans were created equal—all one family.

There was also to be respect for each member of the human family's wider rights. "No disrespecting another human's legal right to possess their own possessions by trying to steal them." True, no one owned the world apart from Yah-weh and the whole of the family of humanity was simply borrowing it from Yah-weh as global tenants. But landlord Yah-weh's rule for letting humanity live in his creation was that no human had the right to try and own another human or his possessions. No human was to act like they were God.

The last two rules were more philosophical but with very practical outcomes. Firstly—"No disrespecting the role of truth." Yah-weh was the basis of everything. He was the fundamental truth underlying Creation. At the heart of Yah-weh's relationship with Family Abraham was promises based on truth—contract. Yah-weh promised to Abraham and he kept his promise. So no member of Family Abraham was to tell lies about other people to gain an unfair advantage. Yah-weh was truth and had built his creation on truth. Lies de-create and de-struct his Creation.

Secondly—"No disrespecting the person Yah-weh has made you to by wishing constantly you were living someone else's life." There was to be no obsession with what you hadn't got—coveting other people's possessions and lifestyle. Life for Family Abraham wasn't to be about being like other people-groups—trying to be like them. This was to live a lie. Yah-weh had made Family Abraham unique and special. There was to be no worship of any other part of Yah-weh's creation instead of the Creator. Each human's ambition was to become the person God made them to be, instead of desperately trying to be the person the rest of humanity seductively coerced them to be.

This last rule loops back to the first instructions clearly stating that humanity works best when it worships the Creator and his plans and directions and doesn't worship other powerful forces or ways of life.

Ten ways to live: ten distinctive clauses in a new contract; ten crucial rules; ten commandments of Yah-weh which have become the core of human ethics. These rules weren't designed as a way for humans to show off to Yah-weh—to prove to him how good they were. These were rules to help save humanity from disaster. They were given by Yah-weh-God who had saved them and had shown he had their best interests at heart. All of these rules must be read in the context of Yah-weh's introduction to his Ten Rules: "Remember—I am the God who brought you out of Egypt—out of slavery. No forgetting that I am the Creator who looks after his creation." These rules were to help Family Abraham remember that Yah-weh didn't want to spoil their lives but save them. These rules gave humans crucial basic information about what their creator Yah-weh was like and what pleased him. What pleased him was seeing his Family safe and successful.

These rules became the small print of Yah-weh's promise to his baby nation Isra-El—the glue that held nation Isra-El together. Everybody was the same. Everyone from Moses to the most average, insignificant, small member of the nation Isra-El had to keep the law.

But the rules still are relevant to us over three thousand years later. The central point of Yah-weh's laws can easily be missed. The point is so obvious to us humans who have lived in the years since Yah-weh wrote on the stones, that we can miss it. The laws point to the central core of Yah-weh: his character; his personality; His Story—who he is; who he always was, and who he always will be—the great I am. At heart, Yah-weh is against all that corrupts humans and makes them forget that they are made by him. Yah-weh is against all that de-creates humans and makes them appear nothing more than another animal, even if a very clever and sophisticated animal. Humans are more than this. Humans are made just like him. Yah-weh is against unfaithfulness: disrespect; cruelty; injustice; materialism, and greed.

These ten rules expanded in time to various laws which ranged from protection of the poor and the foreigner; to health and safety; to marriage; to care of animals; to limiting violence; to the avoidance of sexual exploitation; to respect for the elderly not to mention more productive agricultural and farming practices.[10]

---

10. Deuteronomy 19–25.

But the core is about one thing—Yah-weh is good. He is all powerful. He is all mighty. He is a monopoly. He is without an equal, but he chooses to use his power and freedom to be moral. He could have been an evil dictator. He could have been a despot—a totalitarian evil ruler. He could have been capricious—one day moral, the next immoral; one day good, the next day evil. Instead, he is consistently moral—that is his personality. Yah-weh is good.

Nation Isra-El was going to be great, powerful, mighty and at points, without an equal. But would they be evil and immoral? Humans are great, powerful with almost limitless power to choose evil. But would they follow the maker's instructions and example and be moral? Isra-El's future: the world's future—hanging in the balance before Moses made his way down the mountain. The world was made by Yah-weh to work best when people are moral—when people follow the Maker's Instructions. Yah-weh promised it. And now Isra-El had to keep their side of the contract. The contract was sealed by Moses on humanity's behalf, not by a signature but by the blood of young sacrificed bulls.[11]

Sacrifice of animals had continued to be the way that humans tried to show they appreciated God's instructions and that they meant it when they said they would keep the rules. They sacrificed the life-blood of animals to show their "cross my heart and hope to die" attitude. Sacrifice cost Noah some of his precious animals when he thanked Yah-weh for promising never again to flood the world.[12] It nearly cost Abraham the life of his special son, when he thanked Yah-weh for promising to make his family a great nation—a lamb's blood was used instead.[13] It cost a lamb its life in every household to cause death to "pass-over" before the great escape from Egypt.[14] And by blood Isra-El had promised to keep their side of the contract—to behave like Yah-weh.

To be good.

---

11. Exodus 24:1–8.
12. Genesis 8:20–21.
13. Genesis 22:1–18.
14. Exodus 12:21–30.

## 17

## Broken

THE CONTRACT BETWEEN YAH-WEH and his family lasted intact all but a few hours. Even before Moses had had a chance to tell the baby nation Isra-El the terms of the new contract, it had been broken.[1] The people who were meant to be waiting patiently for Moses to re-appear from the threshold of beyond the Universe, had already broken several of the laws before Moses returned. These people wanted to get on and make their own future without hanging around for Yah-weh to send Moses back down the mountain. Baby nation Isra-El was impatient. Baby nation Isra-El wanted to get on. Baby nation Isra-El had people and gods they wanted to see. In particular they had a few more of Yah-weh's laws to break.

But surely they had learnt to trust Yah-weh and Moses—after all Yah-weh and Moses had just rescued them from oppression in Egypt. But maybe they were just a little bit scared on their own as they waited. They certainly seemed edgy and impatient. They might have thought that Moses had decided to leave them, or dematerialized into the hole in the Universe.

Whatever the cause, Moses was taking a long time. And so the people complained about their missing leader to Moses' brother, Aaron. He suggested they gave him all their gold. And they did: because he was there and Moses wasn't; because he was there and Yah-weh was up the mountain. And Aaron decided to throw all the gold into a fire. And all the gold melted and reshaped itself into an image of a calf—just like that (or so Aaron claimed later, breaking the ninth law and the first and second in one go). Out popped a golden calf—a worship image used in fertility worship by the people living around Family Abraham. This type of worship involved as much random alcohol fuelled sexual activity as possible just to wake up the god of fertility and make sure he or she smiled on you and made your animals and crops fertile, never mind your fellow humans. So they probably broke rule six as well.

---

1. Exodus 32:1—33:6.

When Moses eventually descended down the mountain and saw what they had done, he had a tantrum. He threw down the stones and smashed them. God's stones; God's law—smashed; broken.

What was his brother's excuse? It was all an accident. It always is—it's never our fault. But despite a 70 percent failure rate on the first day of road-trialing the new laws, Yah-weh gave his people a second chance. But only after Moses had persuaded Yah-weh not to tear up his contract with the fledgling nation Isra-El and build a nation on Moses instead.[2]

So, a new set of stones.[3] This time dictated by Yah-weh and carved onto stone by Moses—a new opportunity. But this didn't happen until after the golden calf had been ground up into dust and put into the drinking water and the people forced to drink it. They were made to own their failure—literally. The secret of any success with Yah-weh from now on was going to be drawn from owning up to failure. As a famous believer in Yah-weh would say many hundreds of years later, "When I admit my weakness, then I am strong."[4] This strength was to come through admitting failure; this strength was gained by asking Yah-weh to forgive and forget and give a second chance.

The hardest thing for any human ever to say and mean still is, "I messed up." The hardest words for any human to say and mean continues to be, "I am sorry." But these are hard words which are like music to Yah-weh's ears. A later follower of Yah-weh would say, "If we never admit to being wrong, we are liars; but if we admit and say sorry to our wrongdoing, Yah-weh is faithful and will always forgive us."[5]

And so a journey which took the tiny embryonic baby nation Isra-El to powerful internationally acclaimed nationhood began by Family Abraham saying, "sorry". And so also began the ethical journey for humanity—a journey starting and continuing with God speaking clearly through the Doorway. The Ten Laws were at the heart of a whole growing rule book. Now Isra-El had no excuse about not knowing how Yah-weh wanted them to live.

The Ten Laws and the additional small print didn't end Yah-weh's guidance. Whenever Yah-weh had some more specific instructions for his people, he called Moses. Moses then went into the special Tent of Meeting to speak with Yah-weh. They met in the mobile Doorway—in the special tent that held the heavy golden box now filled with the law stones. This box

2. Exodus 32:9–14.
3. Exodus 34:1–28.
4. 2 Corinthians 12:10.
5. 1 John 1:9–10.

had a special name—the Ark of the Covenant or Contract. Just as Noah's Ark had saved humanity, this Ark was going to save humanity again, not from flood, but from the evil the flood had come to wash away. At the heart of this new baby nation was a great weapon to oppose evil—Yah-weh's law. This law was the terms and conditions of a new contract between humanity and Yah-weh—the moral God.

After Noah's Ark, God had written the rainbow promise of "never again" in the sky: after Moses' Ark, that promise had been set in stone.

# 18

## Our Story or His Story?

THE GREAT, GREAT, GREAT grandson of Judah, Nahshon—the brave paddler up to his neck in the Reed Sea—didn't just live through the great Mount Sinai contract signing event, he appears also to have continued to be a key part of this new moment for Family Abraham. Moses appointed Nahshon as the "Prince of the tribe of Judah"—a great leader but not the prince of Judah promised in Jacob's blessing.[1] But nonetheless he was a vital ancestor of the coming hero—the Super-star of His Story.

However, the most vital thing Nahshon did, that we know about, was to pass on his genes and his destiny to his son. His son had the name, Salmon.[2] Salmon was born on the journey from Egypt to the Promised Land: from slavery to freedom; from extended family to nation. Salmon experienced the highs and lows. He lived through times of hunger, thirst, fighting, fear and opportunities taken and missed. He must have experienced Yah-weh's frustration and anger.

Salmon also experienced Yah-weh's strong guidance. When Yah-weh's special other-worldly "shekinah" cloud lifted up from above the Tent where Moses met with Yah-weh, everyone broke camp and followed, until the cloud stopped again.

In addition, Salmon experienced Yah-weh's protection from other people-groups who didn't like the new kids on the block. Take the battle against the Amalekites for example. When Moses lifted his famous stick with super-natural powers high above his head, the fighters from Family Abraham were successful. The battle raged for a long time, so as Moses' muscles spasmed, he had to sit down and have his arms propped up in position by others.[3] As long as the stick was held high, the power from beyond

---

1. Numbers 2:3.
2. 1 Chronicles 2:11.
3. Exodus 17:8–16.

the Doorway channeled through Moses. Even though Moses' human strength faded, Yah-weh's power didn't fade and baby Isra-El won the day.

Salmon also enjoyed Yah-weh's generosity. From water released out of rock by Moses' powerful shepherd's stick,[4] to weird daily food that appeared on the ground in the morning known as "manna"—meaning in their language, "what-you-call-it," Yah-weh's help kept on powering through the Doorway. Later as a welcome variation of menu, Yah-weh also provided meat that dropped out of the air in the form of birds (quail) exhausted in migratory flight.[5]

Salmon was also protected by a developing legal system; inspired by a worship system; and defended by a military system. All these were built on the words of Yah-weh delivered to them by Yah-weh's Mouthpiece, Moses. Through Moses, Yah-weh gave his young nation a growing list of sensible, practical rules—helpful appendices to his contract with his people. Like what to eat and not to eat.[6] In a pre-scientific age when nothing was known about germs, microbes, infection, and environmental health, Yah-weh kept his people healthy by calling some meat "clean" and other meat "unclean." Largely these rules now can be seen as sensible and healthy, like being very careful about eating seafood and pork in an age before refrigeration.

But it wasn't just an exercise in healthy eating. Yah-weh used his food laws to teach about his own deeper rules of health. To follow Yah-weh was to be a healthy human in every way. Following the maker's instructions—his rules for His Story—was good for you.

Holiness is good for you. Holiness is about being other-worldly. But holiness is also very down to earth. Holiness is about letting heaven break through onto earth to help you. Holiness is about living according to the rules from beyond the Doorway helped by out-of-this-world power—and all this whilst still earth-side of the Doorway.

The Door to heaven through Moses was now ajar. A very pale copy of Eden and Paradise was being slowly but surely replanted on earth. God's Kingdom—his Kingly power extending through the Doorway—was growing through Family Abraham and young nation Isra-El. Soon the new nation would be back in the land promised to Abraham—the land they had lived in when they were the small family of Jacob-Isra-El.

Soon, but not that soon. Due to a massive case of cold feet, the journey lasted years longer than it should have done. It could have been so different. The journey was not very old when Yah-weh brought his nation within

---

4. Exodus 17:1–7.
5. Exodus 16:1–36.
6. Leviticus 11; Deuteronomy 14:3–21.

*our story or his story?* 61

striking distance of his Promised Land. He told his people that this was the land he had promised to give them—a land flowing with milk and honey. This land was thick, creamy and sweet compared to the dry, rocky desert they were stuck in. How could his people resist? But after sending out an advance party of spies to sus out whether the occupying peoples were friendly or not, the spies came back with the good news and the bad news. The good news—the land was stacked full of fruit and good things to eat. The bad news—the people who lived there were giants.[7]

Giants versus Yah-weh—who would win? One of Salmon's descendants would in only a generation or two prove it was Yah-weh—even when Yah-weh's champion was a little unarmed boy.[8] But at the moment, only one of the spies, Caleb, had that sort of trust in Yah-weh. As a result, he became the only spy who would survive long enough to live in the Promised Land. All the rest of the spies would find their lack of faith in Yah-weh's protection a self-fulfilling prophecy. They would die before their journey ended. They didn't want to risk their lives to get into Yah-weh's chosen land and so Yah-weh let them keep their lives but never enjoy the real life he had planned.

Faith in Yah-weh is like that. If we want our story to be His Story then we must keep in step with Yah-weh—keep in tune with our Creator Conductor.[9] If we're not bothered whether to align our story with His Story, our story will always be just that—our story and our story alone. We will exist, but not live. His Story is about discovering that God wants to give us his five star life—abundant life.[10]

So, Family Abraham wandered around the desert for another generation at least. Their wanderings were probably around the Sinai Peninsula in Egypt, though some people think they may have gone as far as Saudi Arabia. By the time they eventually arrived on the edge of their old Promised Land, years and years after they could have entered it, they were more than ready for re-occupying their land. Yah-weh was with them, in the center of their life. But Moses soon wouldn't be.[11] Yah-weh wouldn't let him, possibly because even Moses had become too central—too big for his sandals. Maybe sometimes the people lost sight of the leadership of Yah-weh and acted as if Moses was the leader. Maybe sometimes even Moses lost sight of the leadership of Yah-weh and acted as if he was the leader as well. After all Moses was their King-like leader. Moses was their Go-Between, negotiating on their

7. Numbers 13–14.
8. 1 Samuel 17:1–58.
9. Galatians 5:24–25.
10. John 10:10.
11. Numbers 27:12–23; Deuteronomy 3:21–29.

behalf with Yah-weh—like a High Priest. Moses was Yah-weh's Spokesperson to his people, his Mouthpiece—like a Prophet. But amazingly, Moses wasn't Yah-weh's next star on his bloodline. He wasn't going to be the ancestor of God's special chosen one.

Moses accepted his fate. He saw that Yah-weh in the years to come was going to cause another leader to rise up—a leader who would be the greatest leader ever—the Messiah—a man who would be the greatest Go-Between, linking the whole of humanity with Yah-weh. He would also be the greatest Spokesperson for Yah-weh—a leader modelled on Moses but greater than even him.[12] He would be the one Yah-weh was writing His Story about; the one who would have the ultimate starring role—the Super-star of His Story. Yah-weh had told Moses previously about this special man. He had said, "I will raise up out of Family Abraham a man like you. I will put my words in his mouth. He will by my Mouthpiece to tell the Family everything I command him. Whoever doesn't listen to this prophet will have to answer to me!"[13]

As for Moses, he was allowed to climb another mountain and see the Promised Land from across the river Jordan.[14]. It would be the closest he would ever get to the land of his ancestors. His journey was over and he was soon to die. Instead, Yah-weh's chosen successor to Moses, Joshua, was going to lead the new nation of Isra-El into the Promised Land. But before he did, he sent yet another group of spies ahead to infiltrate and find out the weaknesses of the occupying peoples.[15]

The first great barrier they encountered wasn't giants like the last time, but the walled city of Jericho—a city with massive defense systems and an impenetrable locked door. Jericho—the gateway city to the Promised Land. Finding a blind spot in their security systems was going to be difficult. But the spies found it. Its name was Rahab. Or more correctly "her" name was Rahab.

Rahab lived in the outer defenses of Jericho—in the wall itself. From there she ran a business: not a flower shop; not a hairdressers; not even a beauty salon—more a massage parlor with extras. Rahab was not holy or other-worldly or heavenly. But still she was an ally of heaven. She hid the spies from the Jericho police and sent the pursuing authorities in the wrong direction. She was Family Abraham's very own inside agent in fortified Jericho.

12. Hebrews 3:1–6.
13. Deuteronomy 18:17–19.
14. Deuteronomy 34:1–12.
15. Joshua 2:1–24.

But she was so much more than even this. Unlike Moses, she was going to become part of the bloodline that would produce the great Mouthpiece of Yah-weh—the Super-star of His Story. She was going to hook up with Salmon—a fishy story? No—His Story. Into the special bloodline of Yahweh's chosen family tree came a prostitute.[16] Not only was she a prostitute, she was a foreign prostitute. Why was such an unlikely woman part of His Story? Who knows? Who cares? All that matters is that through Rahab, the Prince of Judah would eventually arrive. All that matters is that through Rahab, the re-taking of the Promised Land would start. All that matters is that through Rahab, the walls of Jericho would fall.

And the gate to the Promised Land would be wide open.

---

16. Matthew 1:5.

# 19

# Kill or be Killed

BEFORE ATTACKING THE PROMISED Land's entrance city of Jericho, there was the barrier of the River Jordan in full flood. But just as the Great Escape from Egypt started with Yah-weh draining a water barrier, it finished with the same—this time not triggered by Moses or even his successor, Joshua, but triggered by the Ark that contained the Law. Noah's Ark had defeated the flood waters.[1] Now the Ark of the Contract would defeat the flood waters of the Jordan.[2]

Yah-weh explained this to his new leader, Joshua, in advance. He encouraged him that he would keep his side of the legal agreement. He instructed him to, "Get ready to cross the Jordan into my promised land. I will give you every bit of ground you set your foot on. Remember: just as I was with Moses I will be with you."[3]

But every legal contract has two sides. Joshua and all the leaders had to keep their side of the contract. They had to keep Yah-weh's Law. Yah-weh was insistent that they all had to, "be careful to obey all the law—don't turn away from it to the right or the left if you want success. This law must be your food and drink, day and night."[4] The small print of this contract was written on the stones in the Ark. Yah-weh would keep his side of the contract and the result would be powerful. Heaven and earth united—like at Mount Sinai.

It was a no-brainer—Yah-weh promised prosperity and success. He ordered that his people should be strong and very brave; not terrified; not discouraged because he was going to be with them all of the way—wherever they went.[5]

1. Genesis 6–8.
2. Joshua 3:1–17.
3. Joshua 1:2–5.
4. Joshua 1:7–8.
5. Joshua 1:8b–9.

Yah-weh's presence on earth was going to be represented by His Story's new central character. Not Moses, or any other human—but the contract written on the stones. As soon as the Go-Betweens carried the Ark to the Jordan with Yah-weh's rule stones in it, the waters of the great river stood up on either side. The message from Yah-weh was obvious. The way forward for Family Abraham was to follow the Law. Follow Yah-weh's words; follow Yah-weh's writings; and even armed up-to-the-teeth, Jericho, wouldn't be able to stand in their way.

But before attacking Jericho, Yah-weh explained to Joshua the strategy. It was an important team talk. To deliver it, Yah-weh entered the world once more. He stepped through the Doorway into human existence as a human—again. But this time not as a guest at Abraham's tent, but dressed as a great commander of an army.[6]

What was the strategy? The commander explained that the Ark containing the out-of-this-world law was to be carried round Jericho's walls, once a day for six days, accompanied by trumpets blowing and followed by the army doing nothing: no fighting; no human intervention.[7] On the seventh day—the holy day—Yah-weh's set aside day—it was to be carried round seven times.

Seven—a powerful number for Isra-El. The seventh "day" was the day when God had stopped working on his new creation—the Universe. This had become the day that marked out God's Family—the day when God's people stopped working. It was called the Sabbath—the Day of Rest—the day when Family Abraham stopped working and took time off to remember that God was in charge of the routines of their lives. This was the day that marked Isra-El out as being different—marching to a different beat—a beat that was other-worldly. This was the day that channeled out-of-this-world power into the every-day—into the every-week. This was the day identified by the rules in the Ark of the Covenant.

God rested on the seventh day after creating his perfect Universe. On the seventh day the entrance to his new land for Isra-El would swing open. And of course it was on the seventh circuit around Jericho on the seventh day that the army and all the people of Isra-El were to stop working and shout instead. No fighting—nothing else but a shout. And when they obeyed, the walls crumbled as in an earthquake. No fighting—just following Yah-weh's rules as they followed behind Yah-weh's rule box.

---

6. Joshua 5:13–15.
7. Joshua 6:1–21.

In the past a water barrier had been overcome. Now a solid barrier was overcome. Bricks had been a barrier to Yah-weh's people in the past—but no longer.

What happened next will attract you and repel you all at once. Yah-weh's holiness is like that. He is awesome. But awesome is a way of saying awe-full and awe-full should be spelt "awful." This word sums up Yah-weh's holiness. No human must be blasé when the outside power of the Universe meets the inside. Family Abraham needed to learn that you don't mess with Yah-weh, even when he has generously revealed his secret name and secret rules to you.

How did they learn this? By the way Yah-weh told them to treat anyone who tried to block, stop, or mess with His Story—they were all to be destroyed. And so after the easy defeat of now defenseless Jericho, Yah-weh ordered every citizen of Jericho to be killed—not raped or tortured—but still killed.

Can such carnage be justified? Remember, it was an age when there was no United Nations; no international Law; no international conventions or court; no developed international diplomatic relationships; no Human Rights. It was just dog eat dog—kill or be killed. Family Abraham was going back to the region where Jacob and his boys had lived before moving to Egypt to find food and the long lost Joseph. But now the Family wasn't small—it was massive in number. It was the embryonic nation Isra-El needing its homeland back. But since the Family members had left their homeland, many people had started to call their home "home." These peoples didn't want Jacob's boys and their families to return. The new challenge to Family Abraham was how to survive long enough to follow Yah-weh's instructions—without being exterminated.

One way forward was to assimilate to the peoples in the Promised Land—to become just like them, instead of just like Yah-weh. But Yah-weh's holiness wouldn't allow this. It would have been the end of His Story: no distinctive people; no role model for humanity; no His Story.

In the midst of the bloodbath, some things had to be saved, in particular, Rahab—Yah-weh's secret agent and her family, not to mention all the precious metals of Jericho.[8] These were Yah-weh's, not the booty of the army—to remind them of who actually won the battle. So, no pillaging—no spoils of war.

And so began a time of battles and wars and blood and gore; mainly victories but also some notable defeats when the people ignored Yah-weh's instructions. It was a time that none of us would have wanted to live through.

---

8. Joshua 6:22–27.

We may well disapprove of the bloodshed. We may well wonder whether Yah-weh behaved morally. We may well wonder whether his plan for showing his world the right way to live was bought at too great a price. But before we stand in judgment over the Creator, let's be careful to remember that many of us still believe that in certain circumstances force is needed for good to defeat evil. Yah-weh was building a force for good that would have to take on evil—a people of Law; a people built on morality and justice. He was building a people who would not survive if they did not fight for their existence. The enemies of this people were certainly not all pillars of morality and goodness. In fact, most of them were violent, cruel and immoral.

But if you still cannot forgive Yah-weh and his new nation, remember that at this point, His Story is still in its infancy—still in its first few chapters. In fact, it is still in its first section.

Section One: The Old Contract—The Old Testament—the pre-quel to the main story. This would turn out to be the foundation of the second section: The New Contract—the New Testament—the main event.

The New Contract would be totally built on the foundation of the old, but introducing the "Prince of Judah"—the human at the end of the bloodline we are following: the human who would complete and fulfil the line we are following; the human who would live in the way Yah-weh truly wanted humans to live; the human who when being tortured and murdered by his enemies for a crime he didn't commit would say, "Forgive them for they don't know what they are doing."[9] No revenge. No fighting. A revolutionary new way of winning by choosing what looks like defeat.

But this revolutionary idea would not have not been possible over three thousand years ago. Family Abraham was not ready to give the world this radical new way of life. Equally, the world was not ready to receive this radical new way of life. We cannot stand in judgment over Yah-weh until after the "Prince of Judah." We must wait until history and His Story moves on over a thousand years. We must wait until the great descendant of the prostitute Rahab.

After the conquest of the Promised Land by Isra-El, Rahab was saved from the destruction of Jericho by hanging a red sign out of her window—not a red light, but a red cord—a sign that her family should be saved from the destruction. After being saved, she then uniquely participated in Yah-weh's plan to save the whole of humanity.

She married one young man we've already met—Salmon.

---

9. Luke 22:34.

## 20

## Follow the Leader?

It wasn't all gloom and doom; blood and gore; battles and fighting. Love and affection also blossomed in between the battlefields. As Isra-El began to settle down in their new home, Salmon met the ex-Jericho inhabitant and Isra-Eli secret agent, Rahab, and fell in love.

The romantics believe Salmon was one of the spies sent to Jericho—one of those hidden by Rahab—saved by her quick thinking.[1] And eternally grateful to her for protection, Salmon's heart was won by her for ever. In return he saved her from her immoral life in Jericho and made her into an honest woman! But who knows how it really happened? What is known is that they met; they married and they produced a child. A child called, Boaz.[2]

Boaz lived at a time of great uncertainty for Isra-El in their new home. This was a time when the war of re-occupation was won but a time when the peace was yet to be won. On top of this uncertainty came an additional dramatic challenge—Joshua died. Joshua—the great military leader—the last human link with Moses their great savior. Who would lead now? Before Joshua died, he renewed again the legal contract between Yah-weh and Family Abraham. In this act he told them straight that their leader was the Lord. He then gave them a history lesson from His Story, highlighting all the main events and Yah-weh's part in them. At the end, the people of Isra-El dutifully responded, "We will serve the Lord."[3]

The "Lord" was beginning to be a title for Yah-weh. It was not so much his name, but his position of power. He was the Lord; their Lord; their Boss; their Chief; their Leader. But this couldn't hide the fact that there was a vacuum of human leadership after Joshua. Vacuums suck in and into this vacuum of human leadership was sucked a succession of leaders. They weren't accidentally drawn in, they were specifically called and empowered by Yah-weh to protect his people by constantly bringing Isra-El and their

---

1. Joshua 2:1–24.
2. Ruth 4:21; Matthew 1:5.
3. Joshua 24:1–27.

enemies under the judgment of Yah-weh's Law. This role gave them a nickname—Judges. They were all flamboyant. They were all colorful. They were all larger than life. They didn't all live up to Yah-weh's high standards; but they all had a vital part to play in His Story.

Take Ehud for example.[4] When King Eglon of the Moabites was trying to oppress Isra-El, Ehud was sent to pay protection money to him. But instead he assassinated him—in the toilet with a sword. King Eglon was so fat, it is recorded that Ehud lost his sword in the King's majestic royal obesity.

Take Shamgar.[5] He tackled the terrorist sea-people (the Philistines) using only a cattle-prodder.

Take Deborah.[6] When the Family of Isra-El was being attacked by the enemy King Jabin, she planned a strategy to defeat the King's army commander, Sisera. She arranged for this plan to be put into practice by Barak her right hand man. Literally her right hand man as it turned out, as Barak wouldn't fight without holding Deborah's hand. In an era when women weren't famed for their leadership, Deborah was the boss. She wore the chain-mail trousers—embarrassing for Barak—an embarrassment that got worse when victory was actually secured by another woman called Jael. She was the wife of a friend of the enemy commander, Sisera. When Sisera ran into her husband's tent to hide from Deborah, Jael killed him as he lay down to hide, pinning him to the ground with a tent-peg smashed through his skull into the ground with a mallet.

Take Samson.[7] He was another special child born by the Lord's direct through-the-Doorway intervention. He was a child dedicated to the Lord for life; a child who in return was to be filled with the Lord's invisible power—his Spirit. [8] He was a child who due to this dedication was never meant to be full of alcoholic spirit, but was—often. He was a child who was to be different—special—shown by him never drinking alcohol and never cutting his hair. His big hair was to be a symbol of his over-sized out-of-this-world gift of strength.

But he was a child who never grew up. A childish man who was selfish—always a servant to his own desires and wants; a childish man who was a violent womanizer with an addictive personality. Samson thought only about himself—not the Lord. If he wanted it, he had to have it: food; women; laughs; fun. Nothing and nobody stood in his way including the

4. Judges 3:12–30.
5. Judges 3:31.
6. Judges 4–5.
7. Judges 13–16.
8. Judges 13:2–5.

Sea People—Isra-El's great new rival people group called the Philistines. He toyed with the Philistines—one moment befriending, even marrying them—the next attacking them with anything that lay to hand—like a donkey's jawbone.[9] In his hand this particular non-conventional offensive weapon killed a thousand men. Samson commented afterwards that he had made an ass of them all.[10]

Some special children grow up to be child geniuses—prodigies. This special child grew up to be stronger than anyone else, but with a will power weaker than anyone else. If he wanted it he just couldn't stop himself going for it. He just couldn't help himself helping himself to it—whatever it was—good or bad (usually bad). Nothing or nobody stood in his way—not even the secret symbol of his dedication—his special promise to the Lord to never have a haircut.

He gave this secret away to a foreign prostitute, Delilah, in return for her attention. She arranged for him to have a short back and sides. The result was that he was honey-trapped; he was ambushed—caught with his guard down (amongst other things). In particular, he was caught with his powerful link to beyond the Universe offline.[11] As he was shaved of his hair he became denuded of his power. He lost his freedom and was led away handcuffed to be made into a circus act for the Philistines. After being blinded, he was made to perform at the Philistines' religious festival. He was weak, but then he did something he might never have done before—he prayed.[12] He talked to God. He talked to the Lord. He talked to his long forgotten Lord. Had he had a conversion experience? Did he utter a prayer saying he was sorry for wasting his gift—a prayer saying he was sorry for not living up to the Lord's gift of life for him? No—a prayer instead for revenge on the Philistine people—to get his own back. His hair had begun to grow again and so had his confidence. Despite being chained to a pillar in the Philistine's Temple dedicated to their created god, he pushed and prayed. And the pillars holding the roof fell down.

It was said that he killed more Philistines in that one act of suicide than he did in all his life. The similarity of his life to a suicide bomber is too close for comfort. He wasn't good—but he was effective. There is no doubt that Samson bought Isra-El breathing space and time to establish themselves in the Promised Land, despite being bullied constantly by their vicious neighbors.

9. Judges 15:15.
10. Judges 15:16.
11. Judges 16:1–22.
12. Judges 16:23–30.

Samson might have been full of the Lord's Spirit but he wasn't full of the Lord's character. Samson wasn't moral. Samson wasn't good. Samson wasn't the leader the Family needed. He was simply your big brother who stops you being bullied at school.

But the Judges weren't all psychopathic loners who happened to be on your side. They weren't all bullies who the Lord used and empowered for one-off rescues. Some were beginning to be inspirational and aspirational leaders. Some started to display some of the leadership and character the Lord needed on earth. Some displayed the Lord's own leadership qualities and character—his Spirit.

Take Gideon, for example.[13] Family Abraham were scared. Every time they tried to settle down to a regular life of planting and harvesting, they were attacked by the Midianites; the Amalekites and other assorted "ites" from the east. They came on raiding parties and fast camels—the blitzkrieg technique of the day. They waited until you had come out of your caves and hiding holes; until you had started to become a little bit confident that the worst was past. And then they hit you—again and again.

They appeared from nowhere with their animals and tents. They were like a swarm of locusts—stealing and eating and using and destroying—everything. They made domesticated bliss in the land flowing with milk and honey impossible. The milk and honey had gone sour.

The Lord decided to use this threat to Isra-El to remind them of their contract with him—to remind them that there are two sides to every contract. Isra-El had to keep their side of the bargain—they had to keep the Law. But first he needed a strong, charismatic, powerful leader to reassure his people.

Step forward Gideon. The Lord decided to open the Door into the Universe once again. This time the Lord stepped through not in human form, but in an alien form known as "angelic." The angel (who was really the Lord) called to Gideon as he was hiding his wheat in a winepress to try and fool the Midianites into thinking he didn't have anything worth stealing. Gideon wasn't exactly stepping forward bravely onto the stage of human history. He was sensible but not heroic. But despite him not being hero-material, the angel-Lord called to him, "The Lord is with you, mighty warrior."[14]

The irony would not have been lost on Gideon: mighty warrior—hiding his wheat; mighty warrior—living with his parents. But Gideon did have enough guts to question the Lord. He asked him why all these bad things were happening to the Lord's Family if the Lord was with them. He asked

13. Judges 6–8.
14. Judges 6:12.

him where the Lord who saved them from Egypt was now. He asked the sort of questions many people have asked the Lord down the years when faced with hard times and certainly they ask them now in the twenty-first century. Gideon was very modern. He was very much like us—questioning God: asking whether God is the Lord; whether God is really in charge. The Lord didn't answer the specific question, he simply asked Gideon to trust him. He rarely does answer our specific questions, even now, he usually simply challenges us to trust him and to prove that trust by following his instructions.

Trust is living by the little faith we have in an all mighty God. But little faith is big in the hands of an all-mighty God—it can even move mountains.[15] The Lord said to Gideon, "Go in the strength you have and save the Family from the Midianites." And just to give him a little encouragement, he added for good measure, "Isn't it me who is sending you?" Enough said you would think. But the Gideon who was brave enough to answer the Lord back wasn't brave when it came to being a mighty warrior. He was brave enough to discuss with the Lord his theories about why the Lord wasn't to be trusted. But not brave enough to test his own theories—just like us. Gideon came up with every reason why the Lord had got the wrong person: he was the most insignificant in his family; his close family was the most insignificant in the tribe; his tribe was the most insignificant in the extended Family Abraham.[16] The Lord's repeated, "I will be with you" destroyed that line of defense. Not to be outdone, Gideon countered with, "Prove it!" He was deadly serious. And Gideon showed this by offering the Lord a sacrifice. He took some of his remaining scarce valuable meat and bread and brought them out to the angel of the Lord. The Lord touched it with the tip of the staff in his hand—heaven touching earth; eternal touching mortal; timeless touching time; the outside of the Universe touching the inside.[17] The result was the same as normal—a mini Mount Sinai. Fire blazed out and vaporized everything including the Lord disguised as an angel.

Gideon panicked. He knew that the created can't mix with the Creator and live. What happened to the meat and bread would happen to him. But the invisible Lord called him and reassured him and gave him a task to destroy his father's altar to the fertility gods worshipped by many of the peoples who lived in the land around where Family Abraham had settled.[18] The altar was dedicated to one god called "Baal". It meant in the local language "Lord."

15. Matthew 17:20.
16. Judges 6:15–16.
17. Judges 6:19–22.
18. Judges 6:25–32.

Gideon's father like so many in Israel was trying to keep God's law but not exclusively. Gideon's father was hedging his bets. Gideon's father was saying that he trusted the Lord, but not giving him exclusive rights. That he ironically had more than one "Lord." He, like many like him, had forgotten Yah-weh's first laws: laws about exclusivity; laws about faithfulness—not wanting your cake and eat it—not "playing away"—or whatever you choose to call it; in a word—commitment. Just like us, Gideon's father and many in Isra-El had commitment issues. The issue being that they didn't like being committed; they didn't like being restricted. Instead, they wanted freedom to choose when and how they were committed to the Lord—just like Adam and Eve. Just like humanity. Just like us.

This half-heartedness was no good to the Lord. His Story needed a distinctive, holy people: to save humanity; to lead humanity by their example; to lead humanity back to the Lord the Creator; to be the Lord's representatives on earth. But the Lord's special people wanted to be ordinary: to be the same as everyone else; to assimilate; to not stand out—just like us. But Gideon was different. Gideon did as he was told by the Lord and destroyed his father's altar to gods who weren't real gods. At night—granted—and without telling anyone he had done it. But still he did it. There was hell to pay next day. But it got Gideon noticed as a man who knew his own mind.

But before Gideon was lynched by the Baal supporters, the Amalekites appeared—again. And something happened that up to this point had only happened very rarely. The Spirit of the Lord—the invisible, eternal, holy power and personality of the Lord—broke into a human being. A human being became briefly connected to the Doorway of the Universe: heaven on earth; the Creator in the Created without destruction of the created. It was a sort of second creation of humanity for a brief moment—the Lord working not only through Gideon but in Gideon.

Gideon became the Lord's mighty warrior. He called Family Abraham to follow him. And they did—thirty-two thousand of them. There was no explanation for this, except that the Lord was true to his promise—his contract. But despite this amazing following, Gideon still was not a 100 percent convinced. He still asked for another trick by the Lord to prove he wasn't dreaming. He wanted the Lord to a make a sheep's fleece left overnight on the floor to be wet with dew and the ground around dry. The Lord complied.[19] No mean feat as this trick broke the so called "laws of nature." Gideon then asked for the same trick the other way round—dew on ground but bone dry fleece. And again the Lord complied.

---

19. Judges 6:36–40.

Miracles to the Lord are just exceptions that prove the rule. The Lord as Creator by definition isn't bound by any laws. The Lord (if he is Lord) must be the Lord of the laws of nature. Science is his plaything—his servant. Scientists at best think his thoughts after him—discover his creative mind. That's not to say that for our sanity, safety and scientific knowledge, the Lord rarely deviates from his normal working practices—our so called scientific "rules." The laws of nature enable us to live in an ordered way in the Lord's ordered creation. If solid objects suddenly without warning became gases or liquids or gravity inexplicably lost its power, human life would be impossible—chaotic—back to the time before God brought order out of chaos. But sometimes the Lord intervenes—rarely and only because the higher purpose of His Story dictates.

And for now it did. Gideon needed reassurance so he could battle against the Amalekites, Midianites and other allied "ites" with confidence. This battle became a blueprint of how to work with the Lord—how to use out of the Universe power on earth. Channeling this rare power starts by not relying on common earthly sense. Common sense says that thirty-two thousand men against the thousands upon thousands of Midianites and Amalekites was hardly a fair fight. So to even it up, the Lord told Gideon to let all the men go who were frightened. Sensible? No—especially as twenty-two thousand legged it. Only ten thousand remained. Now it was so unfair a fight as to be beyond a joke.[20] But still too many for the Lord—he believed he could have the last laugh. So the Lord uses a random selection technique based on how people drank water out of a river: the tongue lappers—out; the hand to water—in. Exit nine thousand seven hundred lappers leaving only three hundred men—against the countless Amalekites and their mates—now laughable odds. Not a fair fight—more a nailed on definite massacre—for humans. But this is the Lord we are talking about. This was His Story. This was to prove who he was: who was the Boss; who was in charge.

The Lord then instructed Gideon to go undercover into the enemy camp to try and find out their battle plan.[21] There he heard that instead of talking military strategy, the enemies were talking about their dreams. Many of them had had dreams of a giant bread roll, favored by Isra-El, rolling down and crushing their camp. The interpretation was obvious even to the Amalekites, Midianites and other "ites"—people who lived by superstition and occult signs. They were going to be crushed big time by Family Abraham.

20. Judges 7:1–8.
21. Judges 7:9–22.

They were spooked before they started. In the end all it took was Gideon and his tiny group of three hundred men of to sneak up to the camp under the cover of darkness to simultaneously blow trumpets, smash clay jars and light torches whilst shouting, "For the Lord and for Gideon' for the desired effect to take hold—mass hysteria: no doubt heightened and brought about by the dream; no doubt brought about by shock; no doubt brought about by the knowledge of how Jericho had fallen years before; no doubt brought about by a loose alliance between the assorted "ites" that made them all very nervous of each other. In fact in the confusion they started fighting each other. But this was victory was only truly brought about by the Lord: by his Spirit; by his human agent; by His Story.

Was this a successful chapter in His Story? Yes—the Midianites left Isra-El alone. Yes—Isra-El did try better at following the Lord's Law. But—there again—no. Isra-El again couldn't commit in the longer term. They were unfaithful. They weren't distinctive. And so the period of the Judges ended with a simple comment. "In those days the nation Isra-El had no King: everyone did as he saw fit." Just like us—a law unto themselves.

After Gideon's famous victory, Family Isra-El tried to make Gideon their King. They tried to make him into a dynasty—with his sons and grandsons becoming the Royal bloodline. They wanted to be like every other people group who had kings! At least Gideon refused. [22] He knew who the mighty warrior was and it wasn't him! It was the Lord. Instead of becoming a royal household, Gideon asked for the gold earrings worn by their defeated enemy and plundered by Isra-El. He tried to give them to the Lord by melting the gold and making them into an ephod—a priestly bit of worship equipment—a key to the Doorway. But this ephod simply became a focus in years to come of superstition. Slowly but surely he and his family were forgotten—even neglected.

As was the Lord.

---

22. Judges 8:22–35.

# 21

## Boy meets Girl

But not all was lost. The Lord might not be into royal dynasties—yet—but when he was ready, he would have his Prince ready. He was already preparing a royal bloodline that would produce the Prince of Judah.

But it wasn't through Gideon. Remember Rahab and Salmon's child—Boaz? Boaz was in the bloodline. But as usual, he needed a child. And as usual, it was all planned.—not by Boaz, but by the Lord. After all, it was His Story.

And so into all the bloodthirstiness, the bullying, the barbarity of the time, the Lord injects romance. Into the unfaithfulness of Family Isra-El he brings commitment. Into His Story enter Boaz and his young bride.[1]

How did boy meet girl? The boy is from Family Abraham, now the nation known as Isra-El and is a descendant of Nahshon and Salmon and of course, the infamous, Rahab of Jericho. Maybe through Rahab, Boaz had romance in his D.N.A. He would have known the stories of his mother Rahab's early years in Jericho (or at least a censored version of them).

The girl Boaz was going to meet and fall in love with was called Ruth. She was like Boaz's mother, Rahab, in that she was a foreigner—a Moabite. She wasn't a child of Family Abraham. But unlike Rahab's colorful past, she wasn't a prostitute—anything but. In fact she was a devoted wife—but not at this point married to Boaz but to another man. In fact she was happily married to another member of Family Abraham even though she was an outsider. But how did this foreign girl meet her Isra-Elite man? Just like many hundreds of years before, the Lord had used famine to write His Story. This time not bringing Joseph and his brothers together in Egypt, but Ruth and her first husband together in a place called Moab. Ruth's first husband was in Moab because his extended family had been forced to leave Isra-El due to food shortages in his hometown—a home town called Beth-Lehem which means "House of Bread." Except it wasn't—it was a house of stale

1. Ruth 1–4.

crumbs. But this famine-struck town called, Beth-Lehem, was going to become famous for providing the world with two of its greatest characters. Both would be Kings of Isra-El in different ways and one of them was going to become known as, "The Bread of Life"—the one to end all famines.[2]

But not yet. Back over a thousand years, our girl meets her boy in Moab. But before you know it—girl loses boy to death. Despite moving to find food, Ruth's first husband died—maybe due to the after-effects of malnutrition. Certainly the famine does seem to have weakened the whole family as after Ruth's first husband dies, her brother-in-law dies. And then her father-in-law dies.

Ruth was left only with her Moabite sister-in-law and Family Abraham mother-in-law. At least Ruth and her sister-in-law were Moabites and were at home in Moab. But Ruth's mother-in-law was a foreigner in a foreign country without any blood relatives left.

As the years went by, the food shortage back in Isra-El receded. There was now nothing to keep mother-in-law away from going back to her homeland of Isra-El. The famine was over. But Ruth's family was over as well. Ruth's mother in law, Naomi, decided to give her foreign daughters-in-law the choice to stay at home in their own land with their own blood relatives. One said, "yes," the other, Ruth, said, "No—you are my family. I will stay with you"—commitment—keeping to contract—even when the contract had become null and void through death. This was true love blossoming amidst the violence and sadness.

Despite her mother-in-law's sensible protests about staying in Moab, Ruth accompanied her back to Isra-El: back to a life of poverty; back to a life without a male wage-earning protector and provider; back to a life where a female's legal and moral earning possibilities were very limited. Two women on their own: two widows on their own. But God had arranged to help them. Through Moses, a couple of hundred years before, the Lord had set up a rule that in Isra-El rich field owners were to leave some of their crops unharvested so that the poor could follow on after the harvesters and pick up the scraps left so that they could have something to eat. This was a rule made up by a caring and sharing Lord and reflecting his character—his way of working. When Ruth takes advantage of God's caring rule, she finds that God provides in other ways as well.

Girl meets boy. Ruth chooses a field to work for leftovers—a field that happens to belong to a long-lost relative of her dead husband's—a single comfortably well off relative, a kind caring man called, Boaz.

---

2. John 6:35.

Boy notices girl across a crowded field. Boaz finds out who Ruth is: tells his men to leave her alone; tells them to drop a little more food than usual. Boaz protects Ruth. But he is older—too old for romance possibly. Maybe he needed a bit of encouragement. And so Ruth's mother-in-law advises Ruth to ask for his protection—in the middle of the night; by lying at his feet where he is sleeping on the threshing floor. Not immoral, but risky and possibly even risqué. But still all part of the way a person in those days was to formally ask for protection from their relative—to sort of be adopted. This was all above board (ish) and it does the trick.

Boy falls for girl. Boy sorts out a few little legal problems with closer relatives which involved throwing a shoe at someone (it's a long story) and seals the deal that very day.

Boy later marries girl. And they all live happily ever after. Even mother-in-law is now set up for life.

This story of boy meets girl is an example of commitment; an example of faithfulness; an example of trusting that our lives can be part of His Story—planned and storyboarded in advance by God. Later Ruth gives birth to a child. He is the next child on the Lord's special royal bloodline—even though the child was half Moabite. His name was Obed. And Obed in his time gives birth to a son called Jesse—the next in the Lord's kingly bloodline.[3] Jesse of Beth-Lehem, whose life would be changed for ever by the visit of one the most famous men in the history of Family Abraham and one of the most famous men in His Story.

Samu-El.

---

3. Ruth 4:21–22.

# 22

# The King-Maker

His Story is full of special, miraculous babies. Samu-El was another of this exclusive club. You know the routine by now: parents unable to conceive; the Lord intervenes and before you know it—baby arrives but with strings attached—the parents had to keep their part of the contract with God.

Before Samu-El's birth, Samu-El's mother, Hannah, was distressed—no children. This is bad enough when you are desperate to be a mother; but disastrous when society placed expectations on women to be mothers. Even more disastrous when you shared your husband with another wife and the other wife was prolific in the baby department.

But Hannah was faithful to the Lord—committed. She kept the contract. And so annually, she went to the center of worship for the Lord. She went to a place called Shiloh where the Ark of the Covenant was now kept—the Holy Box that contained the heavenly contract stones. There, she begged the Lord for a child—year after year.[1]

One year, in desperation, she tried to make a contract with the Lord: "You give me a child and I will give him back to you." El-i, an old man that God used at this time as his Go-Between—his link through the Doorway, saw her wrestling in private silent prayer. But instead of seeing a woman who remembered that the Lord was her Creator; instead of seeing a woman who was hammering on the Doorway; instead of seeing a woman who wanted the Creator to create something unique and special for her—a child, old El-i just saw a drunk woman. This says a lot about what sort of behavior had become common in the worship center in those dark days. It also says a lot about the quality of Lord's Go-Betweens in those dark days as well. They couldn't tell the difference between mouthing silent prayers and mouthing drunken obscenities.

So El-i told Hannah off. Indignant, Hannah explained what she was doing and eventually persuades El-i who gives her his blessing—about

1. 1 Samuel 1:1–28.

time—and in time, Hannah was given what she so wanted—the birth of a baby boy. Samu-El—in the language of Family Abraham: "Heard by God" (El). Of course, Hannah kept her side of the bargain, the contract. So, when Samu-El was old enough, she allowed him to live and work at Shiloh, with the old Go-Between priest, El-i. Samu-El became his apprentice—like a son to him.

El-i's natural sons were corrupt and brought dishonor to their father and to the Lord-God. The Lord-God needed a new successor to El-i. Of course, it was going to be Samu-El—the child of promise; the child of contract.

Samu-El slept by the Holy Box—the Ark. In so doing, Samu-El slept right next to the stones bearing the very words of El-God sent through the Doorway at Sinai. Samu-El was within touching distance of God and the power outside the Universe. He had powerful links—links beyond the Universe—links through time and space.[2]

Some students believe that if they play back a recording of their studies whilst they are asleep, they will almost miraculously soak up information which will help them pass their exams. Whether true or the ridiculous belief of desperately underprepared students, it does seem suspiciously coincidental that when Samu-El slept with his head next to the Ark of the Covenant, amazing things happened through his subconscious. Through his subconscious, the Lord-God opened the Door to beyond the Universe.

It hadn't happened for a long time. So long that Samu-El didn't know what was happening when a mysterious voice boomed out calling his name in the middle of the night. He thought it was El-i. He could be excused. But El-i couldn't. He was meant to be the Lord's Go-Between. When young Samu-El ran into him asking if he had called, he just told the frightened Samu-El to go to sleep. The powerful links were lost on him. Only after the third time of the terrified Samu-El running into him, did El-i start to make the other-worldly connections—that it might just be to do with a miraculously born child's proximity to the most Holy Box in the world. He advised Samu-El to simply next time say, "Speak Lord for your servant is listening"—simple but potent advice—for anyone. And it worked. But not in El-i's favor. The Lord's message to Samu-El was to tell El-i that the Lord was rejecting his sons to carry on El-i's work. He had a new replacement Go-Between on earth—a new improved version—Samu-El. The boy whose name meant "heard by God" had found that he heard God. El-God had his ear.

Samu-El became the first of a long line of people who would hear El-God. And after hearing God they communicated his message to the world.

2. 1 Samuel 3:1–21.

*the king-maker* 81

El-God spoke through these people—they were his Spokespersons, but more than that—they were living, breathing, walking, talking Mouthpieces. Their words and their lives told Family Abraham and wider humanity what God wanted to say. They were voices from beyond the Doorway; voices from beyond the Universe.

A thousand years later, the Super-star of His Story would be a man who became known as "The Living Word of God."[3] But until then, Samu-El was the next best thing—the first of God's megaphones to wake up a sleeping world.

His appointment left no use for the abusive bullying sons of El-i. El-i's sons met their end when they let the holy Ark leave Shiloh and be carried around like a good luck charm into one of Family Abraham's many skirmishes with their enemies. The great enemy—the sea people called the Philistines—had previously decided that Family Abraham's military strength lay in the magical strength of the Holy Box. Unfortunately, so did El-i's sons. They saw it simply as a superstitious talisman but had forgotten that it contained the small print of their contract with God. Instead of obeying what lay inside the Ark, they just thought that if they kept it close to them they would never have bad luck. So it had to go with them into battle. The Philistines knew Family Abraham's dependency on it and not surprisingly took the opportunity to steal it and kill El-i's sons at the same time.[4]

When the bad news of the Ark got back to the old blind El-i, he was so distraught he fell off his chair, broke his neck and died. He was also probably shocked about his sons, but it is clearly recorded that El-i was more upset about the loss of his Holy Box than his corrupt sons. At least he had his priorities right in the end.

The Philistines didn't keep it long. They thought that by having it they would have the Lord's power. But they soon realized that the Lord is awesome and awful—he isn't a magic charm that can be turned on and off. The Lord turned his power against the Philistines and made life hell for them.

And so they sent the Ark back with gold peace offerings as a free gift inside—a sacrifice. The truth was that real power didn't rest in the box, but in the contract it contained. It only worked if you kept the contract written on the stones in the box.

Samu-El knew that and as a result, Samu-El grew into a great leader—inspiring Family Abraham into victories against the Philistines. Samu-El grew into the first great prophetic Mouthpiece of the Lord—hearing the Lord's words and passing them on to the people. Samu-El also grew into the

3. John 1:1–14.
4. 1 Samuel 4–6.

first real priestly Go-Between—speaking to the Lord on the people's behalf and offering the Lord their sacrifices.

A thousand years later, the Super-star of His Story would reunite these great roles for Isra-El and the whole of humanity. He would be a great leader as well as the Living Word of God and the ultimate Go-Between of the Lord—linking humanity and God; connecting the inside and outside of the Universe.[5]

But for the moment, Samu-El was the Lord's man on earth. In fact—he was the nearest thing to a King that Isra-El had. In one of his weaker moments, Samu-El thought so too and tried to make himself into a dynasty, a royal family.[6] But neither Samu-El nor his children were part of the Lord's special bloodline. The people rejected Samu-El's children. Instead they asked Samu-El for a real king—a king like the other peoples round them had.[7] They felt all grown up now—a proper nation and a proper nation had to have a proper king. Samu-El was not pleased. Samu-El told the Lord on them. And the Lord wisely advised him not to take it personally. "It's not you they've rejected—it's me," he told Samu-El. But equally wisely, the Lord told Samu-El to let the people have their freedom like a parent must learn to slowly give his teenager a limited freedom—a freedom that should come with more responsibility.

It wasn't that having a king was wrong—it just wasn't an answer to all their problems. It wasn't that it was harmful—it just wasn't as good as they thought. Not yet at least. This disillusionment with the monarchy would recur until the Super-star King of His Story—the Prince of Judah—would be revealed as the King of Kings.[8] But up to the coronation of this King of Kings, any human king, however great, would be disappointing. But the people had to wait to find this out for themselves.

Samu-El explained this—he put to them the pros and cons.[9] He explained crucially that inevitably power corrupts. A King of Isra-El would end up being like every other king—using his power to force the people into doing as they were told. But he also later explained that a King of Isra-El wasn't like any other king. Unlike all the other kings in the world, the King of Isra-El would have another King over him. He would be subject to this King of Kings just like the rest of Family Abraham. Isra-El already had a king—the Lord himself. The King of Isra-El had himself to be a servant of

5. Hebrews 4:14.
6. 1 Samuel 8:1–3.
7. 1 Samuel 8:4–5.
8. Revelation 1:5.
9. 1 Samuel 8:6–21.

the King of the Universe—under the Lord and his Law. He had to follow the small print of the contract in the same way as his people.[10] No absolute power for their King; no dictatorship; no acting as if they were God—unlike the kings in the nations around. But who to choose? Who was to be the first King ever of Isra-El? Who was going to be the King the Universe's choice as King? Samu-El? No.

Instead, Samu-El was going to have the crucial role of King-maker.

---

10. 1 Samuel 12:13–15.

# 23

# One Nation: Two Kings

SAMU-EL'S GREATEST MOMENT AS king-maker was to "out" the next star in the royal bloodline. Through him the chosen royal bloodline of His Story was to surface again, breaking through from the anonymity it had hidden behind for centuries.

Since the notorious and infamous prostitute turned heroine, Rahab, none of the subsequent members of the royal bloodline had been high profile. None of them would have opened local supermarkets or troubled the editors of the tabloids. Okay, Rahab's son was involved a heart-warming romantic story with Ruth which culminated in the birth of Obed. Obed had in turn produced a son called Jesse who had had lots of sons. But hardly shock horror "A Celebrity" gossip.

In reality it didn't create a big splash when His Story broke the surface of history again. Instead it started with not much more than a ripple. It began when Jesse, the next on God's chosen bloodline, met Samu-El when he visited Jesse's hometown of Beth-Lehem. He was there ostensibly to offer a sacrifice.[1] All the local dignitaries were in a flutter. But the sacrifice was a cover for a secret meeting with Jesse who lived in Beth-Lehem. Through the Doorway, the Lord had told Samu-El that one of Jesse's sons was to be King of Isra-El.

And so Samu-El arrived secretly at Jesse's house with a small horn full of olive oil—oil which was to be poured on the new King as an acted-out sign that the Lord's Spirit and power would be on him. The Lord had given Samu-El strict instructions—the future King was one of Jesse's many sons.

But as usual—there were a few more twists and turns. Like—which son? Jesse had lots. Son One—the eldest—fitted the image profile. Samu-El was convinced and reached for his horn of oil to anoint him. But the Lord spoke to him and in so doing set up an important principle in His Story. "Don't be impressed by his good looks or height. Humans look on the outward appearance; I look inside at the heart—the center of humans."

1. 1 Samuel 16:1–13.

Son Two: same verdict. Son Three: same verdict—in fact same outcome for seven sons. Samu-El was confused and interrogated Jesse, "Have you any more sons you haven't told me about?" It turned out Jesse had forgotten to mention to Samu-El his youngest—Son Eight. Not surprisingly he had been overlooked because he was very young and inheritance always started with the eldest first. Not surprisingly he had been forgotten, because he was looking after all the sheep whilst his older brothers were parading in front of Samu-El in the first King Beauty Contest in Isra-El. Son Eight was surplus to requirements. But the Lord required him. He required the shepherd boy—the one who had the same job as Moses before he became Isra-El's great leader. When Jesse's youngest son was eventually dragged away from the sheep, he was brought to Samu-El. The young man was attractive and impressive, but still very young. But nonetheless, he was the one—David the shepherd boy of Beth-Lehem—King of Isra-El.

Unlikely though it sounded, Samu-El poured the oil on him and the Lord poured his powerful Spirit on him—the Lord's power was injected straight into David from beyond the Universe. What would you expect next—a great public coronation? Not at all—Samu-El had been undercover in Beth-Lehem for a reason. There was already a King of Isra-El anointed by the King-maker, Samu-El earlier—something Samu-El regretted bitterly; something the Lord had sent him to put right by choosing another King.[2]

The reigning monarch was Saul—the first King of Isra-El. He had been chosen by Samu-El earlier. He had even been chosen by the Lord earlier. Had this been a mistake? His Story doesn't tell us why the Lord chose him. He wasn't on the special bloodline. He wasn't particularly special in any way apart from his height and looks.

Sometimes His Story is confusing. Always His Story is far more complex than the story we can read. Beneath the simple storyline are layers upon layers of other stories—individual human stories guided and used by the Lord but not manipulated by him. The Lord gave the first humans the ability to choose—even to choose badly. Humans have never and never will lose that God-given ability to choose. It's what makes being human, special. It makes us like God.[3]

Amazingly though, His Story works with these individual choices, even wrong choices. It redeems bad storylines and gives them happy endings. It can even make the bad choices look like good choices. It's called, "Grace."

2. 1 Samuel 9–10.
3. Genesis 1:27.

Grace amazingly doesn't leave us to drown under the flood of our own bad decisions. God sends a Noah and a big boat to save us. But still we need to choose to get on board. But even if we don't, His Story will not be shipwrecked. Being out of time gives God that ability to look objectively at time—at the infinite possibilities and outcomes and see the one that will further his storyline best.

He gave Saul a chance to be the King of Isra-El. The outcome could have been so good. In fact, in flashes Saul showed what he could have been. But from the outset, Saul had been a disappointment. He looked the part—he was much taller than anyone else. This was usually an advantage to him, but had been a disadvantage when at his public coronation he had cold feet and decided to hide amongst the bags of the visiting dignitaries. His head and shoulders stuck up above his hiding place and gave the game away. But after he was reluctantly crowned as King, he went from being a bashful conscript to being a nailed-on believer, but unfortunately a believer in himself. He was a product of the people's hasty desire to follow the example of the other nations around. And he lived up to that short-sighted desire. He increasingly mimicked the other kings of the other nations around who didn't just believe they were God's gift to their people—they increasingly believed they were God to their people.

After a military victory inspired by his leadership, Saul got the popular vote from Isra-El. They thought he was the King they had been waiting for.[4] But it went to his head. He offered sacrifices—like he were the Go-Between as well as the King.[5] He believed as King he had a special place between the Lord and Isra-El. In fact, he was just their human leader—a king. But soon he believed in himself so much, he didn't follow the Lord's instructions through Samu-El, the Lord's Mouthpiece. He believed he had a hotter line to the Lord than Samu-El. Saul acted as if he were the Lord's Mouthpiece instead.

This was dangerous. The King of Isra-El was not the Lord's Spokesperson or the Go-Between the outside and inside of the Universe. He was just the King—just a human leader. He was under the Lord and the Lord's messengers and the Lord's law.

It all went to Saul's head. The pressure began to tell. Saul became mentally ill. But instead of abdicating quietly, his illness made him believe more and more that he was the Lord's gift to Isra-El. Even though Samu-El had forcibly made it clear that the Lord had rejected him. Saul now was dangerous. At points, he believed he was more powerful than the Lord. He was not

---

4. 1 Samuel 11:1–15.
5. 1 Samuel 12:1–15.

## one nation: two kings

just like God: he was in charge of God. He thought he was in control of his own destiny—writing his own "his story." He thought he was in control of the story of God's people—Isra-El.

The Lord had to intervene. And so into this mess came his intervention strategy—the young shepherd boy, David. After being anointed after Samu-El's clandestine visit to David's dad, this young innocent naïve shepherd boy, David, was thrust into a potential civil war—two Kings in one nation.

But the Lord didn't leave David to struggle on his own. The Lord fixed it so that David's story became His Story. He got David into Saul's royal court, not as a shepherd, but as a visiting musician—becoming harpist to the King.[6] And so David was to be found on the outer reaches of Saul's Royal entourage.

But David needed to have a higher profile if he was to succeed Saul. He needed the people to support him over Saul if Saul was to be removed. And when the opportunity came, it not only made the headlines of the day, but it has become one of the best known, best loved stories of His Story. It has become the story to inspire every person who knows their destiny is great but their way to that destiny is blocked by gigantic problems. The incident?—David versus Goliath.[7]

The battle-lines against the old enemy, the sea people of Philistia, were drawn up—again—each side facing each other across the valley of Elah. But a new way of fighting was developing—one less wasteful on human resources—a fight to the death between a chosen champion from each side. Whichever champion won—won for the whole of his side. End of battle.

The Philistines" champion was a no-brainer. Goliath was pushing nine feet tall—his head would have scraped a soccer crossbar and not far off a basketball net. And he wasn't a skinny beanpole. He was strong enough to propel a javelin large enough to have a metal spike on the end weighing the same as a gallon of water. His bronze armor alone weighed the same as having a lightweight boxer sitting on his shoulders. But Goliath himself was no lightweight—he was a super heavyweight.

Goliath stood and waited for the chosen champion of Isra-El. He stood and taunted Isra-El to find their champion. But strangely, no one moved. King Saul was tall but not that tall. King Saul was slightly mad but not that mad. King Saul was like a rabbit caught in the headlights of an H.G.V. for forty days (which in His Story means a very long time or what seemed like a very long time).

---

6. 1 Samuel 16:14–23.
7. 1 Samuel 17:1–58.

Meanwhile back at the Jesse ranch in Beth-Lehem, David, (still his Dad's odd-jobber when not playing the harp for the King) was sent to the battle lines with food for his older brothers serving in Saul's army. In return David was to bring back news of his brothers to his Dad—hopefully good. On the frontline, David found his brothers cowering, along with the rest of Isra-El. David couldn't understand this. David couldn't understand how a human—however tall and strong—could dare to stand up to the living God. And he said so—much to the annoyance of his oldest brother. David also heard that whoever defeated Goliath would be allowed to marry Saul's daughter. He would become part of the royal family and receive all the fringe benefits that this would bring. David wasn't interested in the financial gain (or the woman for that matter) but as King-elect, he was interested in the power. As the Lord's-elect he wanted to use his power to stop anyone thinking they were stronger than the Lord.

David the musician was now a part-time member of Saul's royal court. As such, he managed to get an audience with King Saul as he sat petrified in his battle tent. But David didn't offer to play Saul a soothing tune. Instead, he volunteered to fight the gigantic Goliath. Saul at first pointed out the obvious mismatch: David—a boy; Goliath—a hardened fighting machine. But David now began to show his heart—his center—what the Lord had already seen in him. David knew the secret of success in His Story—that if you keep the contract, there is nothing to fear. He knew about Jericho. He knew about Gideon. He knew that when the Lord is behind something, then less is more. He knew that the Lord could even use a shepherd—after all he had used Moses. So, David pointed out to King Saul, that the Lord had kept him safe defending his sheep against lions and bears—so what's the difference? The Lord is the Lord. Good point.

Saul, now desperate and completely out of inspiration, goes for it. He put his future and the future of Isra-El in the hands of a young shepherd boy who played the harp for him. At least Saul felt a little guilty. He tried dressing David in his armor. But David rejected it. He was not used to it. It probably didn't fit him. But more than that—it wasn't him. He was a shepherd who trusted in the Lord, not armor. He believed less is more when fighting on the Lord's side. He believed in the Lord of Gideon. And so David did what no one else from Isra-El dared do—trust the Lord and face the giant. He dared to face Goliath—with no sword; no armor; just with a stick—a shepherd's stick like Moses' and with a shepherd's catapult and bag of small stones. Oh . . . and of course, with the Lord as well—something he made sure Goliath and all the armies of Isra-El and Philistia knew as well. When Goliath mocked him and mocked Isra-El for scraping the barrel by sending out a child with sticks and stones, David simply and powerfully replied, "But

I come to you in the name of the all-mighty Lord, the God of Isra-El you have dared to defy! This battle is his—he doesn't need weapons."

As Goliath lumbered forward to swat the annoying fly of David, David put one stone in his catapult and fired it—direct hit—right into his temple. It sank in. Goliath fell—face down. Whether he was dead at this point is a pointless discussion but he certainly was dead after David ran over, managed to pick up Goliath's oversize sword and hack off his head. The Philistines also got the point. They ran. And the army of Isra-El ran after them. And David's fame also ran far and wide. It still does today—three thousand years later.

After this victory, Saul gave David more and more responsibility in his army. He was now a right hand man of the King. Everything Saul asked him to do—he did well. Saul loved him and hated him. He was proud of him and threatened by him. At the time a new pop song was composed—"Saul has killed thousands; but David tens of thousands." When this hit the number one spot in the charts, it angered Saul. And after a reluctant David married one of Saul's daughters, Michal, Saul knew that David was so strong, so inspired, so all action hero, that his own position as King was under threat. The young pretender was established.

Was Saul paranoid? Yes—David's success made Saul's mental illness worse. But no—Saul wasn't imagining things. There again, he didn't even know the half of it—that David was already King in the Lord's eyes—in His Story.

One nation: two Kings—a recipe for disaster.

# 24

## A Proper Nation

SAUL REIGNED. CONFUSION REIGNED. The confusion in Saul's head spilled out into his actions. One day he was for David: the next he was against. One day he needed David: the next he was trying to get rid of him.[1]

Music had become Saul's only antidote to the raging battle in his own head. Music was still David's specialty as harpist to the King. David became Saul's private music therapist. It was a dangerous position for the new young hero. When Saul was angry—he was out of control. Sometimes David's music didn't work—a quivering spear of Saul implanted in the wall behind David's recently vacated head bore witness to this. David ran for safety to his wife, Michal. She advised him to escape—she knew what her father's moods were like. She probably had become quite adept at coping with them over her short life. She helped David escape out of a window and then she made a body shape lump under his bed covers using an idol—a human sized replica of a god not the Lord. The fact that she happened to have a spare idol lying around shows that Saul and his family were into breaking the second of the Lord's rules—they were unfaithful to the Lord. But give Michal her due, she at least used the idol to try and trick the soldiers sent by her angry father the next day. She stuck up for David against her own father and lied that David was too ill in bed to go with the soldiers to see the King. But Saul just ordered for the bed to be brought to him with the bedridden David in it. Only then was Michal's lie uncovered.

David had run to old Samu-El who helped protect him. Even Saul's son, Jonothan, protected David by giving him inside information on his father's state of mind and intentions towards him. But Saul was too unpredictable to predict. There was only one answer—David had to go into hiding.[2] And so began a period of David being an outcast in his own country—the

---

1. 1 Samuel 18–20.
2. 1 Samuel 21–31.

"Robin Hood" years starring King Saul as the Sheriff of Nottingham and David as the fugitive in the forest.

It began with David recovering an old friend—the sword of Goliath.[3] It must have reminded him of the Lord giving him success against massive odds. To mix the folk story metaphors—it was his "Excalibur." David also gathered around him a growing group of fighting merry men discontent with Saul. Anyone found helping David at this time was seen as a traitor and was killed.[4]

David spent his time roaming the countryside, righting the wrongs of individuals and giving help to the poor. In response, Saul took David's wife, Michal, off him. David married another woman instead—a woman he saved from a violent abusive husband.[5] David hid in different places, sometimes disguised. Ironically, at one point, he feigned madness to hide from the increasingly mad Saul.[6] At one point, David even hid with the great enemy, the Philistines.

David used guerrilla tactics, but he was no terrorist against the state. On several occasions he had an opportunity to kill Saul who was pursuing him. Once, Saul was taking a toilet break in the cave that David was lurking in.[7] But even then David would not harm him—after all he was still the crowned King. He would not attack the constitution of his own country. To David, it was like attacking the Lord himself. Each time David confronted Saul, Saul was deeply distressed by his own actions.

But Saul just couldn't help himself. Saul was descending into personal meltdown. He eventually turned to witchcraft that was banned in Isra-El. In the séance that followed, the only person Saul met was the now deceased Samu-El who told him off and said that his situation was self-inflicted.[8]

The final acts of Saul's life were played out on the battlefield—once again against the old enemy, the sea people of Philistia.[9] The army of Isra-El were losing. The Philistines had tightened their net around King Saul. Even his own son Jonothan had been killed. Saul was hit by an arrow and begged his armor bearer to finish him off rather than let him be taken prisoner alive. But the armor bearer was too frightened of the unpredictable Saul and

---

3. 1 Samuel 21:1–9.
4. 1 Samuel 22:6–23.
5. 1 Samuel 25:1–44.
6. 1 Samuel 21:10–15.
7. 1 Samuel 24:1–22.
8. 1 Samuel 28:1–25.
9. 1 Samuel 31:1–13.

refused, and so Saul committed suicide by falling on his own sword—a sad end to a sad reign as the first King of Isra-El.

But the way was now clear for David to become what he was in the Lord's opinion already—King of Isra-El. It was a struggle at first to unite all the factions of Isra-El, but what would you expect for a people whose name means "wrestle"? But in time, David was crowned King and acknowledged publicly as Family Abraham's leader.

But a King needs a castle. And so, David's first act as King was to win a fortress city that was meant to be impregnable. No one could take it. It was a hilltop fortress. The Jebusites who lived there boasted that it was so difficult to attack that, "The lame and blind could defend it." But it fell to David.[10]

The city became a central part of His Story—one of the main characters in His Story. It was a city that was built on Mount Moriah—the hill where Abraham had been seconds away from killing his promised child, Isaac. It was built on land that had been used by the Lord before as the Doorway to the safety and peace beyond the Universe. Its name reflected its history—Jeru-Salem—the place of peace. This would become the site of God making peace once and for all with his creation. But that was to come.[11]

But a thousand years earlier, David engineered peace for Isra-El. For the first time ever, Isra-El was beginning to truly enjoy the land flowing with milk and honey—enjoy the Promised Land. The promise to Abraham had come true. Abraham's family was now a nation—a proper nation with a proper King. This successful King reigned in an inspirational capital city that had the special extra mysterious name of Zion—the name that came to mean the land where God's Kingdom and power touched earth—the Doorway.

But of course, there was just one thing more needed to top off Jeru-Salem's grandeur. The Holy Box—the Ark of the Covenant—needed moving into Jeru-Salem from the place it had rested after being sent back by the Philistines.[12] But for the job, David didn't just call up the local removal firm. He hand-picked thirty thousand men to accompany it and every step of the way David and all of Isra-El worshipped using music and songs. But even despite such meticulous planning and choreography something went wrong. One of the cattle pulling the cart stumbled. One man put his hand out to steady the Ark and instantly dropped down dead. The awful awesomeness of the Lord broke out and reminded them that there was to be no messing with God. David was frightened. He paused—for three months. Three months of great prosperity for the man whose land where the Ark stayed whilst they decided what to do.

10. 2 Samuel 5:1–10.
11. Colossians 1:19–20.
12. 2 Samuel 6:1–23.

And then they tried again. This time before every seventh step (obviously), David sacrificed a bull and a fattened calf and then danced as if his life depended on it. Maybe it did. It was a critical moment—a moment of high drama. Apart from anything else, David's sacrificing was straying into the territory of priestly "Go-Between" duties. He seemed to be setting himself up as something more than the King—something that had contributed to his predecessor, Saul, being removed from the throne.

But God's grace reigned. Slowly but surely the Holy Box made its way into Jeru-Salem with shouts and trumpet blasts and sacrifices, not to mention King David dancing madly. It was placed in a tent in the center of Jeru-Salem.

The Holy Ark was back at the center: the law back at the center; the contract back at the center. David gave bread, dates and raisins to everyone as a celebratory memento and everyone was happy. All was well. Well not all. Michal, the late King Saul's daughter and David's estranged wife, was now back with David again. Back in person, but not in spirit. She despised David's actions. Not his sacrificing, but his dancing. She thought it was demeaning. The King was showing himself up in front of the slave girls. After all he had only been wearing the priestly kit of the ephod. How much this covered isn't known, but probably not much when linked with wild dancing. But David wasn't bothered at all. He was a man of the people—even the slave people. But David saw the problem as deeper than whether his wife thought he had been vulgar. He saw that Michal did not rejoice with the return of the Ark. She did not respect him as King. She did not respect that he was the Lord's chosen one. Her unfaithfulness to the Lord and her disrespect of the Lord's chosen man meant that she forfeited her right to be part of His Story. His Story records that Michal never had any children. She was not to be the mother of the next person in the special bloodline—the bloodline that was now truly royal for the first time. She was not to be the matriarch of the royal family to come. She would miss out on a central starring role in His Story.

But the Holy Box was now safely back in the limelight—back in the center of the nation. It still contained the contract-stones of the Lord produced when the Doorway between earth and heaven opened at Mount Sinai. At the heart of the nation was the heart of the Lord—his desire for a relationship with his people—for humanity to come back home. And certainly Isra-El under the great King David seemed to be touched by heaven. Isra-El began to be fabulously successful and prosperous. Isra-El began to be the super-power in the world.

His Story was now at the heart again of the wider history of the World.

# 25

## The Good, the Bad and the Ugly

DAVID SLOWLY BUT SURELY defeated all his enemies inside and outside of Israel. So what does an all powerful king do when he's no longer needed on the battlefield? He thinks about the different ways he will be remembered when he is dead. One way he might do this is by building great edifices. David wanted to build a fantastic house for the Lord and his Holy Box. He felt bad about the Lord's Holy Box still being stuck in a tent when he was building a brilliant capital city for Isra-El. He also wanted to impress future generations with his magnificent architecture. But the Lord through his current Mouthpiece on earth, Nathan, said, "No"—the Lord didn't need a house before and he didn't need one now.[1]

Instead the Lord offered David a house—a royal House but not a Palace—he already had one of those. This was to be a royal house-hold—a dynasty—a royal family that would make the Lord's promises to Abraham come true; a royal bloodline to be established through David. As for a house for the Ark, the Lord promised that one of David's children would be King after him and he would build a Temple—a home for the Lord on earth designed to house a permanent Doorway from outside to inside of the Universe. He promised that he would not take the Kingdom away from David's family like he took it away from Saul. This contract was solid and binding. This promise was in the line of great promises the Lord had made in His Story so far: to Noah; to Abraham; to Moses, and now to David.

So, what else does an all powerful King do when he's no longer needed on the battlefield and he's got a secure future but isn't allowed to build a massive building? He thinks about art. He thinks about creating great art to be remembered by. King David the harpist was also a good musician. He composed at least seventy great songs. These have become known as Psalms—songs sung to the harp. David's lyrics weren't just simple worship songs to God, but they gave insights into his deep feelings. They spoke about life: about the good and bad; the fair and unfair times; his successes and his

---

1. 2 Samuel 7:1–29.

failures. Some of the most famous words ever written, were written by King David. The twenty-third Psalm composed by King David, the ex-shepherd, starts with David imagining that he is a sheep in the Lord's flock.[2] "The Lord is my Shepherd. I will never be in need because he will lead me to clean water and fresh grass. He will guide me along tracks which are safe. Even if I wander off down a valley as dark and sinister as death, I won't be afraid because the Lord will still find me and use his shepherd's staff to bring me back to safety."

But despite his great songs, David wasn't immune from acting like a senseless sheep himself. He wandered off the right track and needed rescuing—as well as knowing the good and bad times, he also knew the ugly times. So, what else does an all powerful king do when he's no longer needed on the battlefield? He thinks about sex. He thinks about using his great power to conquer beautiful women. For example, like Bathsheba.[3] She was the wife of one of David's trusted soldiers. She was beautiful fully clothed. And naked, I will leave to your imagination. Not that David needed to imagine. His palace overlooked her house and the courtyard where Bathsheba bathed—outside. It was late in the afternoon one day and the warm golden sun highlighted Bathsheba. It was too much for an idle King. He sent for her. One thing led to another and before you knew it, or at least, before Bathsheba's husband knew about it on the battlefield, Bathsheba discovered she was pregnant. What was David to do?—cover his tracks by making sure that Bathsheba's husband, Uriah, came back from the battlefield a.s.a.p. and had a night of passion with his wife—that's what.

Bathsheba's husband was sent home from the frontline on the pretense of reporting to the King how the battle was progressing. After he had reported to the King, David sent him home to have a shower and see his wife. He even gave them room service—a beautiful meal to get him in the mood. But Uriah was a solider. He was still on duty and instead slept on the palace steps because he felt he couldn't luxuriate whilst his fellow soldiers risked their lives for King and country.

Foiled by Uriah's high standards, David ordered him to stay another night before returning. This time David ordered him to eat a meal with him. He made sure that the two of them drank far more alcohol than was good for them. David then sent Uriah home to Bathsheba for a night of passion. But instead, Uriah slept on his mat with the Palace Guard.

Eventually, David in desperation, decided to send Uriah back to the battlefield carrying sealed instructions to the commander of the army to make

2. Psalm 23.
3. 2 Samuel 11:1–27.

sure that he was put in the fiercest fighting. And so Uriah returned holding his own death sentence and inevitably died on the frontline soon after.

When David was told the news, he sent the messenger back to tell the wary commander of the army to, "Cheer up, these things happen in war." No remorse. No regrets. After all he was the all-powerful, successful King. None of this behavior would have worried one of the kings of the other nations around Isra-El. It would have been expected.

Bathsheba mourned—but not for long. She soon moved in with David and they married. And after several months, the baby was born. And they all lived happily ever after—apart from dead Uriah of course—and apart from Nathan the Lord's Mouthpiece on earth. Nathan went to David and reported to him about something that had happened to one of his poor subjects.[4] He reported to David that this subject of his Kingdom had only one lamb to his name. The lamb had become a family pet. It was loved by him and his children. But another rich evil man who lived close by unexpectedly had a visitor and wanted to have roast lamb. But he didn't want to slaughter one of his many sheep, so, as a laugh, he stole the family pet of the poor man, killed it, roasted it and ate it.

When David heard this report, the "steal from the rich and give to the poor" Robin Hood-style King David was out of control with anger. "How dare the rich and powerful steal from the poor and powerless!" David saw himself as the protector of the poor, the righter of injustice and abuse. He ordered Nathan to tell him the name of the rich man who had committed such a heinous crime and he ordered that the man be executed. "You are the man", was all Nathan said. The words hung in the air. Brave man Nathan—brave words to say to a king. The story was a parable—a story with a meaning. And the meaning suddenly became clear to David. He was the rich man who had stolen the love of the poor man's life. Robin Hood had become Sheriff of Nottingham.

How would the all-powerful King react? By his own words, he had sentenced himself to death. Nathan pressed home his advantage. He didn't sentence David to death, but to feel some of the pain that he had inflicted on Uriah and the Lord. His own family would be torn apart. One of his own sons would rebel against him and the baby born to him and Bathsheba would die.

David immediately admitted his fault. And as a poet and musician, of course he had to put his feelings into a musical blog. It has become one of the few Psalms that we can fit chronologically into David's life-story. In it, David pleads with the Lord. "Please have mercy on me. Wipe me clean

---

4. 2 Samuel 12:1–25.

from my dirty life. I have been selfish since the day I was born. I see now what I have done. I can never forget it. Against you only have I rebelled and sinned."[5] Only against the Lord?—what about poor Uriah? But David saw that his crime was not just against one man: it was against humanity; it was against the Lord who had made humanity. He had let the Lord down. He had disappointed the Lord. He was the Lord's great hope for the world. The Lord was going to build Isra-El into a show-nation to reveal to the world how to be human. But in the end, his chosen King of this show-nation was no better than Saul. David had threatened the success of His Story. This aspect of his crime was so massive it dwarfed every other aspect.

Bathsheba's and David's son died soon after birth. Absalom, David's son by one of his other wives, then started a civil war. He rebelled against his father and was only stopped when he was trapped in a tree by his long flowing hair whilst riding a horse in a forest.[6] David's army surrounded him. Then ten of them finished him off. David was distraught twice over. David had learnt painfully the truth that the King of Isra-El was not King of El. El-God was King of the King of Isra-El. David was not a god—he had to live under the same rules as the whole of Family Abraham. He was not above the contract—he had to remember that God was King, not him.

Later, Bathsheba gave birth again—a baby boy again.[7] The Lord through his Mouthpiece on earth, Nathan, called him, "Jedidiah" which meant "The Lord's loved one." It was a name of hope and forgiveness. His parents gave him a personal name as well—Solomon—a variation of "Sa-lem" meaning Peace. For David and Bathsheba, his birth may have started the process of both of them moving from feeling guilty to accepting the Lord's peace. Solomon was also a popular name—an everyday name. But Solomon was far from everyday.

He was the Lord's next star in His Story.

---

5. Psalm 51.
6. 2 Samuel 18:1—19:8.
7. 2 Samuel 12:24-25.

# 26

# Wisdom and Foolishness

David had older sons to other wives who had greater claims to be the next King. But Solomon was the one the Lord chose, even though his mother had been unfaithful and his father was all but a murderer. Maybe the Lord wanted to show that in His Story normal rules don't apply. In His Story there is a rule that breaks all rules—grace: not a girl; not a few words said before food, but the way the Lord chooses to break his own rules. To be precise—the way the Lord chooses to save lawbreakers rather than punish them.

Grace means love—love that keeps on going even when pushed to the limit. Grace is God's love that never runs out even when we don't take the Lord's laws seriously. It's not that the Lord ignores his own rules. It's more that he intervenes when humans break them but not in a way that makes you lose respect for him or makes you think that he is soft and that you can get away with ignoring them. You can't, because the rules are built into how the world works—like gravity. Ignore gravity at your peril as the first intrepid aircraft designers found out. Being successful is about working with the rules and not against them—ignore the Maker's instructions at your peril.

But His Story is packed full of times when the Lord has stepped in and saved humans from the inevitable mess they have chosen by their ignoring of his rules. Grace is God doing something to stop humans getting what they deserve. God showed his grace when he chose to save humanity through Noah, Abraham, Moses and David. David was still a star of His Story, even though he had messed up big time. Grace: when we mess up—God cleans up.

How do you get hold of this special treatment by the Lord? There's no set rule. But one thing you can be certain of: it's always a good idea to be sorry for the mess and not just sorry that you've got in a mess; sorry that you've offended the Lord by spoiling his great plan for humanity as well as just sorry that you've been caught out. David had messed up. He had broken *wisdom and foolishness*

the contract. He was sorry. He was devastated. He apologized to the Lord. And in return, the Lord cleaned up and Solomon became the chosen one.

The Lord was true to his big promise to give David a royal family. He added this big promise to the promise to never again destroy the world through an international flood.[1] He added this big promise to the promise to give Abraham a family with more members than stars in the sky.[2] He added this big promise to the promise he gave Moses to give humanity the secret of how to live a successful life.[3]

And so after a few dicey disputes about succession after David died, the Lord kept his big promise to David and his son Solomon became the next King of Isra-El. Solomon's place in His Story was sealed by his father's trusted Mouthpiece of the Lord, Nathan, and his father's trusted Lord's Go-Between, Zadok, who crowned and anointed him as one of the most powerful men in the world.

But more importantly than that, he was appointed God's man in the world—God's next star in His Story. But what would he do with all the power and riches he inherited from his father David? A key moment came in His Story when the Lord opened the Door of the Universe again and met with the new King Solomon and encouraged him to ask for anything he wanted—anything.[4] Another big promise from the Lord God and backed by his all mighty power. What would you have asked for: success? fame? money? happiness? love?

Solomon asked for wisdom. Sounds a bit disappointing. But remember, in those days being wise wasn't about being old, clever and meaningful. It meant knowing. Not knowing about things, but how to do things. If they had had cars in Solomon's day, a car mechanic would have been thought of as wise. When the car broke down he would know what to do. Wisdom is knowing—knowing what to do and when to do it. God's wisdom is having the Creator's know-how whilst living in his Creation—knowing instinctively the Maker's instructions. The Lord was pleased with Solomon's choice and gave him wisdom.

This out-of-this-world gift was tested early in his reign. Two prostitutes had been living in the same house. Both had baby boys. But one baby had unfortunately died, accidentally smothered by his mother as she slept. Next day both mothers came to Solomon. Both claimed that the one baby

---

1. Genesis 9:12–17.
2. Genesis 22:17–18.
3. Joshua 1:7–9.
4. 1 Kings 3:1–15.

left alive was theirs.[5] How was Solomon to decide? Practical down-to-earth wisdom was needed in those pre-D.N.A. genetic testing days. Solomon grabbed a sword and swung it around his head saying that he would chop the baby in two and each mother could have half—weird but wise. One mother shouted, "Stop! She can have him!" Solomon stopped. Turned and gave the baby to the woman who had shouted. Think about it—that's practical wisdom—knowing what to do and when to do it.

Solomon became known as the wise king. On the back of his wisdom, he became famous for his book of Proverbs and wise sayings—all three thousand of them. It goes without saying that these wise sayings were very practical and very down to earth. For example: "A simple meal of vegetables served with love is better than a rich feast where there is hatred."[6] Maybe Solomon was into veg. Or maybe he had sussed something very simple but true about friendship.

Solomon was also a wealthy King and so his observations on the limitations and dangers of wealth are to be taken seriously: "The wealth you get from crime robs you of your life."[7] "It's better to be poor and honest than rich and dishonest."[8] "Trust in your wealth and you will be a failure, but God's people will always do well." [9] "The tent of a good person stands longer than the house of someone who is evil."[10]

Solomon also had around a thousand women in his life. So he had plenty of opportunity to be an expert on beauty and sex. He observed: "A beautiful woman who acts foolishly is like a gold ring in the snout of a pig."[11] "A woman who sells her love can be bought for very little; but if you go to bed with another man's wife you will pay a high price."[12]

Solomon also was the king of a busy complex kingdom. He knew all about responsibility and work. He wrote: "How long will you lie there doing nothing at all? When are you going to get up and stop sleeping? Sleep a little, doze a little, twiddle your thumbs and suddenly everything is gone, like it's

---

5. 1 Kings 3:16–28.
6. Proverbs 15:17.
7. Proverbs 1:19.
8. Proverbs 16:8.
9. Proverbs 11:28.
10. Proverbs 14:11.
11. Proverbs 11:22.
12. Proverbs 6:26.

*wisdom and foolishness* 101

been stolen by an armed robber."[13] "Having a lazy person on the job is like vinegar in the mouth or smoke in the eyes."[14]

Solomon also needed advisors around him that he could trust in order to run the nation effectively. He had learnt how to spot the people to rely on: "Correct a fool and he will hate you; correct a wise man and he will respect you."[15] "Hatred stirs up trouble; love overlooks other people's wrongs."[16] "No one will trust you if you tell lies."[17] "Gossip is no good! It causes hard feelings and comes between friends."[18] "Good people are kind to their animals, but a mean person is cruel to them."[19]

Solomon also had many children. He believed in good parenting: "If you love your children you will correct them; if you don't love them you'll let them do just what they like."[20]

Fundamentally, Solomon knew that his own wisdom relied on the Lord God: "We make our own decisions, but the Lord alone determines what happens."[21] "Trust in the Lord with all your heart; do not depend on your own understanding. Don't ever think you are wise enough, but respect the Lord."[22]

In fact, Solomon knew all too well that his down-to-earth wisdom wasn't his own. It came from beyond the Doorway—from beyond the Universe. A few years later a wise, deep, mysterious book called Ecclesiastes was written. It reinforced this need for wisdom to be inspired from beyond the Doorway. It poked fun at human wisdom—at wisdom that originated on earth and pretended it could explain the Universe without reference to life beyond the Doorway. Ecclesiastes was a spoof on human wisdom books. In fact the punch line of the book states: "There's no end of books out there— but studying them all will just make you tired not wise."[23]

Ecclesiastes was attributed to Solomon, possibly because he was the wisest man of His Story, or maybe because Solomon's ideas are in it. This book contains lots of amazing ideas and thoughts. It mocks earthly

13. Proverbs 6:9–11.
14. Proverbs 10:26.
15. Proverbs 9:8.
16. Proverbs 10:12.
17. Proverbs 10:32.
18. Proverbs 16:28.
19. Proverbs 12:10.
20. Proverbs 13:24.
21. Proverbs 16:33.
22. Proverbs 3:5.
23. Ecclesiastes 12:12.

wisdom when it says: "God has set eternity into the hearts of humans, and yet humans cannot work out what God has done from beginning to end."[24] The book points out that true wisdom thinks deeply about God's world, but never pretends to know all the answers—only God knows all of them. This Universe doesn't make sense without factoring in what lies through the Doorway. Studying the patterns of life can help us make better decisions but at best it is just a recycling of human earth-based ideas. Ecclesiastes has a recurring phrase about this constant dipping into the pool of collective human ignorance—it is like "chasing the wind."[25] Running around chasing the ever changing breezes is like a dog chasing its tail. It is like meteorologists predicting global weather patterns but being helpless to stop them. Weather forecasters at best are involved in a game of catch-up with the elements. God's wisdom isn't about chasing the patterns to be seen in the human character and human existence, but it is about changing human nature—about getting ahead of the patterns and transforming them. True wisdom only is available to humans when they partner humbly with God who is bigger than the Universe.

But what if God is not accessible to you—locked as he is beyond the Doorway? This inaccessibility to the eternal dimension is always the elephant in the secular room. Human history and human experience are at best confusing and muddled when they refuse to take seriously the through-the-Doorway dimension. They ultimately disappoint as humans are impotent at changing the forces that form the Universe and human experience. Whether we like it or not "there is nothing new under the sun."[26] As humans, left locked out on the earth-side of the Doorway, we are doomed to a circular existence devoid of knowing the meaning of why we are here. All is in vain—ultimately.[27] All this is the message of Ecclesiastes.

Solomon believed that the meaning of life lay beyond the Doorway. But at such an early stage in His Story it was still all but impossible for Solomon to access it in any meaningful way without help. This help was going to be available in the later part of His Story—in a part not yet written. But at least Solomon did know the basics of His Story—that the Lord made everything—that he is the Maker and only by following him can you make sense of your life and see where it comes from and where it could go. This made him the wise king.

---

24. Ecclesiastes 3:11.
25. Ecclesiastes 1:14–15.
26. Ecclesiastes 1:9.
27. Ecclesiastes 1:2.

Not only was Solomon the wisest king, but he was the richest. Amazingly just because Solomon had asked God for wisdom and not for wealth, the Lord gave him wealth as a bonus—as a freebie. Nearly a thousand years later the most famous descendant of King Solomon said, "Search first for what God, the King of the Earth wants you to do and then you will find that King God will give you everything else you need afterwards."[28] But King Solomon didn't just get what he needed. He got far, far, more. Grace again.

He owned twelve thousand horses.[29] Horses were the best and fastest military transport of the day. Also, he owned one thousand four-hundred chariots, which were the tanks of the day. He had an annual income of twenty-six tons of gold. So in today's prices, his income would have put Isra-El as one of our top ten richest countries. And that was just Solomon's income from gold. You can understand why it was said of Solomon that he had so much gold it made silver as common as muck in Isra-El—it wasn't even valued as anything special because there was just so much of it. You probably made your pet's drinking bowl out of it.[30]

Solomon also was a great trader in such commodities as copper. On top of this, Solomon traded in exotic pets like baboons and peacocks. He had a merchant navy that brought him back luxurious woods like sandalwood. All these came from the mysterious land far away called "Ophir"—a land fabulously rich and luxurious. Many have tried to find it since—looking in such diverse places as Zimbabwe, Mozambique, South Africa, Peru, Brazil, India, Pakistan, the Philippines or Australia. No one knows now where it was but Solomon knew then and by his trading alliances and control of trading routes plus his taxation system, he and Israel were rich—fabulously and famously rich. So famously rich that the South-Arabian Queen of Sheba sat on an uncomfortable camel for twelve hundred miles of inhospitable terrain because she just had to come and visit him.[31] She was desperate to see whether the stories told about his wealth were true. She wasn't disappointed.

But through all this, Solomon remembered the source of his power and his wealth—that he was chosen by the Lord. He was the next in the Lord's promised line of key humans on earth placed here to keep his special people true to the contract.

His specialness was seen by the way Solomon was allowed by the Lord to build him a special house unlike his Father, David.[32] This was to be a

---

28. Matthew 6:33.
29. 1 Kings 10:11–29.
30. 1 Kings 10:27; 2 Chronicles 9:20.
31. 1 Kings 10:1–13.
32. 1 Kings 6:1—9:9.

permanent home for the holy Ark box and a focus for the people of Isra-El to show what the Lord meant to them by offering sacrifices. It was built at the center of Jeru-Salem—on the same mount that around a thousand years earlier, Abraham had been a split-second away of sacrificing Solomon's famous ancestor, Isaac,. But Solomon's Temple was an age away from those early days of His Story. Solomon's Temple was even a long way away from the tent that Moses had used for meeting with God. It used rich materials and designs. It used all the materials Solomon's father had left in store for him to use. David might not have been allowed to build the Temple himself, but he had done everything but build it.

The Temple was contemporary but classic. It was a house fit for a King and more importantly—a King's King. It took seven years to complete—true this was six years less than the palace Solomon built for himself, but still it was a magnificent building.

The opening of a new building is always an exciting time and this was no exception. It was grand, memorable and almost overwhelming—aweful verging on awful. The holy Ark box was brought in and placed in its new home. It was accompanied by singers and musicians playing harps and crashing cymbals. There was a one hundred and twenty strong trumpet fanfare. Everyone sang, "The Lord is good—his love lasts for ever."

King Solomon stood and spoke. In the middle of his speech he posed a very important rhetorical question which ironically reveals a fundamental flaw in all Temple building and in fact all attempts where humans try to control God's activity on earth. "Can God really live on earth with humans? The stars, even the farthest stars cannot hold you—how much less this Temple I have built for you." [33]

Solomon remembered. He remembered that His Story is not about humans taming God or controlling God. It is not about building a tower up to God and dragging him down and locking him in a building. It is about God breaking through into his Universe, his world. He remembered that God had chosen his father David and all his ancestors right back to Abraham, because he wanted a nation. Why? God wanted a family on earth to save humanity. And at the center of that family, God wanted a special building—a building which would hold the holy Ark box. This box held the stones forged in the heat of the earth but engraved with words from outside of the Universe: the stones which connected the inside and outside of the Universe; the stones which reminded the people of Mount Sinai—the great Doorway moment of their history.

---

33. 1 Kings 8:27.

This was to be a building which would stand as a reminder that the Lord should be at the center of his family and the wider family of humanity itself. The Temple was to be the Doorway to God for the whole earth, not just for God's people. Solomon in his out-of-this-world wisdom had a wide vision for his people and their new Temple. In his inaugural speech in the new Temple, he pleaded with God that, "When the foreigner comes and prays towards this Temple, hear from heaven, your real home, and do whatever the foreigner asks of you."[34] Why was Solomon asking God to be so generous to the non-Family Abraham person? He went on to explain, "So that all the peoples of the earth may know your name in the same way as your own people—Isra-El." He prayed that Isra-El as a people would become a living Doorway to God who lives beyond the Universe: that Isra-El would save humanity; that through the living Doorway of Isra-El a way of escape would be established—for all humanity.

The building of Solomon's Temple marked the establishment of Family Abraham as a super-power nation with a super-power God. Solomon's vision was truly international. It had gone global. This global vision encouraged the Mouthpieces of God on earth to speak God's words to the other Gentile (non Family Abraham) nations. Famously, the Mouthpiece of God called Jonah, when he tried to run away from this global aspect to his call ended up incarcerated in a great fish for three days until he gave in; admitted his lack of vision and was vomited into obedience.[35] From now on Isra-El and its Temple were going to be the permanent superhighway to heaven beyond the Universe—for all humans throughout space and time.

To mark the grandeur of this global vision, fire fell from the sky and burnt the sacrifices in the new Temple.[36] This was just like Noah's sacrifice of a few of his precious animals after God had saved them from the great flood, but this time not just the sacrifice of a few animals. This time twenty-two thousand cattle and one hundred and twenty thousand sheep and goats, as well as countless fat offerings and grain offerings—all burnt. And as if to show that the Lord was moving in, God's powerful cloud that had accompanied the people of Isra-El in their escape from Egypt appeared again. It must have mingled with the smoke from the burnt sacrifices—so much so that it is recorded that the priests couldn't see what on earth they were doing. They didn't need to. The Lord was running the show.

This would be a good place to leave His Story. Hadn't all of God's targets been met? His Story had gone from failure to success. His Story which

---

34. 1 Kings 8:40–43.
35. Jonah 1–4.
36. 2 Chronicles 7:1–10.

started with humanity kicked out of a garden paradise through the Doorway finishes in a Temple marking the international superhighway Doorway leading the way for the whole of humanity to return to paradise. His Story which started with a small family finishes with a super-power nation—rich, strong and respected. His Story which started with one or two people faithful to the Lord finishes with a powerful wise and committed king praying for all the nations of the world. His Story was now a "once upon a time" story ending with everyone living happily ever after.

But His Story wasn't complete. The global vision had yet to become reality. His Story still had to move from one nation out to the whole of mankind—to every human—everywhere.

But at least Solomon marked a glorious end to the foundational phase. The next phase was now ready to begin. Isra-El was a world super-power with trading links throughout the known world. It was at the center of fashion and ideas. Down these trading routes and links, God was going to be exported.

But His Story is honest—painfully honest. In the later years of Solomon, something went wrong. And the result of Solomon's failure shapes the rest of His Story—slowing it up, turning it in on itself rather than out to the world. A split appears in the family of God—the chosen bloodline that would save the world. What terrible thing did Solomon do wrong that caused such a rift? He put his relationship with a woman above God—or to be honest—his relationship with many women above God. In a re-run of history, Solomon followed in his father's footsteps. You know the wise old saying that the lesson of history is that humans don't learn the lesson of history. Maybe the same is true with His Story. But Solomon's failure wasn't a cruel act of adultery with one woman—like his father's. It wasn't even a ruthless act of manslaughter as a result of a sin with one woman. It wasn't that he abused women or hated women. In fact he wrote one of the most famous love songs ever written to a woman—The Song of Songs.[37] Famous for its tender, romantic, sensual imagery, it is so sexually explicit that Jewish boys have not been allowed to read it until they are thirteen. The love song is stacked full of oriental code words for love-making. Once you know the key to the code it makes your hair curl. On one level it is a natural simple tale of two people in love; on another level it is a sexually charged poem to be sung to a soundtrack of passion. It takes very seriously the power of passionate sexual love and warns the reader on more than one occasion never to awake

---

37. Song of Songs 1–8.

sexual love before it is ready—a warning which many in our society today would do well to heed.[38]

All of this proves that Solomon was a great lover—and God didn't mind a bit. Solomon's failure wasn't to do with his influence over one woman, like David, but instead, the subtle influence his women had over him.[39] His many wives (seven hundred, give or take a few) and the three hundred women in his harem exercised an increasing influence on him as he got older. On purpose he had married women from outside of Family Abraham. He did it for political reasons: to secure alliances and treaties; to secure Isra-El's place in the international political scene of the day. Amongst his royal wives was even a daughter of the Pharaoh of Egypt.[40] The rest were Moabites, Ammonites, Edomites, Hittites and even a Sidonian or two. This went directly and expressly against the Lord's rules that dictated that Isra-El men should marry someone who also remembered the Lord. His people had to be focused—they weren't to have split loyalties—a wise thing to do now even.[41]

But wise King Solomon didn't just forget this—he celebrated his disobedience by building non-Yah-weh places of worship for his foreign wives so they could feel at home. He then went even further and worshipped with them. He made himself feel at home with gods who weren't God—breaking the number one rule given to Moses by God on the holy mountain—no other gods but Yah-weh. Ironic—Solomon had given the holy Ark box containing the ten rules a grand home. He had led the worship at the opening of the home. And then he ignored the rules at the center of the home. And then he turned his back on the Temple he had built and played away at a pagan shrine. He just did his own thing. He forgot why he was King. He forgot who he was in His Story. He forgot what he was meant to do in His Story. He forgot his destiny.

But the Lord remembered and broke through the Doorway and told him that he would tear the Kingdom from his son—not away from Solomon as David's son—that was a solid promise—but away from Solomon's son.

And so after Solomon, His Story splits into more than one track. The united Family Abraham would tear apart into two nations—two nations who claimed to be the true Family Abraham. This would produce two Kings of Family Abraham. But there still could only be one royal bloodline. But

38. Song of Songs 2:7; 3:5; 8:4.
39. 1 Kings 11:1–3.
40. 2 Chronicles 8:11.
41. 2 Corinthians 6:14–16.

even that one royal bloodline would be fragmented into two. There was going to be a public royal bloodline and a secret and private bloodline.[42]

This split in the Lord's special bloodline wouldn't be healed until almost a thousand years later: not until it healed in a rough building a million miles from a royal Temple; not until it healed by a birth in a rough animal feeding trough back in David's hometown of Beth-Lehem—the place where the bloodline had originally turned royal.[43]

This reunification would be in a way that Solomon, even with his super-natural wisdom, could never have envisaged.

---

42. Matthew 1:6–16.
43. Luke 2:1–7.

## 27

## The Right Track?

THE SPLIT IN THE royal bloodline occurred after Solomon died. Solomon's son, Rehoboam, succeeded his father and immediately succeeded in splitting the family nation of Isra-El.[1] King Solomon had taken taxes from the people of Isra-El and other nations. He had used slave labor in his work. He had become dangerously close to behaving how the Egyptian Pharaohs had behaved to Family Isra-El when they had been held prisoner in Egypt a few hundred years earlier. But despite this, Solomon had ruled wisely by consent—he kept the people on his side. But the son of the wisest King was unwise. Even though he was rich, he wanted to be richer. Even though he received taxes, he wanted higher and heavier taxes. And the people rebelled: the people fought against it. Only the area around Jeru-Salem opted to stay with Solomon's son. The rest fought against his rule—literally.

One of Solomon's ex-enemies came back home and triggered a coup. He took off the north of the land. Only the descendants of Judah remained with Solomon's son. At least they had Jeru-Salem and its suburbs—but even this was then ransacked by Shishak, the Pharaoh of Egypt.[2]

It was a mess, but a mess planned-for in His Story. It wasn't a coincidence that only Judah remained with the Son of David. The Lord had written this into His Story many years earlier. He had planned to bring his Special-One out of Judah. Jacob-Israel had made this clear in his blessings to his sons hundreds of year earlier.[3] Now Judah was a separate nation. Judah alone stuck to His Story by siding with Solomon's family. The north left and went off track veering away from the Lord's bloodline. This nation continued—still under the name Isra-El—but it was in name only—it was a pale imitation.

1. 1 Kings 12:1–24.
2. 1 Kings 14:21–31.
3. Genesis 49:10.

The Temple Doorway to the outside of the Universe was in the capital of the south. This capital, Jeru-Salem, was off-limits to the northern imitation. To compensate for its loss, the north invented its own worship center at Beth-El where Jacob, hundreds of years before, had seen heaven opened up as he slept.

But this alternative Doorway had long since closed. This alternative Temple was a fake. It didn't work as a Doorway to the outside of the Universe. It simply tried to be all things to all people. It tried hard to please everybody's religious needs by being open to the worship of all gods. This, by definition, was doomed to failure, because there was only one power bigger than the Universe—Yah-weh. By pretending that there were many gods, the worship center broke the first two of the Ten Rules given to Moses by God himself. The worship in Beth-El broke God's rules of exclusivity and the worship there simply reinforced the closed Doorway.

This was not a good start for the new split-away nation. This second rate copy of the real Isra-El was led at first by a King called Jeroboam. He was the son of a man called Nebat. This King became famous in His Story—infamous more like. Every time his name is mentioned in His Story, it is linked with failure. His name becomes a mantra used whenever any king in the future failed. Each failed king is said to be like, "Jeroboam, son of Nebat, who caused Isra-El to sin."[4] His Story's verdict on this king was that you couldn't get any lower than Jeroboam. Whenever sin is mentioned—Jeroboam is mentioned.

Sin has "i" in its center and sin means having "I" at the center of your life. Sin means rebelling against the Lord and splitting off and doing your own thing—worshipping "I" as your Lord. Sin means splitting away from the Lord's script and trying to write your own storyline to your life. His Story insists that this personal storyline is a fake storyline: a pale imitation of the real thing; a storyline without a happy ending. Sin isn't His Story. Sin is against the God who created the Universe. Sin is doing what we like, not what the Lord likes. At heart it is pointless: it never works; it never succeeds; it goes against the grain of the Universe—the Maker's instructions.

And as if to prove the point this fake split-away Isra-El with its proverbially sinful king didn't work. It didn't succeed. True, it continued to exist for two-hundred years because it is easy to look like you are following God when really you're not. Many religions and worship institutions and their buildings would continue to exist even if the god they promoted was proved to be fake. It is easy for religion to become an end in itself even when it should have ended itself. Religion that doesn't open the Doorway to

---

4. 1 Kings 16:26, 31.

## the right track?

the outside of the Universe is pointless. Worship that has no link through the Doorway is earthbound. It is just cultural—a group of people with a common sub-culture namely—a shared desire to be religious. By definition, earth-based religion helps no one—it has no power because God's not in it.

The new separate northern Isra-El existed but God wasn't in it. His Story was to remind humans why they existed—who was their Creator. The fake northern Isra-El couldn't help further this storyline because they had forgotten themselves why they existed—who was in control of them. The counterfeit Isra-El wasn't on the main track of His Story. It was side-tracked, on a siding going nowhere.

Not that God had lost his feelings for his rebellious family. He gave this rebellious northern Isra-El numerous chances to come back—to rejoin God's family—to get back on track. Grace—again. The Lord sent some important messengers to Rehoboam's successors in fake Isra-El—powerful Spokespersons—his Mouthpieces—his megaphones to wake up his deaf family.

Like El-i-Yah. His name shows his importance. Not many people can boast having a doubly divine name—El and Yah-weh. His name stated the truth he lived for: Yah-weh is El (God). This two-for-the-price-of-one Mouthpiece of God couldn't help but come into conflict with the fake Kings of northern Israel.

One of these kings was called Ahab. Ahab followed Jeroboam son of Nebat in more ways than one. El-i-Yah went regularly to him and told him off.[5] This annoyed the king. Ahab had a nickname for El-i-Yah that meant "pain in the neck for Isra-El" (loosely translated).[6] But El-i-Yah wasn't put off. He told Ahab to get back on track. Fake Isra-El wasn't just on the wrong track: it was like a runaway train; speeding up; heading straight for the bumpers at Nowhere Station. But Ahab and especially his proverbially evil wife, Jezebel, either didn't see or didn't care.

But El-i-Yah did. He tried to snap Ahab out of his suicidal trajectory. He told the King that there would be a drought until Ahab turned back to the Lord. Isra-El would die of thirst if they didn't come back to the Lord. This wasn't El-i-Yah's idea—it was the Lord's. El-i-Yah was the Lord's prophet—simply his Mouthpiece.

No rain fell—for three years. And then it came to a head on a mountain—it always does in His Story.[7] Ahab called his fake "prophets" to the mountain for a showdown. These men were really shaman of the fertility god, Baal. Baal—the god who was meant to make crops grow; animals

---

5. 1 Kings 17:1; 18:1, 16–18.
6. 1 Kings 18:17.
7. 1 Kings 18:19–46.

produce young; and humans give birth. Baal was allegedly in charge of the liquid that made life possible—rain. But this Baal was just a story: a myth; a dangerous piece of nonsense still believed by thousands even though there had been a drought for three years. El-i-Yah had to show Baal up for who he was—a fake. El-i-Yah challenged Baal and his believers to a duel. El-i-Yah challenged Baal and his believers to open up the Doorway to heaven and send a lightning strike of fire down to burn up a slaughtered bull as a sacrifice: to prove himself; to show he could break into the world; to show he could control the natural environment. El-i-Yah in so doing challenged Isra-El to stop trying to think they could be worshippers of Baal and the Lord at the same time. He teased them that they were hopping on one leg and then the other—they couldn't decide which track to take!

Game on. The prophets of Baal went first. They prayed to Baal all morning. They danced wildly to attract his attention—but no lightning strike. At lunchtime, El-i-Yah suggested they might like to shout louder—maybe Baal was daydreaming: or on the toilet; or nodded off; or maybe gone on holiday. Enraged, Baal's boys shouted louder and danced more and more wildly. And then in a desperate bid to attract their god's attention, they self-harmed—slashing themselves with knives hoping that Baal who was meant to be in charge of the essence of life would be impressed with the way they were spattering their life-juice everywhere. This went on all afternoon but still no lightning strike. The bull was still untouched.

Then El-i-Yah took over. He built a barbecue with twelve stones to remind everyone of Jacob-Isra-El's family of twelve sons—the foundation of the true Isra-El. He dug a ditch around the stones and poured three gallons of water over the sliced bull. Everything was soaking wet including the wood which was to be lit. Then when the sun was beginning to sink, he simply and quietly requested that the Lord prove his lordship—that he was the boss—the one in charge.

No razzmatazz. No hype. No showing off. Just a crack of lightning that lit up the darkening sky. Fire streaked down and incinerated the bull, the wood, and even the stones. The ground was scorched and the water in the trench was evaporated instantly and before the day was out, a tiny rain cloud appeared on the horizon over the Mediterranean Sea and quickly blew in land before it doused the ground in torrential rain.

Who was in charge of this world? Who was in charge of life giving rain? The contest answered the question—Yah-weh. He is God. Yah is El—in the language of Family Abraham.

But did Ahab listen? No. Did his cruel hard wife, Jezebel listen? No. Instead, Jezebel put out a contract on El-i-Yah.[8] After the contest, El-i-Yah was euphoric but emotionally drained. When he heard of Jezebel's threats, he was petrified. El-i-Yah ran to the only place he felt was safe. It was another mountain—but this was not any mountain, it was Sinai—God's mountain. This was the historic site of God's Doorway onto earth where he met Moses in the Burning Bush before he later met Isra-El and gave them the ten rules. And God didn't let El-i-Yah down this time. Yet again, God broke through the Doorway and spoke with El-i-Yah. A gale force wind blew up; an earthquake shattered the ground; even volcanic fire raged again—but the Lord didn't use these keys to open the Doorway. He unlocked the Universe by a gentle breeze that whispered words of comfort deep into El-i-Yah's being: meeting his need; encouraging him; revitalizing him; inspiring him. God didn't need wild dancing and massive displays of force to prove he was real. God worked on a deeper level with El-i-Yah—inside him—in that secret place in him that no one else could access, even his closest friend: inside his soul; inside his heart; inside his personality. God entered El-i-Yah through the Mount Sinai inside him. The Doorway to the outside of the Universe was now inside a human.

This was a spoiler for the later chapters of His Story. Eight hundred years of His Story had yet to play out before this would be an offer available to the whole of humanity—an offer that is still open today. But how did the Lord use this radical new Doorway location? He communicated by a quiet whisper. What did the Lord whisper deep into El-i-Yah through the Doorway into his very being? "You're not on your own."[9] And to prove it the Lord gave El-i-Yah some vital statistics—the odds. They weren't thousands to one. The Lord told El-i-Yah, "There's at least seven thousand who haven't yet given in to Baal."

It wasn't the whole world against El-i-Yah—it just felt like it.

---

8. 1 Kings 19:1–18.
9. 1 Kings 19:18.

# 28

## Outnumbered?

EVEN IN SPLIT-AWAY ISRA-EL, there were a good number of people who remembered the Lord. But the sad fact was that even this sizeable minority of people still faithful to the contract with the Lord couldn't save fake Isra-El. It was destined to wither and die. It was an appendix to His Story as an appendix is to a human body. It existed but no one really seemed to know why. It was a place where disease had taken hold—it needed cutting out. The real question in fake Isra-El's case was whether it would be a nice neat key-hole procedure or deep surgery. In the end it was more a slow death. It was a slipping slowly into the comatose pages of world history rather than being the main player in the very much alive His Story.

But that's not to say that there weren't a few His Story highlights on the way to its end a hundred years later. It's not to say that the Lord wasn't faithful to his seven thousand remaining people. The Lord was going to keep his side of the contract for them. He had special plans for them—plans that included sending special envoys to protect them.

Take El-i-Yah's apprentice, El-isha (El-God is the one who saves), for example. El-isha inherited El-i-Yah's spirit and power from God. El-i-Yah passed them to him after he had taken his new assistant on a whistle-stop tour around the historical Doorways between earth and outside of the Universe.[1] Beth-El first—where Jacob had seen the staircase stretching into heaven; Jericho next—where the Lord had appeared as a military commander and told Joshua how to break the heavily defended city just by marching and making a big noise; the River Jordan next—where the waters had parted to allow Israel into the Promised Land. On this re-visit, the waters again stood up on end for El-i-Yah and El-isha to walk through. The trigger for this waterless pathway was not a stick on this occasion, but El-i-Yah's stick-like rolled-up cloak. This re-enacting of one of the Lord's earlier chapters in His Story seemed to unlock the Doorway to beyond the

---

1. 2 Kings 2:1–18.

Universe again. El-i-Yah was instantly caught up into the eye of a tiny but extremely powerful tornado—a whirlwind of dust that made strange shapes of a chariot and horses spiraling up into the sky with El-i-Yah riding them. As the wind sucked him upwards into the sky and out of the Doorway into God's zone outside of the Universe, El-i-Yah's rolled up cloak fell to the ground, trapped on the earthly side of the closing Door. Devoid of its owner, El-isha picked it up and used it to hit the water again. Again, the waters parted. There's an old phrase about how people sometimes take over the "mantle" of their hero. A mantle is a cloak. Here El-isha literally took over the mantle of El-i-Yah. He found that by using it, he had direct contact with God through the Doorway. He could do what his mentor did. He had become another mini Mount Sinai—another place where God touched the earth—a new focus of His Story.

But how was El-isha going to use this new found super-natural power? Answer—to protect the faithful El followers in fake Isra-El. But first this meant protecting the whole of this northern counterfeit Isra-El so that true Family Abraham members in its midst would be safe. This meant protecting Isra-El against their growing enemy, Syria.

Syria threatened to destroy the whole of northern Isra-El. El-isha somehow focused his powers to penetrate the King of Syria's bedroom.[2] Not that he was a peeping tom, but this private room was where the King planned his military campaigns. El-isha eavesdropped on Top Secret Syrian military plans. Long before electronic bugs, El-isha bugged Syria. Every time Syria tried to mount a surprise attack, Isra-El was ready. To the King of Syria, there was only one explanation—a spy, a leak.

The King of Syria got his spooks onto it—his version of MI5—his CIA. But unlikely though it seemed, the most likely answer they found was one man living miles away—El-isha. This annoyed Syria so much that they attempted a surgical strike deep into Isra-El's territory to Dothan—the place where the prophet lived. But as they surrounded the town, El-isha's servant happened to pop outside and look up and see hundreds of enemy troops circling their town on the hillside. They were outnumbered. The servant panicked and ran inside and told El-isha. But El-isha believed that when the Lord was on your side, you are never outnumbered. He knew the stories of Gideon. He knew the stories of his mentor, El-i-Yah. To El-isha the Lord's support made even one person the majority. But El-isha wanted his servant to see this truth for himself: to see the Lord's forces lined up on the other side of the Doorway ready to mount an attack; to have a little Mount Sinai moment of his own; to see earth as if he were looking from outside

2. 2 Kings 6:8–23.

of the Universe in through the Doorway. So, El-isha asked God to open his servant's eyes so he could see with God's eyes. Suddenly, the servant could see row on row of mysterious horses and chariots bright like flames of fire defending El-isha and himself. In comparison the Syrians looked pathetic—outnumbered.

As the foreign soldiers advanced towards the town, El-isha asked the Lord to do the opposite than he had done previously for his servant. And so the Lord struck all the crack Syrian troops blind—blind in a foreign enemy land: lost in a foreign enemy land. They needed help. El-isha offered to help them. He persuaded the helpless and hapless soldiers to follow him as they were blind to his real identity. He promised he would take them to El-isha. This ended up with the Syrian soldiers walking in a human crocodile behind El-isha. El-isha then led the fearsome soldiers by the hand as if they were little children. He led them to the capital city of fake Isra-El called Samaria.

Faced with the sight of this procession of humiliation for his arch-enemy, the King of Isra-El was over the moon—he wanted to kill all of them. But El-isha wouldn't let him slaughter them, but instead got the Lord to open their eyes. And he did. Instead of dying by the sword, they died a death of embarrassment as they realized where they were and who had led them there. To rub it in, El-isha ordered a banquet to be served for them. After eating too much they waddled home to Syria, red-faced but full bellied.

Understandably, not much was heard from the Syrians for quite a while. It took them several years to live it down. This was in fact the second embarrassment the Syrians had suffered. Earlier their top soldier had caught the dreaded embarrassing skin disease called leprosy.[3]

Leprosy was not just a disease—it was the most feared disease. Leprosy left the sufferer disfigured with sores and lumps and bumps. It left the sufferer with festering untreated injuries due to loss of warning pain. Nowadays with early treatment, sufferers can lead a normal life, but in those days, there was a social stigma. You were an outcast—a social pariah. No one came near you because they thought they could catch it off you. You had to live outside in special colonies away from everyone. Lepers had to ring a bell when anyone came near and shout, "unclean!"

That's how you were seen: unclean; dirty; infectious. What a disease for anyone to catch! But for Naaman, the commander of the Syrian army it meant the end of everything: his career; his position in society; his family; his good health. He was so desperate he even listened to his wife's little captured slave girl from Isra-El. In a chance comment, she told Naaman's wife, "It's a pity you don't know El-isha. He has special powers. He'd cure

3. 2 Kings 5:1–27.

my master"—truth from a slave girl—wisdom for an unlikely source. But despite the sensible advice, the truth was that you wouldn't normally let your best friend know you had a skin disease never mind your enemy.

But leprosy wasn't normal. It was the end—the worst thing that could ever happen to you. You wouldn't wish it on your enemy. So, Naaman followed the little girl's advice and came to ask his enemy, El-isha, for healing. Commander Naaman offered El-isha money. But El-isha wouldn't heal him for money or for glory. He simply told him to wash seven times in the tried and tested Gateway to the Promised Land—the River Jordan.

Naaman was frantic; Naaman was begging but he wasn't that desperate. He wasn't going to make a complete fool of himself. He had some self-respect left. The River Jordan to Naaman was little better than a cess pool—an enemy cess pool at that. But to El-isha and to the people of Isra-El it was a place where the Lord had broken through into the world—where God had brought them into their Promised Land. It was the Doorway to God's super-natural power. It had taken Isra-El to the next exciting chapter of His Story and El-isha believed it could give Naaman a future in His Story.

But as far as Naaman was concerned, his next chapter was to pack up and go back home, fed up. But his servants stopped him and spoke sense to him. They pointed out that if El-isha had told him to do something painful, difficult and heroic, like climb a mountain or not eat for a month or save a maiden in distress, he would have done it. All he had been told to do was wash in a second rate river—truth from servants—wisdom from an unlikely source.

They had put their finger on it. We humans like our religion to tell us to do something difficult; something that will make us feel really good afterwards—like we've earned any help we get from our "god" so we can take some of the credit. We like to pay for what we get. But worship of the Lord isn't any ordinary religion. It's about getting what we don't deserve. It's about grace—that rule that breaks the rules. It's about us accepting help. It's about us admitting we need help—when we mess up: the Lord cleans up. Naaman needed to be clean. But he couldn't do it himself. He had to beg the foreign enemy God. He had to have faith in the Lord of Isra-El. He had to bring himself low seven times in the special River Jordan.

After a bit of posturing, he did it and was instantly healed. To show he had got the message, he transported some of the soil from Isra-El back home so that he could worship the Lord on the Lord's land. He didn't realize the whole world is the Lord's—he is the Creator of the whole Universe. His Story was going to make this clear in the chapters that followed. His Story was going to spread throughout the whole of the world through unlikely people like servants and slave girls and even foreign army generals—even foreign army generals who had infectious diseases.

It was a pity that the Kings of fake Isra-El didn't get it. They didn't beg for help—for grace. They went from bad to worse. Unlike Naaman, they didn't come to the Lord's Mouthpiece for help. They didn't follow the Lord's rules—his contract.

They just did their own thing.

# 29

## Barking up the Wrong Tree

THE KINGS OF FAKE Isra-El failed. But that's not to say that their Kingdom was poor, pathetic and poverty-stricken—it wasn't a state in an awful state. To human eyes it would have appeared rich and successful. The rich people lived in massive stone mansions for the winter and sumptuous houses full of expensive furniture in the summer. They laid their pampered lotioned bodies on beds and couches inlaid with ivory. They were too catatonic: too drunk on the wine from their lush vineyards; too stuffed full of the massive amounts of meat they had eaten, to move. Lifting a finger was too much effort. They drank wine not by the glass, standard or large, but by the bowlful. The most exercise they got was strumming on their expensive harps.[1]

How do we know all this?—Amos. Amos was another Mouthpiece of God. He said it how God saw it. He said it how it was. Amos even dared call the rich women in Isra-El, "fat cows"—fat cows who all day ordered their husbands to fill their wine bowls up—rude now and rude then.[2]

Why was Amos so rude, cutting, and politically incorrect? It wasn't that he was bothered that this decadent opulent lifestyle was unhealthy (though it was). What made him angry was that this lifestyle was built on the backs of the poor. He blamed the rich in fake Isra-El for stamping on the heads of the poor. The rich lied in court about their cruelty and paid their way out of any blame. The rich stole from the poor by using dodgy scales ripping off their vulnerable customers. The rich sold garbage for high prices—cutting the food that the poor lived off with rubbish they found on the floor.[3]

What angered Amos the most was that they planned all of this when they were in their fake Temple indulging in their fake worship—trying to look like they were sincerely holy. Even during their fake "holy" worship, the rich were desperate to get out and rip off some poor unsuspecting person.

1. Amos 3:12–15; 6:4–6.
2. Amos 4:1–3.
3. Amos 8:4–6.

How much these people had forgotten that their ancestors had been poor oppressed slaves in Egypt! How much these people had forgotten the story of little David the shepherd being chosen to be the greatest King of Isra-El! How much these people had forgotten that the Lord "looks on the heart of humans, not on their outward appearance."[4]

But the Lord hadn't forgotten. He had a message for these people who should know better: "You make me sick." Through Amos the Lord told the people of fake Isra-El that he hated their fake worship. Their songs made him sick. Their sacrifices made him angry.[5] Instead the Lord wanted justice and right living. He didn't want hypocrites. He wanted people whose lives lived up to their words.[6]

This was a theme picked up over seven hundred years later by the greatest Super-star of His Story. He took the Greek word "hypocrite" from the stage of Greek drama (meaning an actor wearing a mask) to the gritty debating chamber. He was clear that in his day the religious leaders made him sick too—they were all two-faced mask-wearers—looking holy but in reality were anything but.[7]

But back to seven hundred and fifty years earlier, another of the Lord's Mouthpieces went to extreme lengths to get fake Isra-El to listen to the Lord—he married a prostitute. This Mouthpiece of the Lord was called Hosea. And Hosea married a prostitute called Gomer. Hosea claimed that the Lord had given him the desire to marry her—an action that must have been open to question at the very least.[8] Hosea was holy: Gomer wasn't. Hosea believed in faithfulness and loyalty: Gomer didn't. Gomer became a good wife to Hosea for a short time. She even gave Hosea two children. But soon she was lured back to her pimp—back to those who valued her as a commodity and not as a person.[9] Hosea tried to stop her; tried to block her way; tried to reason with her. But he couldn't force her—he loved her—he had to respect her decision. In return for his love and respect: she abandoned her own children; she abandoned her own husband, and went back to her old life—a life of risk and violence and demeaning liaisons.

But the Lord told Hosea to get back out there and find her—to bring her home. By the time Hosea found her, she was a sex slave. The only way he could get his own wife back was to buy her back on the sex slave market—he

---

4. 1 Samuel 16:7b.
5. Amos 5:21–23.
6. Amos 5:15, 24.
7. Matthew 23:13, 15, 23, 25, 27, 29.
8. Hosea 1:2–3.
9. Hosea 2:2–9.

had to redeem her.[10] And what was her redemption value?—less than two hundred US dollars plus a few boxes of barley to sweeten the deal. It was all she was worth—but not to Hosea—he still loved her. But not to the Lord—he still loved her. And Hosea hung in there with her and gave her time to get over her past and get ready for their future together.

Why did the Lord let Hosea love a prostitute? No doubt because she needed rescuing by a good man but also because the Lord wanted humans to know what he is really like: the Lord is into rescuing; the Lord is into redeeming; the Lord is into buying back lost humans—whatever it costs; it's what makes him tick; it's what he is about. Later he was to prove this by showing that he would even pay with the life of his own son.[11]

Redemption costs. Hosea to be God's Mouthpiece on earth needed to know in every part of his body what the Lord felt like seeing fake Isra-El being unfaithful to him—ignoring and breaking his contract with them. He needed to understand what it cost the Lord to commit himself to humanity. He needed to understand what it cost the Lord to commit himself to creating a world of safety and beauty. He needed to understand what it cost the Lord to commit himself to a human family—Abraham and his children. The Lord had committed himself to use Abraham's family to rescue the world whatever the cost. But Amos' brothers and sisters in fake northern Isra-El didn't want to return that commitment—they didn't value his love. Instead they looked to other gods and to luxury and to their own pleasure. They took all of the Lord's gifts and then walked away from him. They were unfaithful even though he had saved them many times—even though he had come looking for them and rescued them from slavery. Still they continued walking the streets of the world looking for another kind of love. They disregarded their contract with God—their marriage contract—their "till death us do part" contract.

But the story of Gomer had a happy ending—she came home—she tried again. But no such happy ending for fake Isra-El. It was all about to end—for ever. It wasn't a surprise. The Lord's Mouthpieces, Amos and Hosea, had spoken publicly that it would end with the counterfeit wing of Isra-El imploding. Weak, unfaithful kings one after another came to the throne and left again leaving the split-away nation vulnerable to attack.

First, the king of the new super-power of the time, Assyria, with the majestic name of Tiglath Pileser the Third, attacked Isra-El and softened them up. Then just over seven hundred and twenty years before A.D. took over from B.C., his successor, Shalmeneser, completely destroyed and

10. Hosea 3:1–2.
11. John 3:16.

dismantled the capital of fake Isra-El, Samaria. He didn't just break the buildings down. He dismantled everything—even the society. He also took many Isra-Elites hostage and removed them to other countries under his power, replacing them in Samaria with people from other lands. These people became known as the "Samaritans."[12] Hated by most as second class and unfit for God's Family—but famous four hundred years later for being surprisingly "good" in a tale told by the Lord's ultimate Star of His Story.[13]

This Super-star was not yet born, but still Amos and Hosea finished their prophecies by seeing a tiny pinprick of hope many years ahead on the furthest time horizon. They both knew that the Lord was insanely faithful and generous and patient. The Lord would rescue. The Lord would redeem. Hosea the lover believed that the Lord would again say to his people, "I will forgive their unfaithfulness because I love them madly."[14] Amos saw a time ahead when the great royal house of King David (which in fake Isra-El was now more like a collapsed tent) would be rebuilt.[15]

But for now, this split-away Isra-El was dead. The Lord had drawn a line under this footnote in His Story. The hope seen by Amos and Hosea would not grow out of this nation of dead diseased branches of Abraham's family tree. So, where would it grow from? What was left of Family Abraham's family tree? Not much—just one branch—Judah. Remember him? Jacob-Isra-El had said to Judah before he died: "The mark of Royalty will not leave you or your children, until the coming of the special King, the one whom all nations will honor."[16]

After the destruction of fake Isra-El, Judah's family was all that was left of Family Abraham. Judah's extended family was centered around Jeru-Salem: a people group still faithful to the Lord's bloodline of David and Solomon; a people group still faithful to the Lord's contract; a people group still looking forward to the special King—the anointed one that all the nations of the world would come to serve.

Judah looked forward to one of their own becoming King—not just King, but the one and only Super-star of His Story.

---

12. 2 Kings 16–17.
13. Luke 10:25–37.
14. Hosea 14:4–9.
15. Amos 9:11–15.
16. Genesis 49:10.

# 30

## Meanwhile Back at the Branch

LET'S REWIND HIS STORY for a moment. Whilst the northern branch of fake Isra-El was in the process of being chopped off and burnt by Assyria two hundred and fifty years after going it alone, what was happening back of the branch of Judah? The southern branch of Family Abraham had continued to be led by Solomon's descendants—the royal bloodline. The greatest achievement of the first king of this line, Rehoboam, as we have seen, was reigning over the break up of Family Abraham. He had indirectly created a North-South divide in the Family Tree of Abraham.

After Rehoboam came King Abi-Yah. He tried his best to reunite Family Abraham by persuading the counterfeit fake Isra-El in the north to join up again with Judah. His "persuasion" involved using four hundred thousand soldiers marching on the North. Quite "persuasive" you would have thought. But northern fake Isra-El had an eight hundred thousand strong army of their own. The ensuing battle left half a million of Isra-El dead.[1] It was a victory for King Abi-Yah but didn't achieve reunification.

Next in line for the Judah tribe was King Asa. King Asa remembered the contract between the Lord and his people. He remembered that God was really the King and not him. And so he did his best to remove the old religions. He even removed his old grandmother.[2] She had to go from being "Queen Mum" because she was into weird religious rites. He burnt her sacred fertility pole and cleared the nation of religious prostitution. Then he built up his army and defended Judah from attack. But his "Achilles heel" was severe foot-rot. Instead of trusting the Lord to be healed, he forgot and trusted his useless witch-doctors instead. Result—death.[3]

After King Asa came King Yeh-Oshaphat—Yah has judged (Yah and Yeh are the same in Hebrew as it has no vowels). Yah-weh judged that he

1. 2 Chronicles 13:1–18.
2. 1 Kings 15:13.
3. 2 Chronicles 16:12.

was a good king. Yeh-Oshaphat continued to attack Baal worship as being false and unfaithful to the Lord. Yeh-Oshaphat remembered that God was really the King. He remembered God's law. He remembered that God had sent his instructions through the Doorway to earth on Mount Sinai. Yeh-Oshaphat sent special agents out to teach the people God's rules and remind them of the small print of the contract again. He wanted his subjects to know that the law given to Moses was the boss, not him—so far so good.[4] But unfortunately Yeh-Oshaphat also had some dodgy friends and he trusted them more than God.

After King Yeh-Oshaphat came King Yeh-Oram. He was King of Judah when El-i-Yah was the Lord's Mouthpiece in the north. In fact, Yeh-Oram was married to the daughter of El-i-Yah's number one opponent and Baal duelist, King Ahab. This marriage was a result of one of the unhelpful friendships arranged by his father, Yeh-Oshaphat. El-i-Yah, the famous northern Mouthpiece of the Lord, didn't like Yeh-Oram. In fact he hated him so much he sent him a famous "poisoned letter."[5] It was to the point. It accused Yeh-Oram of forgetting to follow the good example of his father and instead following his father-in-law. Yeh-Oram was trying to make Judah as bad as fake Isra-El. For El-i-Yah there was nothing worse he could say. Yeh-Oram was a disgrace to the royal bloodline. In El-i-Yah's opinion, Yeh-oram didn't act as if God were King. He had turned his back on the vital truth that for a king to be a good king of God's people—he had to remember even he was under contract to God. And what was Yeh-Oram's penalty clause for breaking the contract? He would die a painful death—and he did (if you call your bowels dropping out painful).[6]

Next came King Ahaz-Yah. He only lasted a year and then something weird happened. At long last, a queen was crowned! Was this a great coup for women's rights? No. She wasn't a young, pretty, fairytale princess with a great future, but a hard bitten, bitter mother of the hapless late King Ahaz-Yah and the daughter of nasty King Ahab and the vicious Queen Jezebel—the same Jezebel who took a "contract" out on El-i-Yah. Her daughter obviously had her mother's genes. Her name?—Athal-Yah. Her name might remind you of Attila as in "Attila the Hun." Her approach to any diplomacy would also remind you of Attila the Hun. Her rule for ruling was simple—oppose her or her son and you die—even if you were family. When her son died after a year on the throne, she grabbed sole power. She killed anyone who stood in her way—grandsons included. God's rule about not murdering

---

4. 2 Chronicles 17:7–9.
5. 2 Chronicles 21:12–15.
6. 2 Chronicles 21:18–19.

didn't seem to register highly on her list of things not to do. After all she was Queen. Who was God to tell her what to do? She'd forgotten big time who was King of Kings. She totally ignored the contract written by God.

Only one male relative escaped her massacre—her grandson, Yeh-Oash. All his brothers were killed by the wicked Queen. But Yeh-Oash was protected by his aunt and his great uncle, who happened to be the High Priest—God's Go-Between. Yeh-Oash's moment came, when after a popular revolution, Queen Athal-Yah was executed to public joy. And her only surviving grandson, Yeh-oash became King.[7] As long as Yeh-Oash listened to his great uncle, all was well because his uncle was the chief Go-Between connecting the people with God. Yeh-Oash ruled with reference to the Ruler of the Universe. He even repaired the Doorway-Temple.

But after his Uncle died, Yeh-Oash's trust in the Lord died as well. He even murdered his caring great uncle's son, the next High Priest.[8] A king killing the Lord's Go-Between: the Lord's appointed representative to link his people with him; the man who stood between the Doorway of heaven and earth? This was nothing less than an attempt to overthrow God's power in the world. Yeh-Oash had forgotten that God was the real King of Kings and that he was contracted to him. He broke the contract spectacularly. He had forgotten that at best he was simply an employee of Yah-weh. This wouldn't end well. And it didn't. Recovering from battle wounds, Yeh-Oash was murdered in his bed by two of his officials who hadn't forgiven him for killing the High Priest.[9]

Yeh-Oash's son, Amaz-Yah, didn't fare much better. He was desperate for another fight with fake northern Isra-El. No one thought this was a good idea except him. After all Isra-El were really family. But of course Amaz-Yah knew best. He was King! But again, he had forgotten that God was really King. After the widely predicted disastrous battle with the northern Kingdom of Israel, Jeru-Salem had a large part of its wall destroyed, and the Temple and the royal palace looted. And then for his pains, King Amaz-Yah was killed by his own side who had conspired against him.[10] Same rule—forget that God's law is King then forget your throne—you've no chance.

King Amaz-Yah, King Yeh-Oash, Queen Athal-Yah, King Ahaz-Yah—all poor monarchs, one after another. They had the crown and the throne, but they didn't have any lasting legacy. None of them register on the Lord's bloodline. None of them acknowledged that God was their Lord—their

7. 2 Kings 11:12–16.
8. 2 Chronicles 24:17–22.
9. 2 Chronicles 24:23–25.
10. 2 Chronicles 25:1–28.

King. None of them acknowledged that he was King of Kings. Yes, they had the right blood and genes but they weren't part of His Story. Significantly, they are all missing on the all important list of descendants of the Prince of Judah who was to come—the Super-star the whole of His Story was building up to.[11] They are all deleted: they are all erased; they are all expunged; they are all as if they had never existed—because they add nothing to His Story.

His Story is far more than blood or genes or human family. The truth is that you can't inherit your place in His Story by birth. Inheritance doesn't work in this story. Having your life-story as part of His Story is deeper and far more mysterious than simply genetic recycling—it is grace.

The next name that was deemed worthy to appear on His Story's list of descendants of the Prince of Judah's is Uzz-Yah. He was an unlikely hero. He was only a young sixteen year old boy when he came to the throne. But he reigned for fifty two years—the second longest serving King of Judah. He was successful at fighting. He was successful at designing weapons. He was successful at making Judah rich. He was successful at running the country well. He was successful at all the things kings had to be successful at in those days. And more important than all of that, he was successful at remembering the key to his power—doing what the Lord wanted—sticking to the contract. His name is the key to his success—Uzz-Yah meant "Yah-weh is my strength." Yah-weh was his source of strength—God was really his King.[12]

So at death, why was he not buried with all the other Kings in Jeru-Salem? Instead, why was he just buried in an ordinary field outside the city walls? The answer is linked to his life—in particular why he lived all alone under a sort of house arrest for years before his death. He was a leper: he had the dreaded skin disease that had afflicted Naaman; he had the disease that made you a social outcast. Should we feel sorry for him? Yes, except that His Story records that he caught the disease on one particular moment when he was doing one particular thing—the one thing as King he shouldn't have been doing. Something that got him banned from the Temple and normal society—he burnt incense in the Temple.[13]

Doesn't sound much but the burning of sweet smelling incense in the official Doorway out of the Universe was a holy replay of Noah's sacrifice of animals after being saved by the Lord from the flood. It was an attempt to tempt God to open the Doorway again. It is reported in the instance of Noah, that the Lord loved the smell of roast meat and opened up his heart

---

11. Matthew 1:8–9.
12. 2 Chronicles 26:1–15.
13. 2 Chronicles 26:16–23.

to Noah.[14] But more than the smell of barbecued meat, the Lord loved the smell of sweet success—of humans following his way and doing the right thing by following his instructions. Ever since Noah's fragrant smelling sacrifice, the Go-Between and his assistants, the priests, burnt incense to try and please God again—to tempt God to open up his heart to them.

So why shouldn't Uzz-Yah have burnt it as well? Because, it was the Priest's job—the job of the Lord's human Go-Between's, and no-one else. Uzz-Yah was just the King. Even the King couldn't appoint himself to stand in the Doorway between outside and inside of the Universe. Uzz-Yah for a brief moment had let his power go to his crowned head. He had forgotten that God was really King and instead had started to believe in his own success—like King Saul over two hundred years earlier.

Pride: an awful disease that we humans often catch—even Uzz-Yah. Pride: thinking we are King of our lives; thinking that we are our own God; thinking that we can tear up the contract with God and make up our own agreement. It is a disease that cuts us off from God like leprosy used to cut you off from your friends and family.

Up to Uzz-Yah's lonely death, he had to watch his young son Jotham rule as King for him. So much for human pride! His son, King Jotham, did all the good things his father had done—except that he wisely kept well clear of the Temple—especially the incense burners![15] The reclusive King Uzz-Yah's grave would have been forgotten very quickly situated as it was away from the royal cemetery—probably overgrown. But his name isn't forgotten. His name is still mentioned as a vital link in the chain leading to the great promised Prince of Judah.[16] This Prince would be allowed to be a priestly Go-Between for God's people as well as King.[17] And he did this with no sinful pride.[18]

Next stop on the royal bloodline was King Ahaz. He reigned in Judah at the time when the split-away fake northern Isra-El was fatally attacked by the new super power Assyria. This all powerful Assyria was hungry for more nations to devour—gobbling up land and nations was meat and drink to Assyria. Who would be next? In comparison to Assyria, Judah was tiny—far too small to fight off the new all-conquering aggressor. If tiny Judah fell to the Assyrian storm-troopers, all of Family Abraham would then be gone—dismembered. It would be end of story: end of His Story; all of

14. Genesis 8:20–21.
15. 2 Chronicles 27:6.
16. Matthew 1:9.
17. Hebrews 7:23—8:2.
18. Hebrews 4:15.

Jacob-Isra-El's sons' families taken apart; Family Abraham wiped off the face off earth; the promise to Abraham cancelled—permanently.

How was little Judah going to survive?

# 31

## Almah, Immanu-El and Pele-Joez-El-Gibbor-Abi-Ad-Sar-Shalom

ONE MAN KNEW—ISA-YAH. His name gives a clue to the answer: In Family Abraham language—Isa-Yah, but in English—Yah-weh is salvation. The answer to Isra-El's safety was—Yah-weh saves!

Isa-Yah was one of the Lord's greatest Mouthpieces on earth—ever. He was activated as a prophet by the Lord in the year that poor old King Uzz-Yah died in obscurity.[1] Uzz-Yah effectively met his end in the Temple surrounded by incense smoke; Isa-Yah met his beginning in the Temple surrounded by incense smoke. No one will know why he was there at just the right moment in just the right place—grace again—His Story and Isa-Yah's story arranged by the Lord to collide.

As Isa-Yah sat in the Temple, earthly reality unzipped to expose the reality that is beyond the Universe. Part of the fabric of the Temple peeled open as if generated by computer graphics to reveal the eternal timeless home of God that is invisible to humans.[2] But this was no virtual reality—this was the real thing. The Temple became the Doorway to the reality in which the Universe sits. Isa-Yah became one of the very few humans who have been chosen to look through it into the beyond.

So what did he see? Through the rip in the space-time continuum, he saw the Lord dressed like a king, sat on a throne with a long robe that flowed out of his heavenly royal court into the Temple. Weird unearthly creatures flitted in and out calling to each other that the Lord was holy—not of this earth. But they also claimed that his power and glory had broken through into earth. It was another Mount Sinai moment. The Temple was now not just a reminder that there is an existence outside of this Universe, it became the portal—the entrance to that world outside of the world.

But this mixing of realities caused paradoxes. The earth began to pulsate and vibrate as the Temple threatened to be sucked into the timelessness

1. Isaiah 6:1.
2. Isaiah 6:1–7.

of heaven. The Temple doorposts shook as they became the threshold to outside of the Universe. And everything was shrouded in thick incense like smoke emanating from beyond the Doorway.

Isa-Yah panicked. Isa-Yah knew that God and mankind can't mix. He screamed in terror that he was a dirty human who was seeing the perfect and pure Lord—the King of everything. The only answer for him was to be inoculated against the harmful effects of timelessness. In effect, to be a little like the alien creatures that flew safely between both dimensions. And so one of these alien flying creatures flew down, took some of the burning coals from the altar for sacrifices and touched Isa-Yah lips searing them to burn off his human impurities: to remove the human weaknesses from his humanity; to make him more heavenly and less humanly.

What then did Isa-Yah hear?—the voice of the Lord God.[3] What did the voice say? "Who will be my lips on earth to speak my words?" Isa-Yah still nursing his blistering lips immediately shouted, "Me! Send me!" And so began his official life as the Lord's Mouthpiece. He wanted to use his painfully purified lips for the Lord.

His role began with a bizarre mission outlined by the Lord: "Go tell the people in Judah: if you don't come back to me—you'll end up like your estranged family in Isra-El—dead and buried; finished!"[4] But according to the Lord, it was a mission impossible. The people of Judah would hear—but not comprehend; they would see—but never understand. Isa-Yah's words would be the final nail in their coffin. They couldn't claim ignorance. They couldn't claim they were in the dark. Their northern sister country of Isra-El was just about to be chopped down like a giant oak by the axe of Assyria. There would be nothing left of God's family tree.[5]

Another flood moment? No, not a full flood this time—God's rainbow promise to humanity after the flood still held. This time, not total destruction: the Lord wasn't totally finished with Family Abraham; the Lord was simply clearing out the deadwood in his people—there was hope. The Lord was going to start again. After the family tree had been chopped down, the remaining stump would sprout new growth: a holy seed; a seed planted by Yah-weh; a new purified people; a new family tree for Father Abraham; a new family tree that would start from a tiny green shoot stubbornly growing out of the dead stump. A stump sometimes called in His Story as "the remnant."[6]

3. Isaiah 6:8.
4. Isaiah 6:9–10.
5. Isaiah 6:11–13a.
6. Isaiah 10:20–22.

Okay—enough of the tree talk. What exactly was Isa-Yah going to do to protect little Judah? It all became clear when the new King Ahaz of Judah was bullied by his northern counterpart, Isra-El, into joining forces with Syria against the world's new super-power, Assyria.[7] Ahaz didn't want a dangerous and wrong alliance with his wayward cousins and old enemy. But he was tempted. After all as much as he didn't trust Isra-El, he feared Assyria more. But Isa-Yah the new Mouthpiece of the Lord intervened. He was told by the Lord to speak to Ahaz and encourage him to ask for a sign that would prove to the King that the Lord was in control and would keep him and little Judah safe.[8]

But Ahaz wasn't into signs. Who knows why? He said he didn't want to "test" the Lord, but more likely he was frightened that the sign would come true and he would feel indebted to Isa-Yah and the Lord—committed to him for life—a fear many of us still have. But you can't stop the Lord that easily. Isa-Yah gave him a sign anyway. The sign?—a young woman would have a child.[9] Not much of a sign—an everyday occurrence in Judah or any other country. Certainly not a super-natural sign unlike Yah-weh's later sign to Ahaz's son, Hezek-Yah, that involved making time appear to go backwards.[10] No, this sign seemed to be just a simple sign about the how long it would take a given child to grow up. When the child was old enough to start to know the difference between good and evil, Assyria would be well gone as a power and threat. Or to put it another way—the threat from Assyria would have disappeared well before the child was even a teenager.

But not everything about this sign was as simple as it seemed: not everything was quite that straightforward. The child was to be no ordinary child: he was to be called "Immanu-El" meaning "God with us." The child was to be no everyday child: he was to eat yoghurt and honey—the food of the rich and royal.

The woman was also no ordinary woman—she is described as an "almah." "Almah" is a word from the old language of Isra-El. And as it is the precise word that Isa-Yah chose to use and as he was the Mouthpiece of Yah-weh, we can be confident that this is the exact word that Yah-weh wanted used. An "almah" was not just a young woman; an "almah" was not just an unmarried young woman; an "almah" was not even a "bethulah" which meant a young unmarried woman who was engaged or contracted to be married to a particular man. An "almah" was a young woman who was

---

7. 2 Kings 16:1–20.
8. Isaiah 7:10–12.
9. Isaiah 7:14–16.
10. Isaiah 38:7–8.

not attached in any way to a man—not engaged; not arranged to be married; not married. So if not married—not attached sexually. This was a society where sexual intercourse only took place within marriage (or at the least, engagement). This young woman was in our language—a virgin.

Now the sign becomes super-natural—more than natural: but touching the natural. Isa-Yah says that the sign to encourage King Ahaz would be that a virgin would give birth to a child. This child of a virgin would be a royal child. By definition, this child would have to be conceived by a super-natural process instigated by God—by El-God at work in partnership with humanity on earth. This child would be Immanu-El—an "El-God with us" human. In the past, God had stretched through the Doorway to give the law. This time, he would stretch through the Doorway to create divine human life—a human life that Isa-Yah was told to give a mysterious very long name: Pele-Joez-El-Gibbor-Abi-Ad-Sar-Shalom.[11] What a name! What a meaning!

"Pele"—the nickname of Edison Arantes do Nascimento, arguably the greatest soccer player ever to have kicked a ball. Pele was his Portugese nickname. It is a strange nickname, but appropriate as it means "miracle' or "wonder" in the old language of Isra-El. What this man could do with the football needed to be seen to be believed! He was a wonder on the soccer pitch. The "Pele" Wonder-child born miraculously to the virgin two thousand seven-hundred years earlier didn't just grow up to be a Wonder-man, he was born a Wonder-child—a miracle from the moment of his conception and birth.

"Joez" means wise. The child born to the Virgin miraculously would turn out to be wise beyond his years: beyond his experience; beyond his humanity. To this day, this man nearly always comes top in all the polls of the wisest people ever to have lived. Not bad for a man who would never go to any university or even any school.

"El"—this boy was going to be the El of Isra-El—yes that El. He would be El-ohim—God. This boy was God on earth—not just his representative, but God himself. Hard to do when God lives outside the Universe. Hard to do when eternal and earthly can't mix. But this boy was going to be unique—able to travel between the two dimensions: to be the link; to be God-man; to be the human Doorway.

"Gibbor" means hero. This child would not just be God on earth popping down to have a look around to check his creation was behaving—but God on earth to save. He would be the world's hero: the world's super-hero but not a batman, superman or spiderman—but the God-man. He would be the Messiah-man to save humanity—divine intervention. This Wonder-boy

---

11. Isaiah 9:6–7.

## *almah, immanu-el* and *pele-joez-el-gibbor-abi-ad-sar-shalom*

would grow up to save humanity from hunger, danger, illness, death—even from humanity's fatal fundamental age-old problem of believing that each of us are our own boss. He would save us from the basic result of our inevitable breaking of the contract between us and God—death.

"Abi-ad" means, Father, in fact "Father of eternity." This is weird. A baby boy is a Father and not just that, the Father as in the "Father of all." He would be God—the originator; the prime-mover. It would later be said of him that, "through him all things were made."[12] He would be known as the means of creation—the way God made everything. But this boy would grow up to say, "The Father of Eternity and I are one" and "If you've seen me—you've seen the Father of Eternity."[13] This talk was likely to get him into trouble—and it did.[14]

"Sar-Shalom"—the Tsar of Shalom, which means, the Tsar of Peace—the Chief of Peace. This Wonder boy would grow up to be able to bring peace to stormy weather, disturbed minds, broken bodies and even dead bodies.

He would be a King. He would be a Wonder-child. He would be God's super-hero on earth. He would use his super-natural powers wisely like a caring Father to humanity. He would be the Prince who would bring peace between the Lord and humanity. He would be the new Prince of Judah—the descendant of great King David who would rule over God's new people with justice and with integrity.

His Kingdom wouldn't just be confined to Isra-El or even Judah or any ordinary earthly kingdom, but the Kingdom of Heaven on earth. Through the Doorway of himself, he would bring heaven onto earth and birth a new nation of humans whose real home would be outside the Universe. This new super-natural humanity would not be just for this world. It would be a nation whose citizens would live in the land beyond the Universe.

This new humanity was to start with one young virgin—one young virgin who became pregnant, not by human means, but by the Creator God creating a child in her. The child would be the seed of God.

A colleague of Isa-Yah—another Mouthpiece of the Lord—gave some more details about the Wonder-child. He even saw where on the map this Wonder-child would be born to the Virgin. Mic-Yah saw it would be in a place we have already met—the place where Samu-El picked David as

---

12. Colossians 1:15–17.
13. John 10:30; John 14:9.
14. John 10:31–33.

King.[15] He would be born in Beth-Lehem—the "House of Bread" which was to become the home of the one who claimed to be "Living Bread."[16]

Not to be outdone, Isa-Yah saw the Wonder-child as becoming like a light shining in the darkness of the land which seven hundred years later would be known as Galilee.[17] This was the part of the country where in fact the Wonder-child did grow up and started to work and become known.[18]

Both Mic-Yah and Isa-Yah knew the Wonder-child born would be the Super-star of His Story—the reason for creation itself. He would be the Doorway for all peoples to enter into God's family—for them to become the new nation of Heaven. Through him, the age-old promise of a gigantic Family Abraham whose number would outstrip the stars in the sky would come true completely.[19]

This great future all began with Isa-Yah offering King Ahaz the sign of the Virgin giving birth to a Wonder-child. King Ahaz heard about this amazing sign given by Isa-Yah and then ignored it: ignored Isa-Yah; ignored the Lord, and instead signed an agreement with the Assyrians.[20] He paid off the Assyrian King Tiglath Pileser the Third. He paid him not to attack Judah. This was financed by him ripping out the silver and gold from God's Temple and handing it over to the Assyrian King. This got the Assyrians off Judah's back but gave the Assyrian King the opportunity to concentrate on destroying the northern Kingdom of fake Isra-El.

Instead of trusting in God, King Ahaz trusted in his own shady dealings with the enemy. Yet again another of the kings of God's people forgot that God was really King and broke the contract God had made with his people and their leaders. He chose short term peace at the expense of long term salvation. King Ahaz wasn't the first nor the last human to make this short-sighted choice.

In many ways, he is just like us.

15. Micah 5:2.
16. John 6:51.
17. Isaiah 9:1–2, 6–7.
18. Matthew 4:12–17.
19. Galatians 3:14.
20. 2 Kings 16:7–8.

## 32

## Caged Bird?

KING AHAZ HAD BOUGHT short term safety to Judah but all at the expense of the nation's riches, heritage and the holiness of the Doorway Temple. But the Assyrians were still greedy for more. Despite the cost paid, little Judah still wasn't safe. King Ahaz had not trusted in God but had trusted an enemy king instead. As if trusting in an enemy king's word more than the word of the Lord's Mouthpiece wasn't enough, King Ahaz fell in love with the gods of the Assyrians. On a diplomatic visit to Assyria, Ahaz was won over by the flashy Assyrian fake gods. Star-struck he came back home and brought these gods and their worship with him. He decided it was a good idea to put an altar to one of these gods right in Yah-weh's Temple itself—right in the Doorway to God's home beyond the Universe.[1] In the special holy portal to beyond the Universe, he shoved a man-made false deity.

Isa-Yah had no time for human created gods. He scoffed at people who cut down trees, put some of the wood on one side to burn in the fire for heat or to bake bread and then used the rest of the wood to carve into an image of a "god." As Isa-Yah pointed out sarcastically, what sort of god needs to be made by a human and then propped up against a wall to be worshipped? After all it is only a block of wood, however artistically chiseled. After worshipping it, the worshipper then has to pick it up and lug it around. The god that was meant to carry the human, ends up being carried by the human—an idle idol—just a burden—a dead weight with the emphasis on dead.[2] All trust in a created thing, or person, ends up the same—a useless dead weight waste of space.

To Isa-Yah, King Ahaz's new gods were bad, but not as bad as some of the religious practices Ahaz had also caught off the Phoenicians. One of these happened to be child-sacrifice. This delightful ritual he practiced on his own

---

1. 2 Kings16:10–18.
2. Isaiah 44:12–20; Isaiah 46:1–7.

son.³ Spot the irony?—God had offered Ahaz a Wonder-child as a sign but Ahaz responded by sacrificing his own child to the fires of the god, Moloch.

But one son survived this less than good parenting—Hezek-Yah. When he succeeded his father, he remembered that God was really King not him. He lived up to his great name: "Yah-weh is my strength." He tore out his Father's D.I.Y. alterations to the Temple. He purified Yah-weh worship by throwing out the other gods his father had introduced. By keeping the contract with Yah-weh, he brought all sorts of success to Judah.⁴ But still the specter of Assyria loomed in the background like a dark shadow. Soon buoyed up by his success, King Hezek-Yah stopped paying the protection money to Assyria that his Father had arranged.⁵ Good. But then instead of trusting Yah-weh to keep him safe, he panicked as the new King of all powerful Assyria, Sennacherib, marched on Jeru-Salem to get his unpaid protection money. This powerful frightening King of Assyria destroyed the outlying towns of little Judah and then turned and marched on Jeru-Salem and surrounded it.⁶ Hezek-Yah lost his nerve and like his father, ransacked any last vestiges of gold that were left in the Temple to pay off the Assyrian monarch—bad.

But Sennacherib wasn't interested in loose change or trinkets. He wanted the big prize—Jeru-Salem. The siege of Jeru-Salem is an event recorded in His Story but also on the lump of stone called "The Prism of Sennacherib." On that stone, Sennacherib boasts that he shut up Hezek-Yah in Jeru-Salem like a "caged bird." He wasn't far wrong. Sennacherib the cat prowled around the bird cage of Jeru-Salem eyeing the juicy budgie called Hezek-Yah. He licked his lips hungrily. His troops surrounded the capital of Judah: surrounded the family of God; surrounded the Temple of Yah-weh; surrounded the special Holy Box with the laws of heaven in it. Where was the promised Wonder-child when you needed him? But this was seven hundred and one years before the birth of the Wonder-child prophesied by Isa-Yah. At this time before the Super-star Prince of Judah was born, Jeru-Salem seemed all alone.

King Sennacherib sent his officials with a message for the King.⁷ "Who are you going to call? Don't bother calling the Lord. He's the one who's told me to come and destroy you! He's angry with you!" Clever tactics—claiming

---

3. 2 Kings 16:3.
4. 2 Kings 18:1–8.
5. 2 Kings 18:7b.
6. 2 Kings 18:9–16.
7. 2 Kings 18:17–37.

to be furthering the divine plot of His Story and hard to prove wrong when you looked at the years of contract breaking by the Kings of Judah.

Sennacherib's officials also had a message for the people of Jeru-Salem. They shouted it to the people listening on the walls of Jeru-Salem. They enticed them to surrender, offering them houses and wealth if they did. "That's a bit better than drinking your own urine and eating your own excrement," they added with bad taste. True but only half true. But a half truth that had enough truth in it to undermine Jeru-Salem and its King—Hezek-Yah. What on earth could the King do? The Assyrian officials shouted over the wall asking the age-old question for all people who believe firmly there is a God but are experiencing a life that is anything but heavenly, "Where is your God now?" And more to the point—"Where was your God when your relatives in Isra-El were destroyed?"

But then King Hezek-Yah did an amazingly important thing. He didn't try and answer this almost impossible question. He did something that makes him a worthy member of the special bloodline of the Prince of Judah—the Wonder-child Super-star of His Story. Something that we should seriously consider doing when faced with impossible odds stacked against us. He went straight to the Doorway of the Lord.[8] He then sent a message right through the Doorway. He shot his S.O.S. straight out of the Universe. How? He used the Lord's Mouthpiece—Isa-Yah. These amazing human Mouthpieces communicated both ways—to the Lord and back again. Hezek-Yah wanted to know what the Lord thought—a good choice always, but especially when you are the leader of the family God.

The Lord's reply through Isa-Yah was short and practical: "Sennacherib will retreat when he gets a message from home. And when he gets home he will be killed—end of siege; end of King."

But did it happen? Of course—if you get a message from the one who created everything, you can trust it. But it wasn't instant. King Sennacherib did get wind of a threat in Assyria and so decided to finish Jeru-Salem off quickly so that he could rush away and sort the problem out at home. He sent a letter to Hezek-Yah giving him one last time-limited offer to surrender. Hezek-Yah knew that if he didn't surrender it was very likely that Jeru-Salem would be destroyed. It would mean the end of Jeru-Salem as the Lord's special center on earth—not an easy decision when you are being rushed.

How do you make such a massive decision instantly? You ask for the best advice you can find. So Hezek-Yah sent another message through the Doorway to the Lord again. This time he even took Sennacherib's offending

---

8. 2 Kings 19:1–8.

letter and spread it out into the Temple. He sent it through the time-lock of the Doorway: straight to the Lord; straight to the focus of the Lord's power on earth. He opened the letter out and prayed.

No King had been recorded as praying in the Temple for two hundred and fifty years, since the time of the great King Solomon. It was high time they did again. It was a simple straightforward plea. It basically said,[9] "You made the Universe. You rule everything. You made the world. You rule the world. See what Sennacherib is doing! Listen to what Sennacherib is saying! He is disrespecting you. Yes, he has defeated many nations, but their gods weren't real—just human myths. Now Lord—do something! Save us! Not just for our sake, but also for your sake—that the world will know that you and you alone, Lord are God!"

Isa-Yah was immediately dispatched by the Lord with an answer to Hezek-Yah's cry for help. He reassured the King that the Lord would catch Sennacherib like a fish—hook him in his mouth and reel him in and drop him back in the net of Assyria.[10] Sennacherib wouldn't have a chance to enter Jeru-Salem—he wouldn't even have a chance to fire one single miserable arrow in anger, because Jeru-Salem was the Lord's city. The Lord would defend it for his own sake, but also in memory of the great King David who founded it and the promises God had made him.

And then, something astounding; something cataclysmic happened to protect Jeru-Salem.[11] A plague swept the besieging Assyrian camp and killed one hundred and eighty-five thousand soldiers. And then the rest ran away. One ancient historian[12] said that they ran away because mice ate all their weapons. Possibly he was trying to say that all the mice were infected with plague and infected the soldiers who died. Who knows, but what is sure, the siege was off. Jeru-Salem never fell to the Assyrians. Sennacherib went back to Assyria and was killed in his fake temple dedicated to the fake god, Nisroch. He was killed by two of his sons. They either used a sword or they used a massive half bull-half human statute. They may have caused it to "accidentally" fall on top of him. Maybe both are true. Who cares? But whichever way, Isa-Yah was right. The Lord was right. And Judah lived to fight another day.

Only one little blip on the horizon (that is if you don't count the fatal illness that Hezek-Yah contracted and was treated by Isa-Yah with the unlikely combination of prayer and an "Elastoplast" of figs)—there was a

---

9. 2 Kings 19:9–19.
10. 2 Kings 19:20–34.
11. 2 Kings 19:35–37.
12. Herodotus (Herod Book II:141).

new growing world power—Babylon.[13] Hezek-Yah, when fully recovered from his fatal illness, received a delegation from this up and coming power. Hezek-Yah was flattered, because they came with get well cards and a present from Merodach-Baladan, the King of Babylon.[14] Hezek-Yah responded to this display of generosity with one of his own—showing the delegation everything: all his treasures and all his national security measures at the same time. Isa-Yah was not pleased. Had Hezek-Yah not learnt the meaning of his name? That Yah-weh was Hezek-Yah's strength? Yah-weh was the best defense policy—not allying with another growing super-power. As a result of Hezek-Yah's love affair with Babylon, Isa-Yah predicted that Judah's security and defenses would later be breached by Babylon and all the treasures stolen not to mention the people. And as usual, the Mouthpiece of the Lord got it right. Just over a century later, Jeru-Salem and Judah were destroyed.

By Babylon.

---

13. 2 Kings 20:1–7.
14. 2 Kings 20:12–21.

# 33

## Lost

JUDAH AND ITS CAPITAL, Jeru-Salem, were to be destroyed by Babylon—but not yet—not in King Hezek-Yah's lifetime. This was his reward for remembering (most of the time) that the Lord was King and for keeping the contract with the Lord.¹

The chopping of the last remaining branch of Family Abraham's tree, started instead in his son Manasseh's reign—Manasseh who infamously got rid of his own son in a ritual child-sacrifice fire.² This very nice man, Manasseh, didn't want anything to do with his father's belief that God was really the King. Instead he went back to non-Yah-weh worship. He worshipped so-called gods who weren't real and re-ordered the Temple to accommodate them.³

Also, instead of trusting the Lord and standing firm against Assyria, he allowed Assyria to bully him. In fact, Assyria couldn't do any wrong in Manasseh's eyes. He did whatever Assyria told him to do. Manasseh broke the contract with the Lord. He rebelled even though his people were the Family of God. Folklore says that part of Manasseh's rebellion, was to cut the Lord's great Mouthpiece on earth, Isa-Yah, in two—with a saw and not as a magic trick.⁴ He may have done this to try and protect himself from the biting criticism that came out of the mouth of this powerful Mouthpiece of God, but his behavior backfired. He had forgotten that Isa-Yah had saved his father from the Assyrians. Unfortunately though, the recently beheaded Isa-Yah was obviously in no fit shape to do the same for Manasseh and inevitably the new King of Assyria treated impotent, pathetic, obsequious Manasseh with contempt. He marched in and attached chains to Manasseh through his mouth and led him to Assyria like an animal.⁵

1. Isaiah 39:1–8.
2. 2 Kings 21:6.
3. 2 Kings 21:1–18.
4. Hebrews 11:32–38.
5. 2 Chronicles 33:10–11.

This humiliating torture brought Manasseh to his senses. In one of the greatest turn-arounds in His Story so far, Manasseh amazingly ate humble pie and threw himself on the Lord's mercy. And even more amazingly, the Lord responded and fixed it so that Manasseh returned back to Jeru-Salem as King—grace again—a second chance, which Manasseh took with all the zeal of a new convert. He rebuilt the security system around Jeru-Salem, including the city wall. But importantly, he rebuilt the central altar in the Doorway Temple—restoring it to focus on Yah-weh rather than the fake gods he had espoused earlier.[6]

But Manasseh's three hundred and sixty degree about turn was too late for the nation. After his death, his successor, Amon, was a chip off the old Manasseh block. He carried on like his father before his father's change of heart. The Lord through his new Mouthpiece, Zephan-Yah, was scathing in his criticism of the state of Judah and the great capital city of Jeru-Salem as a result of Amon's leadership. Through the Doorway came the message from the Lord, "I will reach out and punish Judah and Jerusalem—not a trace will remain of the foreign gods and their priests. Not a trace will be found of those who worship stars from their rooftops, while claiming loyalty to me."[7]

Not a trace left—flood talk again. Talk of destruction of the old to bring a new start. Even Judah the last branch was diseased and needed sawing off. It was a deserved fate, unlike Isa-Yah's. Soon not a trace of King Amon was left. After only two years he was assassinated.

Jos-Yah, his son, was different again—he remembered. He remembered that the Lord was really King. He remembered that the law of the Lord was King—not him. He supported Yah-weh worship. His name means "supported by Yah-weh." And in return, Yah-weh supported him. The Mouthpiece, Zephan-Yah, was more hopeful as Jos-Yah's reign continued. He spoke of a bright new tomorrow for those who followed Jos-Yah's example.[8]

Jos-Yah not only kept the contract with God, he found a copy of the small print of the contract passed on by Yah-weh through the Doorway to Moses seven hundred or so years before. It had been written down in a book that is now called Deuteronomy. But then it was called . . . well, it was called something else, but no one at the time of Jos-Yah knew what it was called because they had lost it.[9] Lost—the vital words of Yah-weh. During the pagan "alterations" of the Temple by Jos-Yah's father and grandfather it had been hidden: forgotten; kicked around the floor; used as a door-stop

---

6. 2 Chronicles 33:12–17.
7. Zephaniah 1:1–3.
8. Zephaniah 3:9–20.
9. 2 Kings 22:1–10.

or covered in thick dust at the back of the furthest recess of the Temple. Lost—the book that clearly recorded the great words of Moses given him by Yah-weh himself: words from beyond the Universe from the Creator himself; words that were to protect Isra-El as they crossed through into their Promised Land. Just before he died, at the end of the book, Moses tells all of Isra-El, "Take to heart all these words. Tell your children to obey them carefully. These words aren't idle or worthless—they are your life!"[10] These vital words—lost. The incredible life-giving words of Yah-weh; of God himself; the Maker's instructions for the world—lost. The book that Joshua was told by the Lord he hadn't to let out of his sight, in fact not even out of his mouth or mind—lost. He had to read it, speak it, think it every day and night and all for one reason only—so that he would put it into practice. These essential words—lost. The words that would make Joshua successful as Isra-El's new leader—lost.[11] Lost and only eventually found in a deep dark corner of the Temple's treasure room by accident as the High Priestly Go-Between was clearing up ready for renovations planned by Jos-Yah to reverse the damage done to the Temple by his father and grandfather.

The discovery sent shockwaves through the royal palace. King Jos-Yah ripped his clothes in mourning. He knew that they had to read the words again—quickly—or death was the only result.[12] The nation would be lost—possibly forever—like fake Isra-El earlier. Jos-Yah sent for advice from the new female Mouthpiece of God, Huldah.[13] She had one verdict—"Lost." It was too late. The Lord was going to cut off the last diseased branch of Family Abraham's tree. Judah had been unfaithful to him, generation after generation. They had not remembered. They had forgotten the contract with Yah-weh—even bringing the worship of non-gods, mythical gods, occult gods into his very home—his Temple—God's official Doorway into his world. The only saving grace would be that it would be after Jos-Yah's time. He wouldn't need to see it. He would be saved the pain.

Despite the hopelessness of the situation, this worthy member of the Wonder-child's bloodline set about cleaning up worship of Yah-weh in his land. He re-instated the annual remembering of the time when the Angel of Death Passed-Over the people of Israel and spared their firstborn in Egypt.[14] He insisted on respect for the special box of the Law—the Ark. He insisted that it was to be left in the Temple and not marched around like some super-

10. Deuteronomy 32:45–47.
11. Joshua 1:7–9.
12. 2 Kings 22:11.
13. 2 Kings 22:12–20.
14. 2 Kings 23:1–25.

stitious talisman. He made sure that Judah worshipped Yah-weh exclusively. Out went the accommodation for male cult-prostitutes in the Temple; out went non-Yah-weh religious trinkets; out went all non-Yah-weh priests—many to death. He even dug up the bones of dead non-Yah-weh priests and burned their bones on their altars—total destruction of the old religions that kept seducing the people of Judah to be unfaithful to Yah-weh. He even attacked witchcraft and its mediums. He was a 100 percent in his support of his Lord Yah-weh and the removal of all that dragged Family Abraham away from Yah-weh.

But Judah was too far gone—lost. The dangerous politics of the day were now fatal for Jos-Yah. In a political attempt to reduce the power of Assyria, Jos-Yah went out to fight Pharaoh Neco the Second of Egypt who was marching to reinforce the Assyrian army. It was brave, but foolish. Jos-Yah, not one to shy away from a battle, disguised himself as a soldier so that he could safely be in the thick of the battle. But a random Egyptian arrow hit him when he was in his chariot, and he was D.O.A. when he got back to Jeru-Salem.[15] Jos-Yah—lost. He was mourned by many, including the up and coming great Mouthpiece of God, Jerem-Yah.[16]

Yeh-o-Ahaz was made King—for three months until the victorious Pharaoh heard and came and took him away prisoner and made his older brother, Yeh-Oyakim, the puppet king. The Egyptian Pharaoh pulled his strings. He had to dance to Pharaoh's tune. [17]

But he didn't dance to the Lord's tune. Yeh-Oyakim followed his brother in not remembering Yah-weh was really King. Jerem-Yah feared that since the death of the reforming King Jos-Yah, the death of the recent welcome move back to obeying God's law was inevitable. This prompted him into a controversial outburst soon after Jos-Yah's death.[18] But he was right and he was nearly killed for saying it. Yeh-Oyakim despised the contract and its small print. He will always be remembered as the King who burnt a scroll of God's words, written down by the new Mouthpiece of Yah-weh, Jerem-Yah—words dictated by the Lord himself through the Doorway. After every few lines were read out to the King, he cut them off the scroll with his penknife and threw them in the fire heating his winter quarters.[19] Every word destroyed—lost.

15. 2 Kings 23:29-30.
16. Jeremiah 22:15-16.
17. 2 Chronicles 36:2-4.
18. Jeremiah 26:1-16.
19. Jeremiah 36:1-32.

Yeh-Oyakim at that time paid protection money to Egypt in the form of silver and gold. But later after Babylon had defeated Egypt, he ended up paying money to Babylon instead.[20] Three years later, Babylon didn't seem as powerful as it had been, so Yeh-Oyakim decided to save a bit of cash and stopped paying Babylon.[21] And Babylon responded. One fateful day five hundred and ninety-nine years before the birth of the Wonder-child, it invaded Judah. Jeru-Salem was surrounded—again.[22] As the siege intensified it was made worse by the immense bad timing of King Yeh-Oyakim—he died. His death forced his son, Jecon-Yah, to the throne.[23] Just for three short months. Then Jeru-Salem surrendered to the Babylonian army five hundred and ninety-seven years before the great hinge-point of World history.[24]

Judah had become a football kicked from one end of the political pitch to the other. Surely the Lord would sort it out again—like before. Jeru-Salem hoped again for one hundred and eighty-five thousand enemy soldiers dying overnight. But not this time—lost. Surely Jerem-Yah would still save the day like his famous predecessor—like Isa-Yah saved King Hezek-Yah when Jeru-Salem was surrounded?[25] Wouldn't Jerem-Yah do the same? But the King's father had just burnt Jerem-Yah's words of warning—lost. The words of God sent through the Doorway should never be treated with disrespect—a warning our contemporary society should never forget. The results are disastrous—eventually. Jeru-Salem had never been totally defeated by anyone since King David had won it five hundred years earlier. But it was different this time. Jecon-Yah was taken hostage, dragged off to Babylon by the famous Babylonian King Nebuchadnezzar the Second—but not only Jecon-Yah—also three thousand of the top movers and shakers of Jeru-Salem.[26] Jecon-Yah had reigned for only three months—three months in the limelight and nothing more—lost.

Or all but lost—his part in His Story was not yet totally over.

20. 2 Kings 23:31–35; 2 Kings 24:1–4.
21. 2 Kings 24:1b.
22. 2 Kings 24:10.
23. 2 Kings 24:8.
24. 2 Kings 24:12.
25. 2 Kings 19:35–36.
26. 2 Kings 24:13–16.

## 34

## Dead and Alive

THE BABYLONIANS MADE THE uncle of exiled Jecon-Yah the new King.[1] He was called, King Zedek-Yah but he wasn't a proper King of Judah—he was just a pretend king made by Babylon. And his kingdom wasn't a genuine kingdom—it was just the decimated remains of the defeated city of Jeru-Salem.

Zedek-Yah lasted ten years—ten years which ended with Zedek-Yah again foolishly cutting his ties with Babylon and entering into a suicidal alliance with Egypt.[2] This was completely against Jerem-Yah's, the Lord's Mouthpiece's instructions and the result was complete disaster as it inevitably is when you blatantly go against the Lord's advice.[3]

Babylon retaliated against the Egyptian alliance and surrounded Jeru-Salem. It laid siege to the capital city, not letting any food in or anyone out to fetch food. The Mouthpiece of Yah-weh, Jerem-Yah, described in his book of "Lamentations" the grizzly scene: "Babies so thirsty their tongues stick to the roof of their mouths; children so hungry they beg but no one gives them a scrap; the usually well-fed so weak they die of starvation in the street; the rich so desperate for something to eat they live on rubbish dumps."[4] Jerem-Yah appealed to the unsympathetic world, "Is it nothing to you all you who pass by?"[5] Even the Lord seemed to turn his back on them—their fate caused by their own bad choices. Some people in Jeru-Salem tried cannibalism. Some people committed suicide rather than die the slow death of starvation. But the greatest pain was the disappointment of their hope dashed in their chosen leaders. Where was Isa-Yah's Wonder-child? Where was the Prince of Judah? Where was the one who would save them and humanity?

1. 2 Kings 24:18–19.
2. 2 Kings 24:20.
3. Jeremiah 37:1–10.
4. Lamentations 4:4–5.
5. Lamentations 1:12.

And then the little that was left of Jeru-Salem fell to Babylon—again—ten years after its first humiliating defeat. The puppet King, Zedek-Yah, tried to escape, like a captain jumping ship before the women and children. But he was caught and before he had his own eyes gouged out, he was forced to see his own children slaughtered. The puppet King Zedek-Yah was taken in chains to Babylon for the rest of his life.[6] Zedek-Yah was never listed as one of the bloodline stars of the Wonder-child who would save humanity. He had no heritage. He has slipped into obscurity.

But would Jeru-Salem suffer the same fate? It was the most likely outcome. Jeru-Salem was totally destroyed. The Temple—the center of Yahweh worship built by the rich wise King Solomon was ransacked, looted and smashed to pieces. The unique special Doorway to God beyond the Universe blocked.[7] The remaining few members of Family Abraham had lost their center: culturally; spiritually; socially. The future looked bleak. Had Project Family Abraham ended? Had King David's royal household been removed permanently from power? It seemed as if the last remaining branch of Family Abraham's tree had been chopped off and burnt. The citizens were shipped off to Babylon leaving just a few poor people behind and even these soon ran off for asylum in Egypt.[8]

Amongst their number was the great Mouthpiece of God, Jerem-Yah.[9] Even he left the sinking ship of Jeru-Salem. It was the end. Jeru-Salem was dead in the water. The hope of an international Family Abraham to save the world was equally moribund—dead.

Or was it? There was a glimmer of hope. The last proper King of Judah, Jecon-Yah, was still alive in Babylon after the first exile ten years earlier. He wasn't just alive—His Story claims he was thriving.[10] In addition, contemporary clay tablets found in an underground vault dug by an archaeologist in Babylon, tell of the rations of food given to a royal prisoner—a royal prisoner who fits perfectly the description of Jecon-Yah. Maybe he was the green shoot growing out of the dead stump of Judah? But Jecon-Yah wasn't the only member of Family Abraham alive. A young twenty-five year old man was with him: a young man with the great gift of speaking the Lord's words; a young man beginning to be the new Mouthpiece of God. His name was Ezeki-El (El—God will strengthen).

6. Jeremiah 52:6–11.
7. Jeremiah 52:12–26.
8. Jeremiah 52:27b–30.
9. Jeremiah 43:1–7.
10. Jeremiah 52:31–34.

Ezeki-El was one of the three thousand leaders of Jeru-Salem taken into exile along with King Jecon-Yah. As traditional nations, Judah and Isra-El might well have been finished. But El-God-Yah-weh wasn't finished yet with his people—or with humanity. His Story wasn't concluded—there were more chapters to be written. Yah-weh opened up the Doorway into the beyond again—this time especially for Ezeki-El. Like Isa-Yah before him, he was privileged to look through the Doorway into heaven. This time there was no Temple as the venue, but instead Yah-weh opened up the Doorway directly into Ezeki-El's psyche.

What Ezeki-El saw in the eternal dimension was almost too mind-blowing for him to describe. It was something like a chariot with four wheels.[11] Not so incredible and fantastic you might think except that each wheel was made up of two wheels set at right angles to each other—it could travel in all directions—wherever needed. Each wheel had rims full of eyes like three hundred and sixty degree sensors. It moved where it sensed a need. Each wheel was driven by a lightning bright creature from outside of the Universe with four faces: one human; one lion; one bull; one eagle. Each alien creature had hooves and wings that touched the next creature. Each alien creature when they flew, sounded like ocean waves crashing on the shore or a large army on the march. Each alien creature moved without turning.

This machine was from the other-world and was designed to be on the move and it was moving through the Doorway! In the driving seat of the chariot sat a human-like creature on a sapphire throne. From the waist up he glowed like hot metal in a furnace. From the waist down he was fiery flames. Around him was wrapped an intensely bright rainbow. Above him was a dome of sparkling ice. The driver was God.[12] This machine was God's ambulance—God's rescue chariot to save humanity.

Despite everything, Ezeki-El saw that God was still in the driving seat of the Universe—not only in the driving seat but Ezeki-El saw that the Lord was on the move again—moving through the Doorway to rescue his people—no longer bound by the Temple walls. God didn't need a Temple. God was with his people—like when they escaped Egypt. God was moving His Story along into its next chapter. It wasn't the end of God's activity through the Doorway.

Ezeki-El panicked like Isa-Yah. He had seen beyond time through the Doorway into the eternal—into what was outside of the Universe. And also like Isa-Yah he was told not to panic but to act. The Lord gave him a scroll

11. Ezekiel 1:1–28.
12. Ezekiel 1:27–28.

with his words on it.[13] But Ezeki-El wasn't to read it: he was to eat it; take it into his very body like a secret message from the Lord beyond the Universe.

The Ark containing the law may well have been completely lost and most likely destroyed at this point along with all the other priceless Temple artefacts of His Story, but the Lord didn't need them—he could make humans into his Ark—containers for his words.

So what did the scroll taste of?—honey: sweet and filling; a gift from the true heavenly land flowing with milk and honey. Energized by this out of the Universe nectar, Ezeki-El became the Lord's Mouthpiece for the depressed and despondent exiles of Family Abraham. His job was to move around giving messages of hope to homeless Family Abraham now scattered throughout the surrounding lands.

Ezeki-El received his unearthly messages at special moments when he was caught up into "out-of-this-world" experiences. Ezeki-El was very down-to-earth about these ecstatic moments. He described them as like being grabbed by his hair by a massive hand and carried away to a faraway place.[14]

One time he was whisked off to a scene of carnage.[15] It looked like a battlefield full of dead bodies. But these bodies weren't soldiers—they were civilians. It was a scene of ethnic cleansing: a holocaust; genocide. The slaughtered bodies lay in a mass grave: in a stomach churning scene reminiscent of a crime against humanity—but not just a general crime against humanity—specifically a crime against one part of humanity—against the whole of Family Abraham. Ezeki-El saw the death of the promise to Father Abraham. His descendants dead and not even buried—the end of His Story. It was a vision of the reality that Ezeki-El had to face every day—the reality that Isra-El was dead and gone. The corpses weren't fresh dead bodies with some hope of resuscitation, but old; ancient; dry; bleached in the sun. The skeletons were of a people beaten and humiliated; dead and gone; turning to dust. Their hope was gone; their future destroyed. They were useless and pointless.

But the Lord hadn't finished with the people of Isra-El. He promised Ezeki-El he would save them: he would open their graves; he would bring them out; he would bring them home. But Ezeki-El had to do something first. He had to say the magic word. As the Lord's Mouthpiece he had to command the dislocated bones to relocate—to reconnect the tendons,

---

13. Ezekiel 2:1–3:3.
14. Ezekiel 3:4–15.
15. Ezekiel 37:1–14.

flesh and skin. And they did—rattling and clicking and popping back into location.

But they were zombies. They looked human—the light was on but there was no one at home. They were empty. At best they were complicated, animated bags of bones—but not human: not made in the image of God; not made with God's breath. They were just bodies—not special—not God's.[16]

So the Lord encouraged Ezeki-El to finish the job off. "Say the word and tell the breath—the Spirit of God's life—to enter them!" And it did. And they were human. And they stood up. And they were reunited with each other—a family of Abraham together again. They were the new Family Abraham ready to be a nation again—alive once more.[17] Not just a people made alive again, but a people with a great new improved, better future—a future that would make even their past look pale in comparison. Ezeki-El was to tell the exiled people of Judah that even though they felt as good-as-dead in their enforced exile in Babylon they would live again. But not just brought back to live the old way of life that had failed—that had resulted in the destruction of everything they relied on and cared for—but in a new way. They weren't going to just be revived like a nation of robotic controlled zombies. But each person would have the Lord's invisible presence, power and Spirit in them. They would receive a special life straight from beyond the Universe—life through the Doorway. They were no longer just to be a human nation but the Lord's nation reborn by power from beyond the Universe. They were going to be citizens of the power beyond the Universe, not just of a world power.

Ezeki-El was totally obsessed with this message of hope for Isra-El. Through him, the Lord explained he was going to rip out his people's heart of stone and replace the center of each of them with his heart of flesh—a heart of flesh pumping God's own life-Spirit around their bodies. These people would be part of God's bloodline—their lives completely inseparable from God's life. God wouldn't have to force these people to do what he wanted, but God's Spirit would make them to want to do the right thing, and give them the power to do it.[18] God's people from the inside out: not outside in. Not robotic and heartless people controlled from forces outside of the Lord but controlled from inside from a heart beating in time with the Lord's.

Heart—as in the heart of the matter: the center; the core. Their human core was to be filled with the Lord. No longer was the Doorway to the Lord to be in the burning bush or the volcano or at the top of the heavenly ladder

---

16. Ezekiel 37:8.
17. Ezekiel 37:10–14.
18. Ezekiel 11:19;36:24–27.

or in the Temple—but in humans: on earth; in the human heart. Each citizen of the Lord's nation was to be an ark containing the Lord's rules written on by the finger of God stretched out from beyond the Universe. Each citizen of the Lord's nation was to be a Temple where Yah-weh lived. Each citizen of the Lord's nation open to the Doorway through which God could visit earth.[19] Each citizen of the Lord's nation was to be a holy set-apart people making up a special nation. A nation where nationality wasn't determined by where you lived, but who lived in you.

And after each individual was renewed, the nation would be renewed by a new leader—a new Shepherd even greater than the great shepherd-leaders of old—Moses and David. The new leader would be the long awaited Prince of Judah.[20]

In the past the Lord had stormed out of his own earthly home—the Temple, in contempt for what was going on.[21] But now the Lord would be happy to return to a radically renewed Temple.[22] But this would be a temple built not of stones and of wood, but heart and flesh. The influence of this renewed Temple would not be limited to worship in Jeru-Salem. Ezeki-El learnt this when once again grabbed by God, he was given a vision of the Temple's new international role when in a vision he saw a dribble of water escaping out from the Temple in Jeru-Salem.[23] This wasn't just a leak of water but God's life seeping out of the Temple—the Doorway of the Universe. Ezeki-El saw this tiny dribble of life-giving water grow to become an ankle-deep stream. Then it was a river that was up to Ezeki-El's waist. Then it was a raging white-water torrent that was too dangerous for Ezeki-El to swim in. The original dribble should have dried up in the hot sun—evaporated; reduced; disappeared—like Isra-El—but like Isra-El's future hope, it reversed the laws of science. The dribble of life-giving water just kept on getting wetter and fuller and more spectacular until it became a torrential river in flood, on its way to the Dead Sea.

The Dead Sea—the lowest point in the dry land of the whole world. At over one thousand four hundred feet below sea-level, it should be under the sea, but it isn't. Water runs in, but can't run downhill any more. There's no more downhill left so it stops and evaporates in the heat leaving salt and minerals. It is well over eight times saltier than the sea—so thick it is almost impossible to swim in. It's a soup. It is impossible for fish or aquatic

19. 1 Peter 2:4–5, 9–10.
20. Ezekiel 34:22–24; 37:24–28.
21. Ezekiel 11:22–25.
22. Ezekiel 43:1–5.
23. Ezekiel 47:1–12.

plants to live in it. It is dead. But Ezeki-El saw the dribble of life-giving water surging into the Dead Sea and making it live—the thick salty gloop miraculously transformed into flowing fresh water teeming with fish and fishermen lining the river banks for miles. Banks that were also covered with trees fruiting successfully every month—their leaves never withering as their roots sucked on water flowing through the Doorway to the center of the Universe—their leaves feeding and healing Isra-El.

But these eternal leaves wouldn't just be for the people of Isra-El. Five hundred years later, Ezeki-El's insight from beyond the Universe, was embellished by a close friend of the future Prince of Judah—the leader of the newly reborn Isra-El. This man had his own extended Doorway experience when he too saw beyond the Universe.[24] Even though he was held prisoner on an island for his support for the Wonder-child, he couldn't be stopped from escaping through the Doorway beyond this Universe—to the Lord's dimension. Whilst there, he saw Ezeki-El's trees.[25] But now he saw them as the reborn trees of life which were available to the first humans, Adam and Eve, before they preferred tasting the fruit of the tree of knowledge of good and evil. These trees now had healing for "all the nations" not just one nation. These leaves were going to pass on their extraordinary super-natural sap to all the nations of the world—life giving trees—drawing on the originator of life itself. Leaves full of life that would heal humans of everything that cut short life including curing the curse of death—the ultimate darkness. Trees that reversed the effect of Adam and Eve's chomping on the fruit of the tree of the knowledge of good and evil in Eden.[26]

The new reborn Isra-El was going to become the Doorway of life to the whole world—the way God was going to heal humans whatever their nationality. His Story was truly going global, as predicted by King Solomon at the opening of the Temple.[27] God's family Isra-El was going to be healed and pass that healing onto the world.

This new chapter in His Story would start with Isra-El. They weren't completely dead. Isra-El was a tiny dribble but it would become a tsunami—not of destruction— but life. Not just to the religious—but even to the fishermen and to all who lived on the fish and the fruit of the trees. Years later, this vision of hope became part of the Feast of Tabernacles re-enacted in the rebuilt Temple in Jeru-Salem. Each morning of the Festival, Ezeki-El's vision of life-giving water escaping from the Temple would be re-enacted as

---

24. Revelation 1:9–10.
25. Revelation 22:1–5.
26. Genesis 3:1–8.
27. 2 Chronicles 6:32–33.

water was taken from the pool of Siloam and poured out in the Temple. It was an optimistic attempt to kick-start God's Spirit to revive Isra-El like the vision of the Dead Sea restored to life. Five hundred years after Ezeki-El, the Wonder-child claimed he could offer this special water to everyone. At the feast of Tabernacles in Jeru-Salem, instead of pouring out water from the Temple, he spoke out: "Let anyone who is thirsty come to me and drink—rivers of living water will flow from inside them."[28] The Wonder-child's friends at the time knew that he was referring to the life-Spirit of God. He was claiming to be the fulfilment of Ezeki-El's vision.

But for now, such a man was only a distant hope to the all-but-dead Isra-El. Never mind water pouring out of the Temple, just having a Temple would have been good. But the tide was beginning to turn. Hope was slowly beginning to grow. Even Jerem-Yah before his escape to Egypt, had also heard the Lord's new plan. He spoke of a time when the Lord would keep his promise and a new shoot would grow out of the branch of King David's family tree; a new shoot who would re-write the story of Isra-El.[29] He wrote to the exiles scattered in far away countries and told them the Lord's words: "Build houses. Settle down. Plant gardens and eat what you grow. Marry and let your children marry. Get involved in the foreign city you are living. Ask God to bless you so that you can bless your adopted city. Be successful because if you are successful, your adopted city will be successful. Make the most of your time away because after seventy years, I will come and fetch you and bring you home."[30] "I have plans for you—not plans to hurt you—but plans to make you successful. I will return for you, if you return to me."[31]

Hope renewed but a hope based on a new contract between the Lord and his people—a completely new arrangement as the old contract had failed. The old one had broken. The old one had been destroyed. The promise made by God through Moses on Mount Sinai was now broken beyond repair—it was defunct. Ultimately it hadn't worked because humans couldn't work it. But the new contract was different. Jerem-Yah passed on the small print faithfully: "The Lord says: 'The days are coming when: I will put my law in their minds; I will write my law in their hearts; they will all know me intimately—from the poorest to the richest; the youngest to the oldest; the insignificant to the powerful. I will be their God, and they will be my people.

---

28. John 7:37–39.
29. Jeremiah 23:5–8.
30. Jeremiah 29:4–9.
31. Jeremiah 29:10–14.

I will let them off for their rebellion and failure and law-breaking—as if they had never broken my contract.'"[32]

This new contract was based on each individual's choice—there was to be no family membership of this new nation. Each person would be responsible for applying for citizenship of this new people whose homeland was beyond the Doorway. Each person would be responsible for applying for God's grace. To make the point, Jerem-Yah quoted a well known saying of Isra-El, "Sour grapes eaten by parents leave a sour taste in the mouths of the children."[33] It was an ancient way of saying that children grow up to be the same as their parents. Jerem-Yah said that this saying was no longer true. Everyone would be responsible for their own choices and not be able to blame their parents, their D.N.A. or their upbringing—a radical idea even now. The new contract was a new start for all humans whatever their background. It was a new beginning—a new agreement between God and humanity.

But who was going to make this new contract possible? Who was going to rescue Family Abraham and give them a future? Who was going to bring the scattered people of Judah back from Babylon? Who was going to make Isra-El a power again in the world?

In the short term, it was a very mysterious, unlikely man: a man who had been spoken about by Isa-Yah several hundred years earlier: a man not part of the bloodline of Abraham; a man not part of the bloodline of the Wonder-child; a man not even part of His Story.

Until now.

---

32. Jeremiah 31:31–34.
33. Jeremiah 31:29–30.

# 35

# The Sequel

Isa-Yah, the great Mouthpiece of Yah-weh, two hundred years earlier, had seen a day when the people of God would be prisoners and refugees in a faraway country. As it turned out it was either a very lucky prediction or it was a fantastic prophecy. Prophecy is not only about bringing out the truth of what is happening but also about what is going to happen. The truth is that if you look through the Doorway into the eternal often enough, a bit of the timelessness of God will rub off on you and help you see around the corner of the future and peek into the not-yetness.

Two centuries before it happened, Isa-Yah prophesied about a time when Isra-El would need rescuing. Inspired by the Lord he told the people that when this happened they would find comfort.[1] Com-fort is an old English word meaning "with strength." The people of Isra-El would be strengthened when they felt weak in exile in Babylon. How?—by knowing that they were coming home. The Lord was coming to Babylon and going to fetch them back from the other side of the desert. Isa-Yah shouted, "Clear a path in the desert! Make a straight road for the Lord! Fill in the valleys! Flatten every hill! Level the rough ground! The glory of the Lord will appear! And his promises never die or fade. He is coming to get you! Just like a shepherd cares for his sheep—he will pick you up like lambs in his arms and lead you back home."[2]

The Lord through Isa-Yah told his scattered people, "I will answer your cries for help. I will come to save you. On your way home, you won't go thirsty or hungry. You won't be burnt by the sun or hot desert winds. I will level the mountains and make roads for you to bring you home."[3]

To dispel all doubt the Lord using Isa-Yah's mouth, added, "Can a mother forget her child? Can a mother not love the child she gave birth

1. Isaiah 40:1.
2. Isaiah 40:1–11.
3. Isaiah 49:8–13.

*the sequel* 155

to? Even if mothers fail—I won't! I will never forget you. Your city will be built faster than it was destroyed!"[4] So—"Leave Babylon! Run away from the Babylonians! Tell everyone that I have bought you back out of slavery like I did out of Egypt—I didn't let you die of thirst when you escaped that time!"[5]

It was true. The Lord was planning a second Great Escape: a second great "Exodus" (as the Great Escape had become known); a son of Exodus; Exodus—the Sequel; another great rescue. [6]

But how was this going to happen? Did Isa-Yah have any prior knowledge on this as well? Yes—it was to be the work of the Lord's servant on earth—a special servant. This servant would be called "the Chosen One"—the Messiah. This servant Messiah would bring justice. This servant Messiah would be gentle—nursing the bruised and bringing back the ill to health; not snuffing out life but fanning life into flame.[7] This servant Messiah would be called by God from before he was born but hidden until the time was right for him to be used.[8] This servant Messiah would bring the light from beyond the Doorway, shining into the created world—a light that would not only illuminate the people of Family Abraham, but also all humans on earth.[9] This servant Messiah would be more famous and powerful than all the Kings ever. He would be powerful and wise.[10]

But this servant Messiah wouldn't be a celebrity with popular good looks. He would be rejected, punished for something he hadn't done. Despite the unfairness of his treatment, he wouldn't complain. Despite his innocence, he would be killed like a common criminal.[11] Only when he was dead would he be treated with respect. Later, he would be buried in a rich man's grave.[12] Later, he would be given life after death.[13] Later, he would be famous and worshipped long after his time on earth.[14] Later, he would become the hope for all who can't keep God's law and need someone to

---

4. Isaiah 49:15–21.
5. Isaiah 48:20–21.
6. Isaiah 43:16–21.
7. Isaiah 42:1–4.
8. Isaiah 49:1–4.
9. Isaiah 42:5–7; Isaiah 49:5–6.
10. Isaiah 49:7.
11. Isaiah 53:1–3, 7–9.
12. Isaiah 53:9.
13. Isaiah 53:10–11.
14. Isaiah 53:12.

take the blame for them; someone who would rescue them from their own mistakes.[15]

But who was this servant? Who was the Messiah who would bring Isra-El back home? It was obviously the same person as the Wonder-man to come, the Prince of Judah. This Super-star of His Story would fit Isa-Yah's profile perfectly. But this long awaited Messiah wouldn't be born for another few hundred years. The need for a Messiah was critical now. Isra-El needed saving quickly if Family Abraham weren't going to be absorbed completely into other people-groups as they lived scattered throughout the world.

Isa-Yah reported that the Lord had told him that he also had a servant Messiah for this immediate job. The Lord had straightforwardly told Isa-Yah, "Cyrus is my shepherd and will do all that I want—he will rebuild Jeru-Salem and a new Temple."[16] Later Isa-Yah reported that the Lord called Cyrus, "his anointed one"—which in Isra-El language was "Messiah."[17] Later again the Lord clearly said through Isa-Yah that, "Cyrus would rebuild the Lord's city and set his exiled people free."[18]

So, who was this Cyrus? It was King Cyrus the Second, otherwise known as Cyrus the Great. He came to the throne of a yet another up and coming superpower—Persia, around five hundred and fifty-nine years before B.C. gave way to A.D. Twenty years later, he defeated Babylon by drying up their river and then using it as a surprise path to enter the city and win a famous victory.

But Cyrus wasn't your typical military king of those days. He was benevolent. He was generous. He was kind. His policy was to rescue all the foreign exiles held captive by Babylon. He not only released the exiles from Babylon but even encouraged and helped them to go back and rebuild their homeland.[19]

This man was God's gift of grace to Family Abraham. This non-Family Abraham man is one fulfilment of the unlikely "servant of the Lord' prophecies spoken by Isa-Yah hundreds of years earlier. By rescuing Family Abraham and making it possible for God's people to go back to their historic promised homeland, Cyrus not only saved Isra-El from extinction—his saving actions also in a small way gave them a glimpse of the nature of the Super-star servant Messiah who was going to be sent through the Doorway to save the whole family of humanity later.

15. Isaiah 53:4–6, 10a.
16. Isaiah 44:28.
17. Isaiah 45:1.
18. Isaiah 45:13.
19. Ezra 1:1–11.

But why was Cyrus the Great so kind to Family Abraham—Isra-El? Why was he so gracious and so generous? Possibly part of the answer might lie in the story of a young man who was one of the first of the bright young things to be taken to Babylon just before Jeru-Salem fell to Babylon for the first time.

The young man's name was Dani-El.

# 36

## You can take the Boy out of Isra-El but not Isra-El out of the Boy

BEING KIDNAPPED ISN'T A good start for any young man. But for the talented Dani-El it turned out to be his moment of destiny. When Babylon was all over Jeru-Salem like a rash, long before Cyrus defeated Babylon, Dani-El was grabbed and dragged to Babylon. But instead of being abused, he was hand-picked by the great Babylonian King Nebuchadnezzar to work in his palace.[1] He wasn't chosen to wash the floor or clean the chimneys, he was hand-picked to become a Babylonian—to assimilate into the culture of Babylon—to be the living proof of "whilst in Rome..." Babylonian style.

Dani-El didn't fight his destiny. He took seriously the great Mouthpiece of the Lord, Jerem-Yah's advice to settle down and be successful even when forcibly away from home in exile.[2] But it's one thing being in Babylon, but another thing being part of Babylon. You could take the boy out of Isra-El but not Isra-El out of the boy. Dani-El had El in his name and there wasn't a chance in El that he would stop following his El-God. Dani-El had principles he wouldn't give up.

One of these was his special diet. In those days, eating food with someone meant accepting them. Eating their food said you were part of their friends and family. This was not a fast-food, T.V. meal culture. Dani-El was not Babylonian and so he didn't want to eat Babylonian food.[3] He was Family Abraham. He wanted to eat his family food. To do anything else would be disloyal to his "Family" and their God. His Family food was from a menu given by Moses to his people, but it had its roots through the Doorway. El-God had told his people what was "kosher." Babylonian food wasn't "kosher." So, the safest thing for Dani-El to do was to only eat vegetables

---

1. Daniel 1:1–7.
2. Jeremiah 29:4–9.
3. Daniel 1:8.

*you can take the boy out of isra-el but not isra-el out of the boy*

and drink water. Dani-El's royal Babylonian minder, had to make sure that Dani-El and his friends were healthy. King Nebuchadnezzar didn't want to waste his time and money training them up only to see them die on him. To be healthy you had to eat. And to be healthy you had to eat the best. Best was the King's food—of course. But it was rich and it was non-kosher. Dani-El's refusal to eat it made his minder sick with worry—if Dani-El started fading away or looking peaky, his minder would end up very unhealthy—dead probably. But Dani-El persuaded his royal minder to let him give his healthy diet a go. Amazingly, soon Dani-El and his three vegetarian friends became ten times healthier and fitter than anyone else.[4] Who said vegetarianism is just a new fad?

So far so good—first hurdle overcome. Not only that, soon Dani-El and his three Family Abraham colleagues became part of the King's trusted group of advisors and counsellors. But this high up position had its difficulties and dangers.

King Nebuchadnezzar had a dream—not a nice dream. It worried him. True, he probably deserved nightmares after what he was doing to Jeru-Salem miles away, but leaving that on one side, he asked his astrologers, magicians, wizards and fortune-tellers to tell him what it meant. They hadn't a clue. They couldn't even hazard a guess. Not surprisingly, as it turned out because the King hadn't told them the dream.[5] No fool this Nebuchadnezzar—he argued that a genuine dream interpreter should know the dream without being told. Nebuchadnezzar wanted to make sure that the interpretation wasn't just a product of the interpreter's mind, but that the interpreter could read the King's mind as well. Makes sense when you think about it but not to his pseudo-psychic advisors—they pleaded that this wasn't fair. In their opinion, it was beyond any human powers and certainly beyond theirs. When they explained this to the King, Nebuchadnezzar concluded that they were all fraudsters and decided to get rid of them all—not to sack them but to kill them (it's what kings could do in those days). Unfortunately for Dani-El and his friends the King decided not just to kill his dream interpreters but all his advisors including Dani-El and co. They were simply collateral damage.

Dani-El heard of his fate. But as the executioners were on their way to execute their fatal orders, Dani-El was busy. He and his friends were begging God "who gives wisdom to the wise and knowledge to the knowledgeable and brings deep and dark things to light," to give them super-natural insight; knowledge from beyond the Doorway; to see into Nebuchadnezzar's

4. Daniel 1:9–16.
5. Daniel 2:1–13.

dream.⁶ And in the darkness of the middle of the night, God brought the dream to light.⁷

Dani-El used his growing diplomatic skills with the executioner and persuaded him to get himself an audience with the King. He was going to describe in detail Nebuchadnezzar's dream. A lot hinged on this moment—like Dani-El's head for example. Not only Dani-El's head and his friends' heads, but also His Story hung in the balance, as we will see.

With his life at stake, Dani-El described King Nebuchadnezzar's nightmare to him. According to Dani-El, the nightmare was of a statue.⁸ It was a statue of a man whose head was gold; his chest—silver; his torso—bronze; his legs—iron. But despite this bling, he had bad feet made of clay. The nightmarish statue stood in front of the King until it suddenly was hit by a rolling rock and came crashing down narrowly missing the King. Despite its fabulously costly metal, its feet of clay couldn't stand the impact. And hey presto—the famous saying about feet of clay was born.

There must have been a moment of intense tension as everyone waited to see if the details of the bizarre dream recalled by Dani-El matched the King's nightmare—to see whether the information Dani-El had received through the Doorway was correct. But Dani-El, not knowing when to quit, piled in quickly with an interpretation before the King responded.⁹ Each metal signified a new kingdom in the world after Nebuchadnezzar's Babylonian Empire. Each kingdom would be destroyed by the Rock of God's Kingdom.

God's Kingdom consists of all the people who remember that God is the real King—it's not a piece of land or a geographical area but the sum of the people who let God's influence stretch through the Doorway and through them into the world. Those people who allow themselves to be a bridgehead for God's "out-of-this-world Kingdom" on earth. God's Kingdom is God's foothold back in his Creation—his foot in the Doorway; his secret army; his nerve-center for his plan to rescue earth. It is as if when God opens the Doorway he always energizes some people. These people then live as if they are part of the land beyond the Doorway, even though they are still inside the Universe. These people sign up as King God's subjects. These people march to the beat of his drum. These people join in God's subversive resistance movement—a secret army fighting to return the earth to its rightful owner—God.

6. Daniel 2:17–23.
7. Daniel 2:24–28.
8. Daniel 2:31–35.
9. Daniel 2:36–45.

Dani-El like the other Mouthpieces of the Lord was beginning to see a time when God would rock the kingdoms of the world. He would build a new Kingdom on earth: greater than any other Kingdom; bigger than one family; bigger than one nation; bigger than geographical or political or ethnic boundaries.

But before that, Dani-El, had the little matter of staying alive after suggesting the powerful Kingdom of Babylon would be toppled and King Nebuchadnezzar's legacy bowled over. Was the dream accurate? It was, and just as amazingly, Dani-El's interpretation bowled over King Nebuchadnezzar.[10] Maybe because it was based on an accurate description of his nightmare; maybe because it referred to events long after Nebuchadnezzar or maybe because it was just simply and self-evidently, correct.

Dani-El was a worthy successor to Joseph—the dream man of old who also impressed a foreign king. Not only was Dani-El saved from the executioner along with his friends, he was given greater responsibility and placed in charge of all the wise men.[11] Even Ezeki-El (the great Mouthpiece of the Lord and Dani-El's contemporary), was a fan of Dani-El's wisdom. At one point he mocks a local King near him and says, "Are you wiser than even Dani-El?"[12]

You would expect that Nebuchadnezzar in the face of Dani-El's God-given gifts and his interpretation of his dream would have learnt his lesson. You would expect him to remember that God is King. Not a bit of it. Human pride is addictive and of all things, King Nebuchadnezzar decided to actually build a statute—a gold statue nearly ninety feet high (just over half the height of the Statue of Liberty) and nearly ten feet wide.[13] The most likely inspiration for the statue was probably the King himself. It certainly was in praise of himself. If so, it was just like his nightmare—though hopefully he designed it without the feet of clay. Was this an ironic choice of artefact to build after his nightmare? If so, the irony was lost on the King.

But it wasn't just ironic—it was dangerous. Not just because the statue might be in danger of toppling over and contravening Health and Safety Regulations (if they had such a thing) but because it was an idol. It broke the special contract between God and humanity—something God would not allow to happen, as Nebuachadnezzar had been warned in his dream. Oblivious to his stupidity, the King ordered that when his band played music, everyone had to fall down and worship the King's handiwork. If you didn't fall

10. Daniel 2:46–47.
11. Daniel 2:48–49.
12. Ezekiel 28:1–3.
13. Daniel 3:1–6.

down in front of the statue you would be burnt alive—so people worshipped it—unsurprisingly. All fell down at the sound of the band, except Dani-El's three friends—Shadrach, Meshach and Abednego. They couldn't. [14] Why? Because this law of the King broke the first and second of the King of King's ten rules written down by God and handed to Moses on Mount Sinai. Abraham's family couldn't worship an idol or anything created—they could only worship the Creator. [15] Dani-El's three friends remembered the Lord. They were loyal to the Lord—and only to the Lord. So when the band played, Shadrach, Meshach and Abednego wouldn't dance to its tune—they opted instead for the furnace. Their view was simple—God could save them. One thing to believe theoretically that God could save them but quite another to believe he would actually save them. But Dani-El's friends had thought about this and told the King that even if God didn't save them he was still God—and they still wouldn't worship anyone or anything else.[16] So there!

And so the three men went into the King's cremator to be burnt alive simply for refusing to worship the powerful leader and his evil delusional ideas.[17] Unbelievable? Approximately six million men, women and children went to the cremators and gas chambers in the Holocaust less than a century ago simply because they were Family Abraham and simply because one powerful leader had delusional evil ideas. Not so unbelievable now? This cremator in Babylon was so hot, it killed the soldiers that shut in Dani-El's friends. But the three friends instead of dying, walked around inside the cremator as cool as cucumbers. At one point, they were joined by another mysterious person who looked like a "son of the gods."[18] It looked like a super-natural being: someone who looked like he was from beyond the Doorway to outside of the Universe; someone who was able to resist super-heated temperatures; someone super-human who then gave his powers to Dani-El's friends. I know what you're thinking—it must be God in human form again. Correct. One day in the future, God would not only be in human form, but actually be human—the Wonder-child who was the God-Man. And he would be found again right in the center of an apparatus designed to kill humans. And this time he would be there to save not just three humans, but all humans.[19]

14. Daniel 3:8–18.
15. Exodus 20:3–5.
16. Daniel 3:17–18.
17. Daniel 3:19–23.
18. Daniel 3:24–25.
19. Philippians 2:6–11.

But at this point in His Story, King Nebuchadnezzar admitted defeat. Dani-El's three friends were still in the peak of health, so the King let Dani-El's three friends out. It is recorded that their clothes weren't even scorched or smelt of smoke.[20] Instead of being incinerated they went back into their positions of power alongside Dani-El. And with Dani-El they continued to advise Nebuchadnezzar and later, Nebuchadnezzar's son, the new King Belshazzar. They used their insider knowledge from the Creator who lived beyond the Doorway of the Universe.

At one point, Dani-El bravely interpreted some weird coded writing that was written on the wall by a scary disembodied hand at one of King Belshazzar's parties. It was a message from God for Belshazzar and his nation of Babylon.[21] The meaning was in the action—the "writing was on the wall" for the Babylonian empire: it had had its time; it was going to be toppled—and it duly was. That same night, King Belshazzar was killed and the non-Babylonian enemy King, Darius the Mede, took over.[22] Not just another king—but just possibly, the King prophesied by the great Mouthpiece of the Lord, Isa-Yah, two hundred years earlier: the King working on behalf of the Kingdom of God; the great rock smashing into the Kingdoms of the earth; the mysterious long awaited Cyrus—the great rescuer of Isra-El talked about many years earlier by the great Mouthpiece, Isa-Yah. In the book dedicated to Dani-El's story you can read, "So Dani-El thrived during the reign of Darius and the reign of Cyrus the Persian."[23] Doesn't this mean that Cyrus came after King Darius and wasn't the same person? Remember though that this is written in Family Abraham language. It needs translating into English. You can just as easily translate it as, "Dani-El thrived in the reign of Darius namely Cyrus the Persian." Darius and Cyrus may well be the same person.

Darius may well be the other name of Cyrus the Great. But why did he have two names? This practice of having more than one name was well known—like the famous King of Assyria we have already met who had the long name of Tiglath Pileser the Third. He was also known simply as "Pul."[24] (Well, wouldn't you want a shorter name than Tiglath Pileser the Third?) There are more reasons why Darius and Cyrus might be one and the same: Darius was sixty-two when he took over Babylon—so was Cyrus; Darius was a Mede—Cyrus was the son of a Median princess. So maybe Cyrus—

20. Daniel 3:26–27.
21. Daniel 5:1–29.
22. Daniel 5:30–31.
23. Daniel 6:28.
24. 1 Chronicles 5:26.

the one seen by Isa-Yah a few hundred years earlier as the friend and helper of the exiled people of Judah—was no other than Darius.

When did Darius come to power in Babylon? Five hundred and thirty-nine years B.C.—the year the kind Cyrus' sneaked into Babylon and defeated it.

Coincidence or His Story?

# 37

## The Real Deal

EVEN IF DARIUS AND Cyrus are one and the same, this still doesn't explain why Darius/Cyrus became the friend of Family Abraham. Why was he so generous to a people of a different culture, faith and God? Why did he bother bringing Isra-El back from exile in Babylon? Bear in mind he was a king at a time when being a great humanitarian wasn't exactly essential on a king's C.V. and getting the Nobel Prize for Peace was not a target to aim for. In fact, he was king at a time when being cross-culturally sensitive was not a vote-winner. He was king when leaders weren't elected—they just ruled with a sharp sword and a powerful army. Any sensitivity was seen as a sign of weakness.

So why the kindness towards Family Abraham? Darius/Cyrus' first action as the new power in Babylon doesn't really help answer this question. It wasn't exactly the action of a modern self-effacing gracious baby-kissing diplomat. It was more the action of an old-style despot. He allowed his advisors to appeal to his vanity—to his pride and his belief in his own power and importance. His advisors persuaded Darius/Cyrus to invent a new law. It was a law designed (allegedly) to give out a clear message to the King's new country that he was the Mr Big. But it was in fact a new law which was designed by his advisors to discredit the foreign upstart, Dani-El, in the eyes of his new boss. What kind of law could have such an effect?—one that ordered everyone in Babylon to worship Darius/Cyrus as a demi-god for the next month.[1] The advisors knew full well that Dani-El would rather die than support a man who thought he was God—demi, semi, or even a tiny bit God. Dani-El who was famous for not changing his diet for a King wasn't going to start worshipping one—whoever he was and however useful he might turn out to be to Isra-El. It was against the created order and the Lord's revealed laws.

So Dani-El carried on as normal praying to the Lord—not daily, but three times daily—and also not in secret. He was at home, granted, but he

1. Daniel 6:1–9.

flung his windows open towards Jeru-Salem.[2] Catching Dani-El disobeying the King was like taking candy off a baby. The jealous colleagues of Dani-El told the new King on Daniel. They grassed him up to Darius/Cyrus.[3]

Immediately, Darius/Cyrus was aghast at his own stupidity—appalled at his own pride. He knew that Dani-El was his key man—trustworthy and honest. Dani-El was already a hero to Darius/Cyrus. He knew the potential of the man: he knew the integrity of the man; he knew that the man's stubbornness was not his fatal flaw but his greatest gift—a gift he used for the King. But Darius/Cyrus had fallen for the oldest mistake in the book of human experience. He had fallen for the oldest mistake in His Story—pride—making yourself God; forgetting that even though you might be a king, you are not God.

Darius/Cyrus was angry at how his jealous advisors had got an honest, indispensable man like Dani-El into trouble. But all was not lost. Maybe he could give him a royal pardon—after all he was the King. But as was pointed out gleefully by his advisors, no law made by the King could be changed. It was the law that laws made by the King couldn't be repealed.[4] They were set in stone for ever. This left a stark choice to Darius/Cyrus. The King was between a rock and a hard place—lose Dani-El or admit his mistake and lose all respect as the greatest most powerful king in that part of the world.

Darius/Cyrus felt he had no option but to punish Dani-El. But problem number two was that the "punishment" was to be thrown into a pit full of starving lions. Lions have over the years eaten a fair few humans, the most famous being the lions of Njombe that ate over one thousand five hundred humans in 1932. Even as recently as 1991, one lion became infamous in Zambia for eating six people. In addition, between 1990 and 2005 in areas of Tanzania, five hundred and sixty-three humans have been attacked by lions and many have been eaten. It has been estimated that as many as seven hundred people every year are eaten by lions. In the past keeping a pride of lions was like having an attack dog as a pet. It was a way of showing your strength and keeping your enemies away. They were even kept at one point in the Tower of London by the King of England. But in Babylon and the surrounding countries of Dani-El's time, the lion was truly symbolic of kingship. If you kept them—you were the King of the King of the Jungle.

It was these animals that Dani-El faced. It was this show of majestic, beastly power that Dani-El had to survive. This wasn't just a punishment but an execution—there was no way out. At least in the end Darius/Cyrus was

2. Daniel 6:10.
3. Daniel 6:11–13.
4. Daniel 6:14–15.

big enough to dare to see that he was on trial here as much as Dani-El. His last words to Dani-El before ordering Dani-El's descent into the big cats' pit were, "May the God you always serve—serve you now!"[5] It wasn't a taunt but a prayer. He was asking for Dani-El's God to find both of them a way out of the King's pride of lions that the King's pride had got them into—and all this from a man who wasn't meant to have faith in God. But it was surely a vain hope—or was it?

The King spent the night in his palace too worried to eat, too worried to sleep, too worried even to be "entertained."[6] As soon as the first rays of dawn light pierced his palace window, he rushed to his pit of lions. Hoping against hope he called out, "Dani-El are you there?" He expected to only hear the purring of content, well-fed lions. But instead he heard the confident, very much alive and uneaten voice of Dani-El. "Yes, O King—my God sent a special messenger from beyond the world who shut the mouths of the lions. God knows I am innocent!"[7] And the King now also knew Dani-El was innocent. The King was beside himself with happiness. He got his number one expert advisor back in one piece and he had been given a clear sign that the people of Isra-El had a very powerful protector and helper—El God.

Darius/Cyrus knew exactly what to do—he had to support Dani-El's God because he was real—he was the real deal. The most powerful King in the world was now a believer in the El of Dani-El. As for the King's advisors who had tried to trick the King into getting rid of his wise man, the King decided that what was good enough for Dani-El was good enough for them. But this time, the human pet-food was torn apart and eaten by the royal big cats before it had time to touch the floor. If he needed more proof that it was wise not to go against Dani-El's God, Darius/Cyrus now had it. And so he sent out a message to all his empire, "People everywhere in my Kingdom must respect the God of Dani-El: he is the God who is real; he is powerful; he is outside of time; is beyond the Doorway but he does amazing things on earth!"[8] For the first time ever in His Story, the God of Family Abraham was respected internationally. The promise to Father Abraham was coming true. From that point on Darius/Cyrus knew he had to protect God's family—Isra-El. He released all the exiles in defeated Babylon and even helped them rebuild their lives and their country.

So was Darius/Cyrus the one prophesied by Isa-Yah two hundred years earlier? Was he the one who would rescue God's scattered family and

---

5. Daniel 6:16.
6. Daniel 6:17–18.
7. Daniel 6:19–22.
8. Daniel 6:26–27.

their land from disaster? Was he the one seen by the great Mouthpiece of God a couple of centuries previously? Undoubtedly. But was Darius/Cyrus the special servant—the chosen one—the Messiah—the Wonder-child? Was he the special one that His Story had been building up towards? Wise Dani-El would no doubt have said, "No." He would have seen that even though Darius/Cyrus was great, there was a far greater servant of the Lord on his way in the future—an even greater rescuer and savior of God's family and people.

Later, Dani-El had another amazing vision from beyond the Doorway. A vision of someone he called a, "Son of Man"—his name for a "super-human." This title for the "super-human" was one used five hundred years later by a man who knew Dani-El's vision from beyond the Doorway. He used it to describe himself—time and time again. It was his most popular way of talking about himself. There is no doubt that this man saw himself as the "super-human" seen by Dani-El.[9] This man is the Super-star of His Story—the long awaited Wonder-child. Dani-El described this super-human "Son of Man" as, "riding on the clouds of the sky" before being crowned as King of the Universe by the "Ancient of Days"—Dani-El's title for the eternal God. [10] This super-human "Son of Man" would be a king with total power: total glory; total authority over all peoples, nations, ethnic groups, and religions—for ever.[11] He would be a real human but more than human—super-human.

Whatever Dani-El thought of Darius/Cyrus he didn't think this of him. This "Son of Man" was someone greater than even the great Darius/Cyrus. In fact, someone more amazing than any person who had lived on earth so far—greater than even the greatest stars of His Story or any human we have already met in His Story. After his arrival, everything and everybody would be second best. And leading up to his arrival, the stars of God's bloodline would seem just ever so slightly disappointing.

They would be all stars of His Story but all living in the shade of the future advent of the long awaited Super-star—the special servant "Son of Man."

---

9. Matthew 16:13–17.
10. Daniel 7:13.
11. Daniel 7:14.

# 38

# God's Signet Ring

DARIUS/CYRUS MIGHT NOT HAVE been Dani-El's super-human "Son of Man", but he was a God-send to Family Abraham. What was left of the scattered remains of Family Abraham was in a bad way—a long way from home and a long way from their God (or so they felt).

We know their state of mind at the beginning of their foreign exile by the lyrics of one of their songs. One of their chart-topping songs went, "By the rivers of Babylon we remembered Jeru-Salem and cried. We sat down in protest and refused to play our music. We hung up our harps on the trees and refused to sing. When our kidnappers taunted us with, 'Go on sing us one of your songs!' we said, 'How can we sing when we've nothing to sing about stuck in this land!'"[1] The song had a less than uplifting chorus about anyone who dared to be happy and sing a cheerful song should have their hands cut off and their tongues glued to the top of their mouths.[2]

But Darius/Cyrus, the new best friend of God, gave this depressed people new hope. He put a new song into their mouths. He released them from exile and encouraged them to make their way back from Babylon to Jeru-Salem. He even helped attempts to rebuild the shattered Temple in Jeru-Salem—the blocked Doorway to beyond the Universe.

But there were lots of problems: lots of enemies; lots of people who didn't want the old superpower back home. But despite the drawbacks, the Temple started to be rebuilt. This was thanks in part to Haggai, the new Mouthpiece of God, who told the people that it was wrong to concentrate on rebuilding their own houses before rebuilding the Lord's house. He criticized them for being more interested in their own front doors than the front Door to beyond the Universe.[3] Haggai famously said that until they did the right thing: their purses and wallets would seem to have holes in; their fields would harvest little; their stomachs would ache with emptiness and their

---

1. Psalm 137:1–4.
2. Psalm 137:5–6.
3. Haggai 1:1–11.

clothes would never keep them warm.⁴ Until the Lord was made number one in their lives: they would never have enough; never be content; never be happy. If they tried living without reference to God their lives would feel dead and would always be ever so slightly disappointing. Many people still witness to the same phenomenon today. In response, they still turn to God.

The recent returnees also turned to God and listened to Haggai. These people wanted to be content. They wanted to be happy, so they gave their time, skill and resources and the Temple was rebuilt under the leadership of another significant man, Zerubbabel.⁵ Zerubbabel was made Governor of the Persian province of Judah by Darius/Cyrus. Zerubbabel was an able man—but much more than that. He was the grandson of Jecon-Yah, the King of Judah who was dragged off into Babylon—the last proper King of Judah—the last part of the bloodline of the Prince of Judah—the bloodline of the Wonder-child. The bloodline—re-surfaced. The Mouthpiece, Haggai, said the Lord's nickname for Zerubbabel was, "the Lord's signet ring."⁶

A signet ring in the past was used to make a unique impression on wax used to seal up documents. It was a sign that the document was genuine and carried the king's authority. Haggai said Zerubbabel had King God's authority on earth—his man in His Story—his star. Zechar-Yah, Haggai's fellow Mouthpiece of the Lord, had a special personal message from the Lord to Zerubbabel. It was a special piece of advice from the greatest power of the Universe and beyond, "Don't even think of doing anything by your own power or your own strength, Zerubbabel, but do it by my invisible Spirit empowering you from through the Doorway."⁷

Zerubbabel didn't just have God's authority—he had his power. Was this man the special one? Was he the Wonder-child—the end of the bloodline? No. Just the next star in the long bloodline stretching back to the great King David—the Super-star's most famous ancestor.

Or was he? Jerem-Yah, the famous Mouthpiece of the Lord from years before, had said about Zerubbabel's grandfather, King Jecon-Yah, "This is what the Lord says, 'Record this man as childless—none of his children will prosper—none of them will sit on the throne of King David or rule Judah anymore.'" Not just an empty threat, but an inspired word from beyond the Doorway. According to the Lord, the bloodline of Jecon-Yah would never give birth to another King of God's Family.⁸ Jecon-Yah's grandson, Zerub-

---

4. Haggai 1:5–6.
5. Haggai 1:12–15.
6. Haggai 2:23.
7. Zechariah 4:6.
8. Jeremiah 22:24–30.

babel, though important, was not a king. He was only Governor of Judah. He was an important key-player in His Story, but not that important. Things weren't as special as they had been. Nothing was quite as it was. And certainly no one rivalled the great King David of old. And even more certainly, no one was living up to the prophecies of a Wonder-child, a super-human super King, who would be like great King David but even greater—a King whose Kingdom wouldn't ever end but be eternal. Zerubabbel did a good job—but not that good a job. It was all more than slightly disappointing.

But maybe the let-down was because the time hadn't yet come: more patience needed; more waiting needed. The Lord's Mouthpiece, Zechar-Yah, at this time saw a Savior coming—a Prince of Judah on his way—not your usual kingly person on a stallion or in a heavily armed chariot, but one riding into his capital city, Jeru-Salem, on a donkey.[9]

A donkey—not exactly the transport of choice for a great, rich, powerful, military king. This future King obviously would be so great—he wouldn't need to show off or brag. He would be humble—he would ride on a donkey.[10] This future King would get rid of the war horses and chariots because this King's victory would mean that there would be international peace across all seas and lands.

Was this dream of Zechar-Yah just a naïve desire for "world peace" as meaningful as the desires of Miss Universe pageant contestants? Yes—for the moment—because Zerubbabel wasn't that good.

And quite wisely, he didn't ride into the wild, semi-derelict Jeru-Salem on only a donkey.

---

9. Zechariah 9:9–10.
10. Matthew 21:1–11.

# 39

## Miss Star of Persia

DESPITE ALL OF HIS great leadership skills, Zerubbabel wasn't going to be the ancestor of the Wonder-child. In keeping with Jerem-Yah's damning prophecy about the descendants of Jecon-Yah, the bloodline that came directly from him reflected a growing sense of anti-climax. Zerubbabel's son was Abiud.[1] He may have been an amazing human being, but we will never know, because no one at the time ever wrote about him, or his children's children: Eliakim; Azor; Zadok; Achim; Eliud; Eleazar; Matthan; Jacob. All names that are famous for not being famous: notable only for being ordinary; notable for being non-entities on the world stage; notable for being the boring end of a previous long line of exciting people—generation after generation of names—just names; no stories; no amazing personal stories; no His Story stories.

That's not to say that everyone at this time was ordinary or that a general greyness had cast its sickly pallor over Family Abraham people in general. There are some amazing stories at this time. One of these surfaced around five hundred years after King David and five hundred years before the world's time-clock clicked round from B.C. to A.D.

Despite Darius/Cyrus' help and reassurances, some members of Family Abraham didn't want to venture back to repopulate the wild dangerous Jeru-Salem. They opted to stay in far-flung countries. But like Dani-El earlier, they didn't want to assimilate to the culture—they didn't just want to make themselves comfortable in their new adopted foreign homes—instead, they made names for themselves.

Bizarrely, one of the most famous people who made the most of her time in exile was a woman. Nothing strange in that, but this was a woman who made a name for herself by entering a national beauty contest—Miss Persia and not just entered but won. This beauty contest was no pageant though. It was a way of finding a new queen for the king. The king was King Xerxes of Persia (modern day Iran). King Xerxes was the king who followed

---

1. Matthew 1:13–15.

on after the benevolent King Darius/Cyrus. Who was the woman? Esther, a name that means "star"—a name she lived up to. She wasn't one of the stars of the bloodline of the Wonder-child, but her story shone brightly at the time of a dark threat of genocide for Family Abraham. She is the only woman of history who has ever stopped a holocaust by undergoing a year of beauty treatment and of course, by being insanely brave as well.

She replaced King Xerxes' Queen Vashti. Vashti had been removed from her position after she refused to be paraded in front of the King's guests at a lavish party wearing her crown.[2] Was she just a bit touchy about her regal wardrobe? Not if you believe that she was ordered to appear, wearing only her royal crown and nothing else. Such independence of thought was a bit ahead of its time nearly five hundred years before the beginning of what we now know as A.D.—especially for a woman.

So, Queen Vashti is removed by Xerxes—but who to replace her with? King Xerxes, as a man, thinks a beauty contest would be a good idea. He would. And so he sends his spies out to find the most beautiful young women to replace his opinionated ex-wife.[3]

The orphan Esther is caught up in this Royal trawl for pretty young women. When she is forcibly selected for the finals, she doesn't reveal that she is Family Abraham not Persian. Her legal guardian—her older cousin Mordecai, had advised her that keeping quiet about her nationality would be a wise move. Her Family Abraham name was Hadassah. But wisely she let herself known by her Persian name—Esther.

Mordecai and Esther's ancestors had of course been dragged out of Jeru-Salem by King Nebuchadnezzar of Babylon when he took Jecon-Yah prisoner back to his court. Mordecai, like his ancestors, had been successful at keeping himself and his family safe in a foreign land. This sixth sense had made him aware of new rumblings against Family Abraham. Many of his wider family were beginning to be too successful. As has happened many times since, Mordecai and Esther's people provoked jealousy and suspicion by their success.[4] In fact, just as had happened in Egypt around a thousand years earlier at the time of Moses, was happening again. Family Abraham was beginning to be blamed for the country's problems in which they were living. Some of the indigenous population felt that they had outstayed their welcome. Family Abraham needed someone on the "inside." Cousin Mordecai decided it should be Esther.

2. Esther 1:10–12.
3. Esther 2:1–4.
4. Esther 2:5–11.

Esther was prepared for the contest by a long series of beauty treatments. In fact, one year's worth. All this time, she lived in the King's harem.[5] After a year of preparation, the King called for her, and fell for her. She won.[6] She became the new Queen—a young innocent, non-Persian Queen of Persia. Her cousin kept close to her and listened out for trouble. But he didn't reveal to anyone else that he was related to Esther.

As he was keeping close to the Palace, he overheard about a coup—a plan to assassinate the King. He reported this to Esther who reported it to the King.[7] As a result of the intelligence, Mordecai had gathered, the traitors were executed. The King was saved.

Later, Esther's cousin found out about another plan, but this time not to harm the King but to harm all the Family Abraham members in Persia.[8] This plan was the brainchild of the new Prime Minister of Persia. He planned to commit genocide. Mordecai again told his cousin, Esther.[9] Coincidentally, the first of Abraham's family planned to be executed was actually Esther's cousin Mordecai. This was for refusing to bow down to the big-headed, pig-headed, racist Prime Minister. Like Dani-El and his friends Mordecai could not worship another man. The Prime Minister was livid: he loved power; he loved the trappings of power; he loved people worshipping him.

To save her cousin, Esther knew that she had to speak to the King. To save her people, Esther knew she had to speak to the King. To do this she had to reveal her true identity at a time of great racial prejudice. To do this, she had to stand up and be counted when ethnic cleansing was about to start. Mordecai reminded her that maybe she had ended up in the royal palace for just, "such a time as this."[10]

Such a time as this—His Story's perfect timing. His Story—storyboarded, scripted and planned by God. His Story: God intervening from beyond the Doorway to save his people—to rescue his Family. But Esther knew the Persian law that anyone who went before the King without being invited would be killed—get it wrong and the King would be displeased. You didn't displease the King—not if you wanted to keep your pretty, beauty-contest winning head on your graceful shoulders. You had to pick your moment or pick your headstone. She might have been chosen for such a time as this, but she still needed perfect timing.

5. Esther 2:12–14.
6. Esther 2:15–18.
7. Esther 2:19–23.
8. Esther 3:1–6.
9. Esther 4:1–11.
10. Esther 4:12–14.

Add to that risk, the danger of going to ask the King to overrule his chosen Prime Minister and national policy. It was a mission impossible—especially as the King, in a weak moment, had agreed to the slaughter. But up against these odds, Esther showed she wasn't just a pretty face.

She didn't rush. She decided to ask the God of her ancient Father Abraham, for help. She decided to ask other members of Family Abraham to ask God for help. There was only one way to do this—to fast: to diet; to not eat or drink for three full days; to show how serious they all were; to show that the threat was more serious than the most basic need of humans—food.[11] After three days, she invited the King to come to her for a banquet, including, of course, his best friend, the Prime Minister. She wasn't the first or the last to know that the way to a man's heart is through his stomach.

It went well. The wine flowed well. The King enjoyed his meal so much he said Esther could have anything she wanted from him.[12] The Prime Minister enjoyed his meal so much he became convinced he had been specially invited because really Esther fancied him and that he might get anything he wanted from her.[13] Pride—again. Hundreds of years before this, wise King Solomon had said, "Pride comes before a fall."[14]

And he was right in the Prime Minister's case. Esther planned another meal for the King and his favorite Prime Minister. This time, it followed hard on the heels of a special awards ceremony arranged by the King. The Prime Minister thought it was going to be for him, but instead the King remembered he had not publicly honored Mordecai for saving him from assassination earlier.[15] And of course he asked his trusty right hand-man, the Prime Minister, to arrange it and be the M.C. The award ceremony was like a living death to the Prime Minister: honoring the man he hated; honoring a member of the people he hated; honoring the man who had refused to bow down to him. After this, the Prime Minister was beyond anger—he was twisted with hatred for Esther's cousin and all his race—he was consumed with pure bigotry and racism. He consoled himself by building a massive gallows on which to hang Mordecai.[16] He consoled himself by the thought of another meal served by his secret admirer, Esther. Of course, he didn't know she was Mordecai's cousin or that she was Family Abraham as well! If he had, he would surely have choked on Esther's cooking.

---

11. Esther 4:15–17.
12. Esther 5:1–7.
13. Esther 5:9–12.
14. Proverbs 16:18.
15. Esther 6:1–14.
16. Esther 5:13–14; 6:12–14.

At this meal, Esther literally took her life in her hands. The King, again full of fine food and fine wine, offered her anything she wanted. So at this point, she spilt the beans at the meal and pleaded for protection for herself and her people from the evil Prime Minister.[17]

Esther waited to see whether she had won the beauty contest for, "such a time as this" or whether this was the last time she would be alive. The King must have looked at the Prime Minister: the King must have looked at Esther—and put the two together. He was overcome with anger and left the room.

Meanwhile, the self-absorbed Prime Minister, saw his chance. He made his move on Esther. Despite her newly revealed ethnicity, he pleaded with her to show her secret love for him and ask the King not to be angry with him. He got on his knees and hugged her prostrate body as she lay on a couch.[18] Just then the King returned. Talk about timing. The King must have looked at the Prime Minister: the King must have looked at Esther—and put the two together. He was overcome with anger and called for his Prime Minister to be executed. Not only was he trying to exterminate Esther and her people, he was also trying to assault her first. He had to be got rid of—hanged—quickly.

But there wasn't a scaffold ready—or was there? Just by chance there was one—a very tall one—one reserved by the Prime Minister for Mordecai—one he wouldn't be needing any longer. It was used instead to hang the Prime Minister.[19]

Ironic? Justice? His Story? Whatever your view, Esther saved her people from slaughter—despite being many miles from home. The King declared that Esther's people were allowed to protect themselves against racist attacks and assaults—and they did. Esther's victory has been celebrated by Family Abraham ever since. Her timing was impeccable.

It was God's timing—His Story.

---

17. Esther 7:1–6.
18. Esther 7:7–8.
19. Esther 7:9–10.

# 40

## Learn the Lesson of His Story!

Esther kept Family Abraham safe in Persia. Esther's bravery meant that Family Abraham was allowed to grow stronger in Persia.

Equally, Dani-El, with the help of Darius/Cyrus, kept Family Abraham safe in Babylon and helped many of them to return home. Family Abraham as a result grew stronger in Babylon and around Jeru-Salem.

The news of such victories must have fed into the general rising excitement that this was the beginning of a new golden era for Isra-El: a new land flowing with milk and honey; a new Promised Land; a new time of success unprecedented since King David and King Solomon; a new era when just maybe the Wonder-child, now servant-Messiah-man, would appear and defeat all Family Abraham's enemies and set up a permanent Kingdom on earth reflecting the world beyond the Doorway.

But the reality was that even if the great new Prince of Judah appeared, he would have had no place to reign over. Despite the Temple being in the process of being renovated, its setting, Jeru-Salem, was still in a mess. More than anything it was wide open—vulnerable to attack. It needed defending. To do this, it needed a wall and someone to build it. Cue one man—Nehem-Yah. This was a man with an existing important job. He was the Royal Wine Taster—in fact the Wine Taster to Artaxerxes, King of Persia—the King who reigned in the Persian Empire after the husband of beauty contest winner, Queen Esther. But don't visualize Nehem-Yah as just a well-connected wine-waiter or royal smellier—he was a bodyguard for the King like the man who takes the bullet for the President.[1] He tasted all of the King's drink to check it wasn't poisoned—to stop the King being assassinated.

This top security man was from Family Abraham. He was another trusted successful Family Abraham man who was miles from home but doing a good job by making the best of a bad job, but now a man who felt the call of God to go and defend his family home—Jeru-Salem. Like Esther: he

---

1. Nehemiah 1:11b.

bravely went to the King and asked for help; like Esther, he asked for the Lord's help to persuade the King; like Esther, he was successful. [2]

Nehem-Yah was sent by the King to be Governor of Jeru-Salem. The Kings of Persia—Darius/Cyrus, Xerxes and now Artaxerxes continued the policy of support and help to Family Abraham—all in their way serving God.

Despite attacks from the locals who didn't want to give up the land they had come to enjoy for themselves, Nehem-Yah set about his task.[3] He asked God for help but also posted guards and watchmen.[4] He was down-to-earth as well as remembering that he needed out-of-this-world help. This hybrid approach insisted on half his builders wearing swords and the other half building like mad. Under his inspired and practical leadership the wall was rebuilt—in fifty-two days.[5]

But still a Temple and a capital city don't make a nation. The heart was not right—the glue that held the nation together. Another royal helper was needed. A man named Ezra was ready in the wings. King Artaxerxes sent him also to Jeru-Salem.[6] Ezra was probably one of the King's advisors with special responsibility for Family Abraham affairs. Ezra's specific task was now to get the special Family reunited—to rebuild the Family into a nation again: organized; working together; and building on the basis of the rededicated Temple, five hundred and fifteen years before B.C. turned into A.D.

They kept building—come what may. And what came were scurrilous accusations from those who lived around Jeru-Salem: from those fearful of losing their lands to the growing Jerusalem; from those fearful of living next to the increasing power of the old super-power; and from those who just plain hated the returning Isra-El.

These hysterical neighbors appealed to the next King of Persia who had the old Royal name of Darius. But this new Darius, encouraged by Ezra, simply checked the old royal history books and found his namesake predecessor, Darius/Cyrus' historical message to his subjects—the one that ordered them to support Dani-El's God and his people. This support was to include helping to rebuild the heart of Jeru-Salem—the Temple.[7] So, no

2. Nehemiah 2:1–9.
3. Nehemiah 2:10–20; 4:1–12.
4. Nehemiah 4:13–23.
5. Nehemiah 6:15.
6. Ezra 7:7–28.
7. Ezra 5:1—6:12.

contest—even from the grave Darius/Cyrus was still helping God's people. The new Darius couldn't break his law. Isra-El had God and King on their side.

But there was a deeper battle raging for the hearts and souls of the new nation. The Lord's Mouthpiece of the day, Malachi, told Family Abraham that the problem was that even though they were back home in body and mind—their spirit; their heart; their loyalty was miles away.

The Lord through Malachi asked the returnees some rhetorical questions, "Do I not love you? "Was not Esau Jacob's brother, but I didn't choose him—I chose to love Jacob—your descendant instead!"[8] This appeal to the returnees to see themselves as part of a very special chosen Family, didn't seem to be making them act in a special way. They were back in the heart of their historic homeland but their hearts weren't back at home with the Lord. The Lord said through Malachi that he hated their shoddy, slapdash approach to worshipping him—of showing how much the Lord was worth to them. They had the Temple back to sacrifice animals in, but they simply chose to sacrifice the flea-bitten, weak animals that were barely alive instead of their best animals as the law demanded.[9] It was no sacrifice to them—simply a way of getting rid of diseased weak animals no good for anything. Noah had started sacrifice with his last few endangered animals, vital for his food, vital for the sustainability of humanity.[10] But Noah's descendants were using it as a form of glorified recycling. The Lord said they were robbing him—not giving their first 10 percent of all they earned or grew but giving him the leftovers, the loose-change that was weighing their pocket down—not the crisp bank-notes warm out of the cashpoint.[11] They wanted to worship the Lord without it costing—without it changing their life. Bottom line was that they didn't value the Doorway to the beyond any longer. It was down their list of priorities—near the bottom of their personal To Do Lists.

They were disloyal to the Lord and this lack of keeping their promises infected their marriages. They were disloyal to their marriage partners as well. It was simply symptomatic of their unfaithfulness to the Lord.[12] The Lord said, "Judah has been unfaithful." The Lord even said that the people were tiring him out with their many complaining words but no faithful action. They were ready to blame God for all their problems, but couldn't be bothered to take their relationship with him seriously. Funny how humans

8. Malachi 1:2–3.
9. Malachi 1:6–14.
10. Genesis 8:20–21.
11. Malachi 3:6–12.
12. Malachi 2:10–16.

ignore God and don't value his friendship until things go wrong and then he gets all the blame! Nothing changes.

So why did the Lord want to give Isra-El another chance back in Jeru-Salem?—because the Lord never changes. He had promised to work through Family Abraham—and he would. But they needed to return to him—to stop being unfaithful, disloyal and disrespectful. The return from exile was meant to be a new start for the nation. But they were just carrying on like before. They hadn't learnt the lesson of His Story—to stop reliving the mistakes of the past.

Ezra was clear what was needed: God's law needed resurrecting; the special instructions and rules given by the Lord through the Doorway at Sinai; the Unique Selling Point of the nation.[13] In particular Ezra insisted on Family Abraham not marrying outside of the Family.[14] At a time of great mixing and Isra-El being spread far and wide, Ezra wanted to bring the Family back together in a distinctive way—to stop the Family being dysfunctional: pulled in different directions; watered down.

This wasn't meant to be racist. It was meant to be about keeping God's family together—to try desperately to re-create the days of old when Family Abraham was self-sufficient: when Family Abraham was separate; when Family Abraham was one united family like in the good old days—days which possibly didn't ever really exist but had become a dream for the future.

Faced with Ezra's potent teaching and hardline rules creating an inspirational vision of a new future, the returnees to Jeru-Salem admitted they had messed up time and time again as a Family. They confessed their faults and entered into a new agreement to be different this time.[15] They knew they needed a complete new start. They needed the great hope of the Messiah and his Kingdom. The Lord's new Mouthpiece, Malachi, spoke about a day in the future when there would truly be a total and complete new start: not a recycling of the old; not a return simply to the good old days, but a forging ahead into a new radical future. The rubbish and dross of the old would be burnt away like silver in a furnace. The dirt and stains of the old would be bleached out like linen in strong laundry soap.[16]

When would this happen? Family Abraham had been waiting for so long! And how would they know it was really appearing? The Mouthpiece of the Lord, Malachi, said that before the Lord opened up the Door again he would first send a very special messenger to earth to get everyone ready so

---

13. Nehemiah 7:73—8:18.
14. Ezra 9:8–12.
15. Nehemiah 9:1—10:39.
16. Malachi 3:1–4.

that they didn't miss the portentous moment. But who would be this special envoy—this heavenly warning? According to Malachi it would be no other than the Lord's old Mouthpiece, El-i-Yah.[17] Yes, the El-i-Yah who had lived four hundred years earlier—the El-i-Yah who hadn't died, but had been collected by horses and chariots from beyond this Universe and transported back beyond the Doorway.[18] El-i-Yah back again through the Doorway revived to usher in a new era: a new age that Family Abraham were looking for but hadn't found; a new age that Family Abraham wanted so badly but which had eluded them so far; a new age which would be radical; a new age which would be awesome and aweful.

Malachi revealed that this new age would be inaugurated by a person he called, "the sun of righteousness." This amazing sun-like person "would rise with healing in his wings."[19] He pictured this special person's effect being like the sun's rays—solar wings stretching down to earth. These solar wings wouldn't be destructive like a modern solar storm knocking out the earth's satellites but instead they would bring healing. Malachi said that this special person would be like sunlight on earth—coming from the outside of the earth but entering earth to bring new life to the whole of creation. In the light of this "sun of righteousness" the people would have a new start—like calves escaping from the dark demonic abattoirs and skipping into lush green fields on a bright new sunny morning, beating their demonic butchers.[20] Malachi's vision of the future would be picked up a few hundred years later by the Super-star of His Story when he would describe himself as being like the sun—"the light of the world."[21]

Some of us are sad because of S.A.D. (seasonal affective disorder). Our brains crave bright light in the winter. Our brain's chemistry is addicted to the sun's rays. It is estimated that 2 percent of people in Northern Europe suffer badly from it, and as many as one in ten suffer to some degree. Malachi said that on this future day of sunshine, none of us would be sad any longer. Light from beyond the Doorway would stream into our Universe and into our lives. On this day, dysfunctional Family Abraham would function again—the hearts of the parents would be turned to their children; their children to their parents: unity; harmony; one big family—one big Family Abraham. This rising of "the sun of righteousness" would open up an opportunity for all who wanted to be part of this one big newly extended

17. Malachi 4:1–5.
18. 2 Kings 2:11.
19. Malachi 4:2a.
20. Malachi 4:2b–3.
21. John 8:12; 9:5.

Family Abraham. This day would mark the sunrise of the last day—the beginning of the last chance for humanity to return to living again as part of God's Family in his Kingdom.

But this great "Day of the Lord" (as it had started to become known) was still frustratingly further ahead—like a mountain peak that seemed to keep evading the tiring mountaineer—behind each apparent summit there seemed to be another summit. This new summit was the great day seen ahead by many of the Mouthpieces of the Lord in the years before.

For example, it was the great day also seen by the mysterious Mouthpiece, Jo-El. Jo-El had been inspired to speak God's words after a disastrous famine had hit Judah. It was caused by a mega-swarm of locusts that stripped bare every plant.[22] Jo-El described them as a powerful invading army that no defense, no weapon could repel. This natural disaster may well have been at the time that the people had started returning to Jeru-Salem—just as they had started to get their house in order, disaster struck.

A swarm of locusts can have forty to eighty million locusts packed into every half square mile of it. A swarm can stretch over four hundred and sixty square miles. Each individual locust can eat its body weight in plants every day. A swarm can easily eat over two hundred thousand tons of plants every day. Jo-El described the swarm of locusts as the Lord's "shock troops." The Lord wanted to force Family Abraham into getting back to him by destroying their food—to create an enforced, unrequested, national fast.[23] Just as Esther had fasted before approaching the King, the King of Kings wanted his people to fast to get them into the right attitude before approaching him. He wanted them to be forced back—jolted back into being true to him.

Why?—because the great "Day of the Lord" was coming: a day seen by other Mouthpieces of the Lord in the years before; a day which would be radical, painful and destructive; but a day which would bring in God's new plan—the start to the climax of His Story. This was a day for which Family Abraham had to be ready and through them—the whole of the world. Jo-El describes it as the day when the Lord would step into his world: a day which would make Judah and Jeru-Salem great again; a day which would make Judah and Jeru-Salem the center of the world; a day which would make up for all the bad things that had happened to them. This day would make the hard times that the locusts had eaten worthwhile.[24] But more than anything, this day would see the Lord do an amazing new thing. He would pour his

---

22. Joel 1:1–7; 2:1–11.
23. Joel 2:12–17.
24. Joel 2:25–27.

*learn the lesson of his story!*

invisible, super-naturally powerful presence through the Doorway.[25] This power wouldn't just be a special gift for his Mouthpieces, Go-Betweens or kings (as in the past), this would be for children and the elderly; for servants as well as the free; for women as well as men.

Through this power—wonderful amazing things would be set in motion that would eventually climax in the end of time and the final closing of the Doorway.[26] This would be a time of harvest in a new special way—to make up for the harvests the locusts had eaten: a harvest of people; a harvest for the world; a harvest of humanity—an opportunity to be harvested into the barn of a new Promised Land flowing with milk and honey.[27]

The Lord's offer of his powerful presence would be for everyone who called: everyone who was desperate; everyone who was not too proud to ask for help. This would be a harvest of His Story—a completion—a happy ending.

But not yet. It was a day in the future—a day that would be brought in by the long awaited special one, the Wonder-child, the Messiah—"the sun of righteousness."[28] His appearing would be the climax of His Story. It would be the destination of the bloodline central to His Story: the bloodline starting with Adam; the bloodline restarted by Noah; the bloodline focused on Abraham and his Family; the bloodline finely tuned by Jacob and his boys—the one family nation; the bloodline that surfaced as a royal bloodline through David's descendants. But a bloodline that since the demise of the royal bloodline was now so anonymous—it was invisible, unknown and underground.

This bloodline was waiting for its rebirth. But first El-i-Yah had to reappear back through the Doorway from beyond the Universe.

---

25. Joel 2:28–32.
26. Acts 2:1–21.
27. Revelation 14:14–20.
28. Malachi 4:2a.

# 41

# Hammered

Lots of history for the next four hundred years up to A.D.—but precious little His Story. His Story records the historical events of this period only in coded visionary messages originating from beyond the Doorway and received by Dani-El before the events took place.[1] Only Dani-El touched on the apocalyptic stormy events that would swirl around the central eye of Jeru-Salem during these four hundred years. Only Dani-El saw that one earthly kingdom after another would vie with each other to rule God's city and the world. But despite his great visionary skills, even Dani-El didn't fully understand all of God's messages given to him about this confusing time.

The only clear fact was that El-i-Yah was nowhere to be seen—four hundred years of silence from beyond the Doorway—not even any Mouthpieces of God. His Story seemed to have hit an unscheduled interval—a pause. There was activity and action but the history that was being written and the action that was being played out was not commented on from beyond the Doorway in real time. It were as if God was holding his breath. The history of Judah and its capital city, Jeru-Salem, became one of disappointment after disappointment; frustration after frustration; occupation after occupation; false dawn of "the sun of righteousness" after false dawn.

After the repopulation of Jeru-Salem and Judah and the rebuilding of the Temple and the city walls, a utopia might have been expected. Whilst Persia continued in the tradition of Darius/Cyrus to look after Jeru-Salem, things were at best okay. But two hundred years after Darius/Cyrus, the Greek leader, Alexander the Great, defeated Persia and Jeru-Salem was taken over by him. When he died, his Kingdom fell apart and Jeru-Salem was up for grabs—again.

It was run next by Egypt, then Syria. In fact in one seventeen year period, control of Jeru-Salem changed seven times. This wasn't good; but it wasn't too bad. The bad really came when one Syrian leader—Antiochus

---

1. Daniel 7–11.

Epiphanes—took over just over one hundred and fifty years before the era known as A.D. He decided to sacrifice a pig on the Temple altar and force the priests and the people to drink pig's blood (as you do— if you want to offend every single person in Family Abraham, that is).

A pig in the Temple—the Temple made unclean; non-kosher. A pig which was not be eaten or sacrificed by Family Abraham, killed in the traditional Doorway to heaven. This was one of the most offensive actions imaginable: it was desecration; it diseased the whole of the Temple—fouling the Doorway to beyond the Universe. It caused a shockwave down His Story which was still reverberating when the Super-star of His Story was alive. He described the eventual ultimate destruction of the Temple as being on the same scale as the tremors caused by Antiochus Epiphanes' pig. It was like the end of the world.[2]

After his pig, Antiochus Epiphanes then used his diplomatic skills to ban worship of Yah-weh—in the Temple of Yah-weh. Instead, he changed the Temple of Yah-weh into a Temple to Zeus—the Greek king of all gods.

History was not going well for the newly re-formed Isra-El and its capital city. Where was His Story? Where was El-i-Yah?

And then the fight back began. Family Abraham revolted under the leadership of Judas the Maccabee and his brothers. Maccabee means "hammer" and he and his brothers "hammered" the obnoxious Antiochus. They managed to win back the Temple off him. They won back their freedom and gave themselves independence (with a little help from the Roman senate and Roman people). The Maccabee family developed into the Hasmonean dynasty which in turn grew in strength until sixty-three years before what we know as A.D.

Cue the Roman Empire. It occupied the land and Jeru-Salem is taken over again. The Romans eventually made a man called Herod, into King. Herod desperately wanted to be proper Family Abraham but he could only trace his bloodline back to Esau the hunter and not to his brother, Jacob who became known as Isra-El. Herod looked like a king in the royal bloodline—but he wasn't and Family Abraham knew it. Herod had another failing—he was a madman. Herod would show the depth of his madness just at the point when after almost four hundred years of silence, His Story and the special bloodline would resurface. The Doorway was about to crash open after four centuries of being locked shut. When re-opened, Herod would have a villainous part in the second part of His Story in a role which is infamously celebrated every year since.

King Herod—the child murderer.

2. Mark 13:14–20.

# 42

## One Small Stepson for a Man: One Giant Leap for Mankind

AFTER FOUR HUNDRED YEARS, the silence was over. His Story returned to impact on human history. The Doorway to beyond the Universe opened again but this time in a new, radical and unique way. This time it caused the royal bloodline of the Wonder-child to be re-energized—reborn—literally—and all through one man—the great, great, great, great, great, great, great, great, grandson of Zerubbabel (give or take a great)—the last person of note in the Wonder-child's bloodline. Zerubbabel—the last significant man on the bloodline—the grandson of Yecon-Yah, the last bona-fide real King of Family Abraham before Jeru-Salem was destroyed by the Babylonians.

The rebirth took place through this many times great grandson of Zerubbabel—a man called Joseph.[1] This Joseph may have been named after the famous special child from His Story who over a millennium and a half years earlier had grown to be a famous leader in Egypt. But despite his famous name, this Joseph was still a complete unknown—for the moment. But don't be fooled. This Joseph did have royal blood. But he wasn't in any sense—royalty. He was an ordinary young man and also a young man with a problem. His girlfriend was pregnant—but not by him.

While he pondered his possible reaction to this news, it happened—the outside and inside of the Universe reconnected for the first time in four hundred years. Where did the Doorway appear this time? You'd imagine it would be in the Temple rebuilt again by King Herod as a desperate begging ploy to be accepted as Family Abraham's real King and royal benefactor. But you'd be wrong. It wasn't even in a geographical location you could pin on a map. Instead it opened in Joseph's subconscious. The Lord opened up the Door and connected the outside of the Universe with Joseph's mind.

1. Matthew 1:16.

*one small stepson for a man: one giant leap for mankind*

For such an auspicious and significant moment, the Lord's words were surprisingly practical. "Carry on with your marriage. Despite what it looks like, your fiancée is still a virgin. She is pregnant by God's invisible power."[2] A strange "first contact" after four centuries of silence, but a contact that made sense if you knew the back story of His Story. The Lord continued, "Your fiancée is going to give birth to a unique son: the special son; the long promised Wonder-child; the new child King; Immanu-El; El-God on earth."[3] At long last the birth of Immanu-El—the child seen by Isa-Yah seven hundred years earlier.[4] The child from beyond the Doorway was about to appear—the child who would have a foot either side of the Doorway—human and divine. The child who would become the Human Doorway to beyond the Universe—his very body bridging the temporal gap. He would grow up to be the Messiah-man who would reconnect God with humanity: the one hoped-for; looked-for; longed-for for over a thousand years.

This unique once-in-a-lifetime of a universe child would be given an ordinary name that has become very special—Yeh-shua (in the Hebrew language of Family Abraham). To the English speaking world he would become known as Jesus (using the Greek and Latin versions of Yeh-shua).[5] To the Arabic world he would become known as Isa.

One in ten boys in Family Abraham were called Yeh-shua when this Yeh-shua was born. It was the fifth most popular male name of the time. Yeh-shua was the shorter version of the Hebrew name "Yeh-oshua" meaning "Yah-weh who saves." And for this one time only, the meaning of the name was totally going to reflect the one bearing the name. The popular name now had found its real home. The name would never be viewed the same again anywhere in the world.

Joseph took the Lord seriously. Like so many of the stars in His Story beforehand he let God be his Lord—his boss—and he married his pregnant fiancée. But he never made love to her until after the child was born.[6] He had absolutely no genetic connection with the Wonder-child. The child was not his son biologically despite the fact that through Zerubbabel and Jecon-Yah, Joseph was in the bloodline that stretched back through the Kings of Judah to Solomon and through him back to the great King David. And it didn't end there. Through David Joseph was connected to Jacob otherwise

---

2. Matthew 1:18–25.
3. Matthew 1:22.
4. Isaiah 7:14.
5. Matthew 1:21.
6. Matthew 1:24.

known as Isra-El and back from him through to Abraham himself—the human Father of God's family.

Joseph's ancestors were the spine and backbone of Family Abraham and His Story. As well as being the royal family of Isra-El. But despite this great heritage, Yeh-shua-Jesus was not genetically part of the royal bloodline through Joseph. At best, Yeh-shua-Jesus was Joseph's stepson—no D.N.A. connection. It was as if Jerem-Yah's words about Joseph's royal blood ancestor, King Jecon-Yah had come true. Jerem-Yah had said of Jecon-Yah—the last proper King of Judah—"Record this man as childless—none of his children will prosper—none of them will sit on the throne of David or rule Judah anymore."[7] To Jerem-Yah this meant that the great promised Prince of Judah would not be a descendant of Jecon-Yah. And true to the great Mouthpiece's words, the unborn royal Wonder-child had arrived from beyond the Universe without being in the D.N.A. bloodline of Jecon-Yah even if he were a member of one of Jecon-Yah's descendants' families. The Wonder-child was not the son of King David's descendant, Joseph, but his stepson.

But if the true bloodline from Abraham through great King David stopped at Joseph, how could Joseph's stepson Yeh-shua-Jesus be seen as part of the royal bloodline—how could he be related to the great King David? What connection did Yeh-shua-Jesus have with the royal bloodline of His Story? The answer is: by being a genetic descendant of another branch of the royal family tree—another branch of God's Family Abraham royal bloodline—one that had remained secret for hundreds of years; one that hadn't been written about in His Story so far but was still there under the surface waiting for the moment to break through into His Story.

The moment of breakthrough had come.

---

7. Jeremiah 22:28–30.

# 43

## Tzippori or Nazareth?

HIS STORY IS THE story of a royal bloodline: a bloodline through the Kings of Isra-El and Judah; a bloodline through King David's son, Solomon. But in the lists of King David's children, there is an older brother than the rich, wise King Solomon—another son who has the name of Nathan.

Nothing is known about Nathan which is not a surprise because human history is biased towards kings and rulers—they make and write history. But Nathan, despite his royal blood, never became King. He lost out to his younger brother, Solomon, probably due to his father's affection for Solomon's more famous (or maybe, infamous) mother, Bathsheba—or was it the mysteries of His Story at work again?

But His Story didn't cast aside the older son of David. His Story is different to most records of history. His Story often uses unknown people as its Stars. Nathan is one of those unknowns—one of the overlooked. All that is known is that he had a son called Matthatha; who had a son called Menna; who had a son called Melea; who had a son, Eliakim; who had a son, Jonam; who had a son, Joseph; who had a son, Judah; who had a son, Simeon; who had a son, Levi; who had a son, Matthat; who had a son, Jorim; who had a son, Eliezer; who had a son, Joshua; who had a son, Er; who had a son, Elmadam; who had a son, Cosam; who had a son, Addi; who had a son, Melchi; who had a son, Neri; who had a son, Shealtiel; who had a son, Zerubbabel.[1]

Zerubbabel—that name again. For a brief moment this secret Davidic genetic bloodline collides with the official public royal bloodline.[2] We have already met Governor Zerubbabel who brought back the returning Family Abraham to Jeru-Salem from Babylon—the one God called his signet ring.

But after this brief co-habitation, the two bloodlines bounce apart again. The public royal bloodline, we have already followed, goes through Zerubbabel's son, Abiud, whiles the secret genetic bloodline goes down another of Zerubbabel's sons, Rhesa. After Rhesa, the unknown line goes

1. Luke 1:27–31.
2. Matthew 1:12.

through his son, Joanan; who had a son, Joda; who had a son, Josech; who had a son, Semein; who had a son, Mattathias; who had a son, Mahath; who had a son, Naggai; who had a son, Hesli; who had a son, Nahum; who had a son, Amos; who had a son, Mattathias; who had a son, Joseph; who had a son, Jannai; who had a son, Melchi; who had a son, Levi; who had a son, Matthat; who had a son called Heli.[3]

At Heli His Story pauses to take a breath. Heli was an unknown man and an unknown father but not a father to an unknown child. Who was his child? To find out we have to ask an ancient historian called Luke, who researched the true genetic bloodline of Yeh-shua-Jesus. This ancient historian and biographer said that Joseph was only "thought" to be the father of Yeh-shua-Jesus, the Wonder-child.[4] In that one word, "thought" Luke showed that he knew that Yeh-shua-Jesus' father wasn't really his father but only his stepfather though everyone treated him as his father. Luke is telling us that in his view Yeh-shua-Jesus didn't have a human father because he was the Wonder-child born to a virgin.

But also Luke the historian records that the closest Yeh-shua-Jesus had to a genetic male father was his maternal grandfather—Heli—the Heli at the end of the unknown, secret Davidic genetic bloodline. Luke wants us to see Heli as the Grandfather of Yeh-shua-Jesus and the father of the mother of Yeh-shua-Jesus; father to arguably the most famous woman of all time—Mary—the mother of Yeh-shua-Jesus.

Women weren't important in bloodlines in those days and even Luke avoids putting Mary's name into his genealogical family tree of Yeh-shua-Jesus. Instead he puts Mary's father and his ancestors into the family tree. Ironically though, this omitted woman became the most famous part of Yeh-shua-Jesus' genetic bloodline—Mary daughter of Heli who through her father, was genetically descended from King Solomon's older brother, Nathan. This meant Mary was also genetically descended from King David himself. And through David she was genetically descended from Jacob—the man known as Isra-El. This gave Mary the honor of being genetically part of God's chosen royal bloodline as well as her husband.

But for now Mary was a misunderstood teenage girl falsely accused of being unfaithful to her partner, Joseph. Mary was a poor young mother-to-be who was trapped in poverty. She may well have come from the city of Tzippori known as the "Jewel of Galilee" but there were no jewels in Mary's purse.

Her home city, Tzippori, had been made the capital of the district of northern Isra-El (Galilee), by mad King Herod. The city's name meant

3. Luke 3:23b-27.
4. Luke 3:23.

"bird"—fitting for a mountain city set high up the mountains in the clouds. King Herod's son, Antipas, made it his home and lived in a palace there. He was always developing his city and upgrading it. It was a beautiful, wealthy city—the largest and most important city in the whole of Galilee. It was Jewish but built to the most up to date Roman and Greek fashions. It had all sorts of luxurious buildings including a four thousand seater amphitheater. This theater may have been built by the young Yeh-shua-Jesus helping his stepfather, Joseph, who was a joiner. Hundreds of joiners must have been used to build its stage one hundred and fifty-six feet wide and twenty-seven feet deep. Tzippori had shopping precincts and residential areas; it had reservoirs of water—one holding over a thousand gallons. It was impressive. Mary might have lived in this impressive city. Joseph might have worked in this impressive city. Mary and Joseph might have met in this impressive city. But together they were too poor to live in it. Instead, by night they lived three miles away in a slum town housing the poor workers who made their living by day in the luxurious capital city.

The slum town was called Nazareth. There was a saying of the time, "Can anything good come out of Nazareth?"[5] Probably the best answer was the cliché, "Yes—just the main road." Each day there would have been a queue of poor workers on this road trying to make their way into work in the rich city on their doorstep. Tzippori and Nazareth were only three miles apart: Tzippori and Nazareth were a million miles apart. Nazareth was also an eternity away from the outside of the Universe but Mary of Nazareth became the mother of the Doorway to the outside of the Universe. She became the most unique human Mount Sinai: the Virgin mother promised by Isa-Yah; the Virgin mother to the royal child, Immanu-El—El-God with us. Yeh-shua-Jesus of Nazareth was living in Mary who in turn was living in the poverty-stricken slum town of Nazareth.

El-God—slumming it on earth.

5. John 1:46.

# 44

## The Asylum-seeking Peasant King

YEH-SHUA-JESUS MAY HAVE SPENT his embryonic months in Nazareth safe inside his mother Mary, but he in the end, he wasn't born in Nazareth. The ancient Mouthpiece of God, Mic-Yah, seven hundred years earlier, had insisted that the Wonder-child was going to be born in Beth-Lehem. This was a key qualification for the Wonder-child.[1] It was appropriate, obviously—Beth-Lehem was the ancient home town of the great King David.

King David was the key ancestor of the Wonder-child. But despite being genetically connected to David through his mother, Mary, and socially connected to David through his stepfather, Joseph, neither parent was living anywhere near the Davidic hometown of Beth-Lehem. Both parents were stuck in Nazareth with no prospect of living in Beth-Lehem. Why would a poor pregnant young woman and her new husband leave their poor dwellings in their poor town and set off for another historic town around eighty miles away? It is very unlikely that they had any close family there—it was simply their ancient ancestral home. So His Story was heading for a disappointing and confusing ending if this super-natural virgin mother and her Wonder-child parted company in Nazareth.

But His Story is interactive. It interacts with history so that earthly history supports His Story. History plays the supporting role to His Story's main character and out of the blue a census is called by the Roman authorities.[2] The Romans wanted to know how many people were in their Empire—probably for tax reasons, if nothing else. But this was achieved by everyone returning to their ancestral homes to be counted. Everyone had to return to the towns and villages from where their families originated.

Mary and Joseph were forced by a Roman Imperial dictat to travel eighty miles back to Beth-Lehem—no doubt against their doctor's advice (if they had one) and certainly against all modern-day humanitarian objections.

1. Micah 5:2.
2. Luke 2:1–7.

Despite traditions, it is very unlikely that they could afford a comparatively expensive donkey. The likelihood is that they walked—eighty miles—and Mary pregnant. But they made it to Beth-Lehem—to the birthplace of King David a thousand years earlier—the right town at the right time.[3]

To make sure His Story had a satisfactory ending, God even fixed the actions of Caesars of the great Roman Empire. We shouldn't be surprised—after all the Wonder-child to be born would later become known to his followers as the "King of Kings."[4]

After two thousand years of build-up in His Story, Yeh-shua-Jesus was born: not in a hospital; not in a home; not in a five-star guest accommodation but in the animal quarters of a guest house due to Beth-Lehem being so full.[5] After a millennium of family tree branching, there were too many descendants of the household of David to fit into Beth-Lehem. Even in an age of much lower human population, Beth-Lehem was still packed. The density of population meant that the Wonder-child promised by Isa-Yah seven hundred years earlier had to be born in the parking spot for animals used to transport David's descendants to Beth-Lehem—in the equivalent of a first century garage—possibly on the ground floor below bed and breakfast accommodation.

How do we know he was born in such a deprived place? Because Yeh-shua-Jesus was placed in a feeding trough—a wooden or stone box used for animals' hay—the first century equivalent of a petrol pump. You fed your transport with it.[6]

The Wonder-child was in the royal ancestral home of the great giant-slayer, King David; in the long prophesied Messiah's birthplace but in a food box for animals—not a great start in anyone's estimation. But remember: this human walking-talking Mount Sinai; this living Doorway to beyond the Universe; this living stairway into heaven; was also the servant Messiah-child of God who would get his hands dirty to rescue humanity.

Seven hundred years earlier, Isa-Yah had seen that this Wonder-child would suffer. He saw that this Wonder-child would be "a man of sorrows"—a servant of humanity taking on human suffering even though he didn't deserve any of it.[7] Isa-Yah saw this Wonder-child would not behave like a celebrity or live like royalty. His royal status and connection to the royal bloodline would be hidden. He would be misunderstood and maligned.

3. 1 Samuel 16:1–13.
4. Revelation 1:5; 19:11–16.
5. Luke 2:7.
6. Luke 2:7.
7. Isaiah 53:3.

His unique contribution to humanity would only truly be noticed after his death.[8]

God's child came down to earth with a bump. He left all his inherited glory beyond the Doorway in order to be down-to-earth down on earth.[9] A later follower of Yeh-shua-Jesus pondering on His Story noted that, "Even though he was rich, he become poor so that through his poverty, humanity might become rich"[10]—a transfer of riches through grace.

You don't have a Wonder-child from God breaking into the Universe everyday so despite the down-to-earthness of the surroundings, it was still a moment of celebration for those in the know. That meant mainly—the non-human messengers from beyond the Universe who were everywhere—celebrating.[11]

It's what you would expect when the outside and inside of the Universe start to merge: when the eternal time-locked Door existing since the first human man and woman is breached; when the locked and guarded Door into Eden is smashed open; when the created and the Creator start to mix; when mortal and immortal collide. The non-human sightings took place out on the hills around Beth-Lehem.[12] Shepherds, (the proud descendants of the shepherd boy King David and the great rescuer, Moses) were the main spotters. The shepherds were told by these non-human messengers from beyond the Universe that the Wonder-child had been born.

But on a practical note—how to spot the right baby in the crowds? There may well have been lots of young babies in Beth-Lehem. But he would surely be the only new-born baby in a cattle trough.[13] It was a giveaway; it was unique—like the child. It was good news—after four hundred years God was on the move again. His Story was alive and well and kicking in Beth-Lehem.

The shepherds ran into Beth-Lehem and found the unlikely Prince of Judah, Son of Man, Son of God in the feeding trough. The shepherds told Mary and Joseph about the non-human contact and their message.[14] Mary was reassured. Mary was amazed. Mary was quietly content that the weird out-of-this-world message she had received before she was pregnant was coming true. She, like Joseph, had experienced the Doorway opening

---

8. Isaiah 52:13—53:12.
9. Philippians 2:5–11.
10. 2 Corinthians 8:9.
11. Luke 2:13–14.
12. Luke 2:8–15.
13. Luke 2:10–11.
14. Luke 2:15–20.

## the asylum-seeking peasant king

up right in front of her before Yeh-shua-Jesus' birth—in fact right at the beginning of her pregnancy. An out-of-this-world messenger, with the name of Gabri-El, had stepped through the Doorway and told her that she was the Virgin mother predicted by the great Isa-Yah seven hundred years earlier.[15] Her child was to be the famous and mysterious "Immanu-El." She was going to be the mother of the Wonder-child. She was going to be the mother of the King who would even make great King David's empire look pathetic. Her child was going to rule over a Kingdom that was eternal, timeless, out-of-this-world—a Kingdom that would stretch beyond the boundaries of time and space. Her child would be King of the inside and the outside of the Universe. For the first time since Adam and Eve rebelled and rejected God's Kingship, outside and inside of the Universe would be linked permanently—the Doorway opened again.

But after the euphoria of the birth of this child, reality would have set in. The new parents were miles from home. Joseph wasn't earning whilst they were in Beth-Lehem. They had another mouth to feed. They had to keep the Messiah alive. What if they couldn't feed the one who was here to save humanity? All hope would be lost for humanity—after hundreds and even thousands years of waiting.

They needed money. They needed to win the lottery. They needed a windfall of cash. They needed destiny to smile on them. They needed supernatural help. And just on cue—some strange men saw some strange astrological happenings. They witnessed out-of-this-world messing with our world's reality.[16] These men were probably from Mede—the same place as the earlier great savior of Family Abraham, Darius/Cyrus. But what was certain, they were "magi"—magic men who spent their life watching the stars and planets interpreting their movements and brightness. They were men desperately seeking truth: men desperately trying to glimpse through the Doorway; men desperately trying to break out of this planet to understand the power behind all the planets and stars to find the King of the Universe.

And one day they thought they had found him. They found an astronomical event with astrological significance that pointed to a great King of the Jews.[17] Some people say it was an unusual auspicious event like the lining up of Jupiter, Saturn and Venus. This happened seven years before B.C. changed to A.D. If it was this, it seems weird because B.C. is meant to end and A.D. is meant to start at the birth of the baby Yeh-shua-Jesus. His birth has become the hinge on which the door of time swings. Before

---

15. Luke 1:26–38.
16. Matthew 2:1–2.
17. Matthew 2:2.

him—"B.C."; after him—"A.D." B.C. means "before Christ" using the Greek word for "Messiah." A.D. means "anno Domini," which in the language of the Roman Empire meant "in the year of the Lord"—the Lord in question being the King of the Universe—Yeh-shua-Jesus.

So how could the Wonder-child be born seven years before B.C. ended and A.D. began? How could he be born before his own birthday? Human historical failings—that's how. The early historians who calculated B.C. and A.D. were out with their timing by a few years. But this shouldn't make us question the truth of the event. Remember just because you don't know someone's exact birthday, doesn't mean you doubt their existence (I hope).

Some people say the special sky sign seen by the magi was Halley's Comet—but that would probably have moved too fast and too early. It shot past in 11 B.C. There was another comet in 4 B.C., which is feasible, but a bit late. Mad King Herod who was alive when Yeh-shua-Jesus was born, died in 4 B.C.

Some people say it was a Supernova. The Chinese at this time recorded the birth of a star in our galaxy—a very rare event. A new star shines with an intensity a billion times brighter than our own closest star—the Sun. Sounds good—a new star for a new King.

Who knows exactly what the magi saw but whatever they saw made them believe that there was a new King born onto earth. They believed the stars broadcast the news. Some people go further and believe that stars affect history—that astronomical events have astrological significance. But seven hundred years earlier, Isa-Yah made it very clear what the Lord thought. He relayed the Lord's thoughts when he said, "Look up at the stars! Who made all these? Who makes them shine each night? Who knows all their names? My hands stretched out the Universe—I'm in charge of the stars!"[18] The star wasn't the star. The Lord was the star—and for Super-star baby Yeh-shua-Jesus—the stars came out.

By using the stars, the magi eventually arrived in Isra-El but not immediately at Beth-Lehem. For all their brilliance, they had to have a bit of help to find Yeh-shua-Jesus. The stars had pointed to a King in Isra-El. So they went at first to Jeru-Salem—the capital, and then to the place where they logically believed they could they find information on royalty in Jeru-Salem—the royal palace. And in the royal palace they bumped into King Herod. So soon King Herod got involved in the search.[19]

Getting the King involved in finding the new royal baby seemed common sense. But common sense isn't always sensible. Instead of finding the

---

18. Isaiah 40:25–26; 45:12.
19. Matthew 2:1–7.

## the asylum-seeking peasant king 197

new Wonder-child, they found the old, twisted, bitter, mad King Herod. They found paranoid Herod—suspicious that everyone was plotting against him. He didn't trust people and people didn't trust him. He wasn't the real proper King. He was kept in power by the Romans. Deep down Herod knew he had no real power and so the little power he had, he held onto insanely. His insane fear about people plotting behind his back had caused him to execute his wife. He had also executed two of his sons. He also executed his step-brother. The Roman Emperor Augustus joked about him that it was safer to be his pet pig ("hus" in Greek) than be his son ("huios" in Greek) because at least his pet pig lived longer. This amazingly offensive jibe at the desperate wannabe-"kosher" Jewish King, no doubt increased Herod's mad desire to hold onto power whatever the cost.

So when the Magi turned up at his door asking where the new Royal Jewish baby was born, all of Herod's insecurities would have come rushing to the surface. But he was a diplomat as well as a despot. He pretended to be interested. But his interest was to kill the potential child-rival rather than show respect to him. He called together his advisors who remembered the prophecy of the Mouthpiece Mic-Yah, that the special King would be born in Beth-Lehem.[20] After hearing this message, the Magi set off after agreeing to Herod's request for them to come back and tell him when they had found the new baby King because obviously Herod wanted to show his respects to the newly born king! Pigs and flying come to mind.

The Magi, aided again by some stellar navigation, found the baby Yeh-shua-Jesus in Beth-Lehem.[21] And then the magi fulfilled their destiny in His Story. They showed their respect by giving Yeh-shua-Jesus fabulously expensive gifts: gold—the precious metal of kings; frankincense—an expensive resin used for perfume and medicine; myrrh—another expensive resin used in religious embalming rituals but also used as an antiseptic for healing.[22] Baby Yeh-shua-Jesus was set up for all that was to come—symbolically but also practically. Soon he was going to need the priceless gifts as a refugee and asylum-seeker in Egypt.

Herod had decided to kill the new royal baby as soon as the Magi came back and reported on his location. But the Lord had other ideas. Before the Magi headed back to Herod to give him the exact co-ordinates of his juvenile rival, they were contacted by the Lord directly through the Doorway into their sub-conscious dream-minds. As a result, they wisely decided to

20. Matthew 2:4–6; Micah 5:2.
21. Matthew 2:9–10.
22. Matthew 2:11.

miss out on a repeat visit to Herod on their return journey.[23] But not knowing an exact location of the baby king didn't put Herod off—he simply used the sledgehammer to crack a nut approach. He killed every Family Abraham boy under two years old in his Kingdom.[24] Mad?—yes; evil?—yes; unbelievable?—no. In fact, totally consistent with the behavior of mad Machiavellian Herod and the treatment of Family Abraham in the past. Thirteen hundred years earlier, Moses had nearly been exterminated by a similar decree from another despot.[25] And so Yeh-shua-Jesus was not only born into poverty, he was also hunted down by the King.

It was time for another through the Doorway intervention. An out-of-this-world messenger whispered into Joseph's subconscious that he had to leave with his fledgling family and escape into Egypt. And so, Yeh-shua-Jesus with his mum and stepdad escaped mad Herod by running into Egypt[26]—a place of safety for the first man called Isra-El over a thousand years earlier[27] and now a safe haven for the most eagerly awaited man of Isra-El. Yeh-shua-Jesus and his mother and stepfather were on the run. They were homeless—stateless. How did this peasant couple survive in a new country? No doubt with thanks to some fabulously expensive gifts that had come to them via the stars themselves!

And of course from the one who put the stars in place and knew them by name.[28]

23. Matthew 2:12.
24. Matthew 2:16.
25. Exodus 1:22.
26. Matthew 2:13–15.
27. Genesis 46:5–7.
28. Isaiah 40:25–26; 45:12.

# 45

## Lost and Found

EXILE FOR GOD'S FAMILY: a common theme in His Story for Family Abraham. And just as a change of King triggered a return home for Family Abraham in the past, so it did again. Mad King Herod died. Another non-human visitation from beyond the Universe broke into Joseph's subconscious and announced the news.[1] The young family returned—but not to Beth-Lehem—back instead to shanty town Nazareth.[2]

Life continued. But the next part of His Story jumps to when Yeh-shua-Jesus was twelve years old. On their annual trip to Jeru-Salem on the Pass-Over festival, Mary and Joseph lost the Wonder-child.[3] Losing a child may be regarded as a massive misfortune; losing the Wonder-child looks like carelessness on a cosmic scale. Lost—one Messiah! Lost—one successor to King David! Lost—one Savior for humanity! Mary and Joseph didn't realize their loss until they were nearly back home in Nazareth a day later—a whole day later—the embarrassing and excruciating loss caused by a false assumption that he was travelling with friends. But he wasn't.

They raced back to Jeru-Salem and retraced their steps into the city. Wisely they went back to the Temple. Found—one Messiah! Found—their son and God's son chatting with the teachers of God's Law: a twelve year old asking difficult questions of lawyers; surprising the teachers with his answers; a twelve year old on his own far from home but totally at home—unusual. True, many twelve year olds can be unaware of the anxieties that they are causing their parents and Mary and Joseph were normal parents with a normal response. They were so relieved at finding him they were angry. "Why have you put us through this?"[4] But Yeh-shua-Jesus' answer was anything but normal. He simply and succinctly answered his mother.

1. Matthew 2:19–21.
2. Matthew 2:22–23.
3. Luke 2:41–52.
4. Luke 2:48.

"Why did you need to worry? You knew I would be at home in my Father's house."[5] Lost but found at home amongst family—his real father—God.

In a way the true holy of holies was back in the Holy of Holies. Since the destruction of the Temple by the Babylonians, the special box containing God's handwritten laws had disappeared from out of the tiny room at the center of the Temple called "the Holy of Holies"—the official focus of all Doorway activity. The Ark had been lost in the mists of time. It remains lost to this day. It continues to excite normally sober and academic archaeologists. Many theories have it in many different places, from as far away as Ethiopia to as close as below the Temple Mount in Jeru-Salem; from the west of the River Jordan to the east of the River Jordan. What is known is that it has not been seen for over two thousand years. This special box was at the heart of the small Temple room known as the Holy of Holies. But now at the heart of King Herod's newly refurbished Temple, was emptiness—a vacuum. The room was just a shell—it had lost its meaning.

But not on this day—Yeh-shua-Jesus—the living, breathing Word of God was in the house. He wasn't just a Mouthpiece of God's word or a God's Go-between pleading on behalf of humanity to God. He was God. He was going to embody and personify everything God had ever wanted to say in His Story.[6] The amazing truth was that God was back at home. God had not left his house for ever.[7] The Doorway in the Temple was open again.

But Yeh-shua-Jesus didn't just embody the law of God like the special box had contained the law. He obeyed it—especially the fifth law.[8] He respected his parents. He left with them and honored them.

We hear no more in His Story of Yeh-shua-Jesus until around eighteen years later. These eighteen years probably were years when Yeh-shua-Jesus fulfilled his role as the older son of the family, in caring and providing for his mother and his younger step-siblings—like any first-born Family Abraham son should when the Father of the house was not around. In these eighteen years, his stepfather, Joseph disappears—dead presumably.

But after eighteen years, Yeh-shua-Jesus' younger siblings were old enough to support their mother and family. Yeh-shua-Jesus was now free to be the person he was created to be—the Savior of the World. But how do you start such a colossal mission?

With a big splash!

5. Luke 2:49.
6. John 1:14; 1 John 1:1; Hebrews 1:1–3a.
7. Ezekiel 10:18.
8. Exodus 20:12.

# 46

## U-Turn

IF YOU WANT A big splash you need a celebrity—in this case one celebrity above all—El-i-Yah. But where was the old Mouthpiece of God when you needed him? Had there been any sightings of El-i-Yah returning through the Doorway to usher in the new Messiah? Yes and no. The promised warm-up act to the Messiah hadn't literally returned through the Doorway as promised,[1] but someone that suspiciously looked like him and reminded lots of people of him had turned up.

He was a weird recluse—a rough man who lived rough in the desert. His name was Yeh-ohanan, better known now as John. Like Yeh-shua-Jesus, his birth had been unlikely—born to an ancient barren mother who was a distant relative of Mary.[2] He had grown up to be a weird loner who ranged around the uninhabited desert areas in the land of Family Abraham. He lived out on a limb. He was a throwback to an age gone-by. He didn't fit into the new Greek and Roman fashions of the day. He wore animal skins. He ate locusts. He ate wild honey that he found.[3] He was just like the Lord's Mouthpiece of hundreds of years before. He was just like El-i-Yah—and it hadn't gone unnoticed. To all intents and purposes—it could have been him—seeing that El-i-Yah hadn't died but had been sucked through the Doorway into beyond the Universe alive ready to return to announce the Wonder-child—now Messiah-man. John fitted perfectly the picture of the man who would introduce the Messiah-man to humanity.

Before his trip through the Doorway, El-i-Yah had lived on the edge of decent society. He made comments about it: attacking it; trying to reform it and make it better; trying to make it more like the place God wanted it to be—not "limping" between God and false gods. El-i-Yah was hated by the King and his Queen, Jezebel. El-i-Yah wasn't nicknamed, "the Troublemaker"

---

1. Malachi 4:5; 3:1.
2. Luke 1:5–25, 57–66.
3. Matthew 3:1–4.

by the King of Isra-El, Ahab, for nothing.[4] John too was uncomfortable—he didn't just dress like El-i-Yah, he also let his frustration and disappointment with God's family show. He was disillusioned. He believed that after God's people had returned from Babylon, they had gone soft. They had stopped being truly Family Abraham. They were more interested in fitting-in than standing-out. They "limped" between fashion and keeping the family honor. They were born Family Abraham, but like Esau hundreds of years before, they didn't value their birth right.[5] They were no better than every other nation. They had been given an awesome advantage—God had chosen to save humanity through them—but they weren't bothered. What was needed was something radical to get them back in line because an axe was poised ready to chop down on the Family tree of Isra-El again[6]—unless they agreed to change their behavior radically and undergo an initiation rite so fundamental it was like being born again.

In those days, if you weren't of Family Abraham blood, you could be adopted into the Family by going through an initiation ceremony: a washing away of your old life; a burial under the water; a breaking of the waters and a rebirth into a new life as a child in God's family. If you weren't part of the blood Family, through a ceremony of going into water you could be adopted into it. John took this rite and put a radical new spin on it. He said that all those who were truly Family Abraham through their blood needed also to go through this conversion rite. They had to opt in to what they already thought was there's by right.

So John developed this symbolic action of conversion and pushed it to its limit. He forced the Family Abraham volunteers to stop breathing as he shoved their whole body under the water of the River Jordan, closing down their senses served by their eyes and ears, holding them down until their lungs burned and their heads spun and they panicked about being drowned. Only then he allowed them to burst up through the surface and take their first painfully desperate breath of their new life—like a baby's first crying breath after emerging from its mother into the bright lights and sounds of life.

John was clear what this meant to the members of Family Abraham who queued for hours to be almost drowned. He said that because Family Abraham had devalued their birth right so much—they had to be born again into the Family again. They had to go through the convert's ceremony of water. And they had to do it in the River Jordan—the old gateway into their Promised Land—the turnstile into God's promises to Abraham.

---

4. 1 Kings 18:16–17.
5. Genesis 25:29–34.
6. Matthew 3:7–10.

And so a water ritual that became known as "baptism" was invented. "Baptism" means being completely soaked and drenched and overwhelmed. A "baptized" ship is flooded out with water—sinking only to rise again as a new and watertight vessel.

Amazingly John had caught the mood of a nation. Family Abraham was disappointed. Family Abraham was disillusioned. Family Abraham was frustrated. Family Abraham wanted to be born again. Family Abraham turned out for John's weird baptism in their hundreds. After their return from exile in Babylon and the rebuilding of their nation, capital city and Temple, they had hoped that utopia was on its way. They had hoped for the climax of His Story. They had longed for a complete new start. They had longed for a new era. They had longed for the Wonder-child. They had longed for the King who was like great King David but even greater—not just his Son but also his Lord.[7]

And so when John called them to be baptized, they came out to him in their hundreds. They queued by the River Jordan—the ancient gateway to their "promised land"—the way to a brighter new tomorrow.[8] They wanted to cross the river again into a new future. They wanted to be like Nahshon—diving into the Reed Sea and wading up to their noses to find a new exciting future.[9] They wanted to be like their ancestors walking through the River Jordan on dry land ready to take over a new Promised Land flowing with milk and honey.[10] They wanted to come home from exile again and have a second chance of re-building Isra-El after years in Babylon. Isa-Yah had talked about the exiles coming back from Babylon, but their return hadn't seemed to fulfil his optimism. It fell short of what Isa-Yah had promised.[11] And so John's message struck a chord. Everyone who came to be baptized had swallowed their pride. They had all "repented—made a "U-turn." All of them had chosen to take their lives in their hands and cross the forbidden central reservation and head down the other carriageway towards God's Promised Land.

John was big on U-turns. He told everyone who came to him to make one—everyone who wanted to say sorry for their abuse of their birthright—even soldiers and the traitorous tax-collectors came to John.[12] It was like

---

7. Matthew 22:41–46.
8. Matthew 3:1–6.
9. Exodus 14:21–31.
10. Joshua 3:14–17.
11. Isaiah 35:1–10; 49:8–26; 51:1–3.
12. Luke 3:10–14.

everyone wanted a new start. And John obliged by baptizing them all. John did nothing else but baptize. It gained him the nickname of "the Baptizer."

And so they queued to be baptized by John—the weird El-i-Yah look alike. Maybe they remembered the old prophecies of the ancient Mouthpiece of Yah-weh—Malachi—who said that El-i-Yah would introduce God's super-King to the world.[13] For all intents and purposes—El-i-Yah was here. But where was the Messiah?

And then Yeh-shua-Jesus turned up in the queue for the big splash.

---

13. Malachi 3:1; 4:5.

## 47

## Big Splash

YEH-SHUA-JESUS CHOSE JOHN'S BAPTISM to break into the public arena to create his "big splash" and claim his throne as King of all Kings.[1] But why was he baptized? Did he have something to turn away from—something to be ashamed about? No, he wanted to show his solidarity with the rest of Family Abraham—to show that he did value his birth right. But his desire for a new start was bigger than joining in the national soul-searching—it was to mark the beginning of his mission: to show that he did understand his destiny; to show that he understood that he was the Wonder-child. Amazingly, John recognized him publicly to the crowds as, "the Lamb of God."[2]

Many lambs had been sacrificed since Noah had first sacrificed some of his precious cargo of animals as a sign of thanks for God's rescue.[3] Many lambs had been sacrificed since the lamb was killed instead of Abraham's only special chosen son, Isaac.[4] Many lambs had been sacrificed since Yahweh's people had smeared lambs' blood on the doors of their houses in Egypt to keep them safe from the passing-over of the angel of death.[5] Many lambs had been sacrificed in the Temple of Isra-El. Many lambs were still being sacrificed in the Temple. But this Lamb of God was the lamb sacrifice to end all lamb sacrifices—literally. Not long after his death no more lambs would be sacrificed in the Temple as the Temple would not exist. Later Yeh-shua-Jesus would be known by his followers simply as, "The Lamb."[6] His followers believed that all the sacrifices were leading up to this one—the final and greatest one when the chosen son of Abraham: the miraculous son; the son

---

1. Matthew 3:13–15.
2. John 1:29–31.
3. Genesis 8:20.
4. Genesis 22:13.
5. Exodus 12:21–23.
6. Revelation 5:6, 8; 7:17; 14:4, 10; 15:3; 19:9; 21:23; 22:1; 22:3.

of a Virgin; the Wonder-son; God's Son; was to be sacrificed on earth.[7] The Creator was going to be de-created—killed by his creation.

John tried to block Yeh-shua-Jesus' baptism because he knew who he really was.[8] He pointed out that Yeh-shua-Jesus was too great for baptism. Instead Yeh-shua-Jesus should baptize the people but not with dirty river water but with "out-of-this-world" power.[9] John also said that Yeh-shua-Jesus was too great for baptism by another human. John wasn't worthy even to tie up his sandals—not even worthy to be his slave.[10]

But Yeh-shua-Jesus—the Son of Man-kind and the Son of God—insisted on baptism and when he broke up through the surface water, the Universe tore open like a sea parting: not the waters of the Reed Sea; not the waters of Jordan but the Universe itself turned into liquid and separated.[11] It was a re-run of the Creation.[12] It was another Mount Sinai moment.[13] It was another Burning Bush moment.[14] The Doorway to beyond the Universe was wide open. And out of the open Door came a strange unearthly creature—a visitor through the fissure in time; through the split in reality. It was from beyond; from timelessness; from outside the Universe. Those standing by thought it was something like a dove. But that was because they had never seen God's super-natural power and personality assume a visible shape.[15] Just like the dove to Noah spelt a new land; a new life; a new beginning,[16] this dove marked the beginning of Yeh-shua-Jesus living the life he was born to live. This dove-like shape also spelt a new unity on earth between the outside of the Universe with the inside—a rebirth; a recreation for the Universe. At the beginning of the Universe, God's power hovered like a mighty bird over the formless sloshing, primeval, liquid molten earth and squeezed it into shape.[17] Now God's power hovered again—bringing a new world order into being.

The strange dove-like creature landed on Yeh-shua-Jesus. The new creation had begun. But for the moment, it was limited to the

---

7. Hebrews 10:8–14.
8. Matthew 3:13–14.
9. Matthew 3:11.
10. John 1:26–27.
11. Mark 1:10.
12. Genesis 1:1–4.
13. Exodus 19–20.
14. Exodus 3:1–22.
15. Mark 1:9–11.
16. Genesis 8:6–12.
17. Genesis 1:1–2.

Wonder-child—Yeh-shua-Jesus. In him, humanity was reunited with the power of God for the first time since the first humans messed up. Yeh-shua-Jesus was the new human—the new model human—humanity as it was meant to be.[18] Now the power and personality of the greatest Being in and beyond the Universe was in an adult human on earth. Humanity and deity united—totally one—totally powerful in a new way. This was a rebirth for humanity—a second chance for humanity. Yeh-shua-Jesus was the prototype of new humanity. He was the second type of human being—a type to supersede the old Adam model.[19] Here was a human with God at its heart.

In case the immensity of the moment was not noted, a voice boomed from through the Doorway—a word emanating from outside of the Universe. "You are my child—I am thrilled with you!"[20] The baby born into poverty now revealed as the Universe's Wonder-child—the grown up Wonder-child now revealed as God's "love-child"—his love gift to his Creation.

This was Yeh-shua-Jesus' confirmation that all the stories passed onto him by his mother regarding his special birth were true. But more than that, it was the confirmation that he was the Super-star of His Story—that all of His Story had been leading up to himself. This personal confirmation was also a public confirmation. Yeh-shua-Jesus' baptism was the big splash that signified that His Story was in its final chapter. After countless millennia, God had revealed the trailblazer of his newly recreated humanity. God once again looked at his creation and thought it was good.[21]

Nothing else needed to be said.

---

18. John 1:32–34.
19. Romans 5:12–17; 1 Corinthians 15:22, 45.
20. Matthew 3:17.
21. Genesis 1:4, 10, 12, 18, 21, 25, 31.

# 48

# Kingdom

THE HEIR TO THE Royal Bloodline had come to claim his throne. The Son of God had come to claim God's Creation back. The Wonder-child—now Messiah-man—was fulfilling his destiny planned since the beginning of time. The Prince of Judah had been crowned as the new King of God's People—the new leader of Family Abraham. The long hoped-for Super-star of His Story was about to start his mission.

The first words in books of great authors are always remembered. "It was the best of times: it was the worst of times" will always be remembered as Charles Dickens' first line of his "Tale of Two Cities"—a line which draws the reader inexorably into the story. Some first lines are mysterious as well as memorable, such as George Orwell's "1984" that begins with, "It was a bright cold day in April, and the clocks were striking thirteen." Famous words: instantly recognizable.

But beating all of these first words for intrigue and mystery are the first words of the author of new humanity himself. Yeh-shua-Jesus, after his baptism declared, "The Kingdom of God is so close—you can almost touch it!"[1] And with this tantalizing phrase he began his adult contribution to "His Story." His words explained his sudden burst onto the public stage. He followed up with an instruction which was a logical consequence of his advent. "So, change your way of thinking—believe the good news!" It was a call to U-turn. It was a follow up to the message of John the Baptist but now with a more positive twist. His words were redirecting Family Abraham away from concentrating on the bad news to now believe the good news. They were to start to believe the unbelievable after they had U-turned. They were to dare to expect the impossible; in a word—to hope again. It was a call to think out-of- the-box: to think out of the Universe; to think through the Doorway beyond the Universe. It was a call to see Yeh-shua-Jesus as the super-natural King of Isra-El.

1. Mark 1:14–15.

This needed some imagination. The non-educated, illegitimate child of a poor joiner from the slums of Nazareth didn't look the part. He didn't look like the glorious climax of the royal Messianic bloodline. Yeh-shua-Jesus' kingship didn't have the trappings of obvious power. A year or two later, when he came to claim his throne in God's capital city Jeru-Salem, he didn't ride a stallion or sit in a chariot but instead he rode on a donkey,[2] as predicted by God's Mouthpiece, Zechar-Yah, hundreds of years before.[3] This obviously wasn't your usual royal mode of transport. When later he was interrogated by the Roman Governor, Pilate, Yeh-shua-Jesus said his Kingdom was, "not of this world."[4] This King saw himself as out-of-this-world—from beyond the Doorway of the Universe. But his Kingdom was of the people—he claimed that it was so close to humans that they could reach out and touch it—just like they could reach out and touch him. He was Immanu-El—"God with us." His Kingdom may have been close to humans but this didn't mean it was in their face. It was only clear when you looked for it in the right way. It was unlike any human Kingdom ever experienced before.

The hiddenness and enigmatic nature of his Kingdom was emphasized by a lot of his teaching. His stories appeared down-to-earth, simple and obvious but actually they were deep and coded. Their full meaning was only obvious to those who didn't just hear them but also listened to the hidden message.[5] Yeh-shua-Jesus' trademark ending to his stories became, "If you have ears to hear—then hear!"[6] It was his slogan—his mantra. He appealed for ears attuned to his underlying motif—like hearing and understanding Beethoven's famous repeated revolutionary message in the first four Da-Da-Da-Dums of his Fifth Symphony.

One of Yeh-shua-Jesus' most frequently subliminal subversive messages in his stories was that of his Kingdom being invisible to the normal senses. It could only be seen on the super-natural spectrum—with the eyes of faith. The eyes of faith could see past through the hiddenness and see the truth that Yeh-shua-Jesus' Kingdom was like a seed growing hidden in the ground—like an insignificant small seed that apparently dies and decomposes.[7] But the decay is in fact the necessary prelude to its real life as the seedling breaks through the rotting husk of the seed and through the ground surface into a

2. Matthew 21:1–11.
3. Zechariah 9:9.
4. John 18:36.
5. Mark 4:10–12.
6. Mark 4:9.
7. Matthew 13:31–32.

glorious plant—a plant full of seeds ready to reproduce throughout the field.[8] Yeh-shua-Jesus' group seemed insignificant and small—with no royal court or army. On top of this, within three years he would die. But his death wasn't the end but the beginning. Out of his death would grow an international, timeless Kingdom—a Kingdom that would break into the world and spread throughout all lands and time. In fact, this was the victorious Kingdom supernaturally seen by Dani-El years before.[9]

To be a citizen of this secretive, seditious Kingdom, you didn't have to be important or influential. In fact, according to Yeh-shua-Jesus you had to be like the most insignificant humans of the day—children.[10] In Yeh-shua-Jesus' day, children were seen as only potential-adults. The respect and honoring of childhood would have to wait for another two thousand years until reformers like Dr Barnardo and Lord Shaftesbury realized that children needed protecting. Many of these childhood reformers followed Yeh-shua-Jesus' teaching. They followed Yeh-shua-Jesus' example and changed the world forever. They believed that Yeh-shua-Jesus was right when he told off his colleagues for attempting to bar children from visiting him and apparently wasting his time. He ordered his colleagues to let the little children come through to him.[11] To Yeh-shua-Jesus, children were as important as adults.

This wasn't just sentimentality on Yeh-shua-Jesus' behalf but the core of his teaching about entry into his revolutionary Kingdom. Yeh-shua-Jesus taught that, "The Kingdom of God belongs to children."[12] He told people that the only way to be a part of his super-natural Kingdom was to enter it like a child.[13] Children trust. Children believe. Children are more likely to believe in the unbelievable—in magic. Children see the unseen whether it be the unwanted monster under the bed or the invisible friend. Children are more naturally attuned to life beyond the obvious; to life beyond the Doorway. Emotionally healthy children usually believe in goodness and happy endings. Yeh-shua-Jesus believed that nothing should rob our children of this belief. He said that anyone who abused children should have a massive stone tied round their necks and they should be thrown into the sea.[14] These direct words of gentle Yeh-shua-Jesus are sometimes forgotten. Maybe it is high time we remember them again.

8. Matthew 13:8.
9. Daniel 2:44–45.
10. Matthew 18:1–5.
11. Mark 10:13–16.
12. Matthew 19:14.
13. Matthew 18:3.
14. Mark 9:42.

According to Yeh-shua-Jesus, adults shouldn't rob children of their childhood—in fact, adults should follow the example of children and believe themselves in happy endings. They should swallow their grown-up cynicism and world-weariness. He told those around him, "Put searching for my Kingdom as your first priority in life and then you will receive everything you need for this life from beyond the Doorway."[15] Adults need to trust in good news again, not in a childish way but in a childlike way. Adults need to know they have an invisible friend and do this without being embarrassed—thinking they are childish or feeble-minded failures.

The good news that Yeh-shua-Jesus shared through his teaching was that this Kingdom of new life was now close by—so close you could touch it. The outside and inside of the Universe were as close as they had ever been. The gap between the inside and outside the Universe was not even paper thin—it was occupying the same space.

It was so close—it was accessible to humans. And every new recruit who joined Yeh-shua-Jesus' royal Kingdom gave the Kingdom more power on earth. Like a resistance movement in occupied territory, Yeh-shua-Jesus wanted his Kingdom of followers to liberate the world—to rescue it from the power of the created and return it to the power of the Creator. He wanted humans to become the visible dimension of the invisible Kingdom. When quizzed once as to what humans should ask God for, he said, "Say this, 'Our Father who lives beyond the Doorway outside the Universe may your name be respected on earth! May your Kingdom break through onto earth and may your wishes come true here on earth as they come true beyond the Universe. Please give us here on earth what we need to work for the Kingdom every day. Please show us grace when we disobey your Kingdom orders. Help us to show the same Kingdom grace as we let other people off for their bad behavior towards us. Please protect us when we are tempted to live our lives without reference to your orders or when we are bullied by the enemy to go against you.'"[16]

These words in previous generations have been learnt off by heart by many adults. But they shouldn't be treated as a religious mantra but as more of a manifesto for God's resistance fighters. They remind Kingdom fighters: to follow the commanding officer's orders; to fight for the Kingdom of heaven on earth; to make the Creator's wishes come true on earth; to bring heaven on earth.

But how can heaven break into earth through humans? How can the Kingdom grow through humans? Basically, Yeh-shua-Jesus' message can

---

15. Matthew 6:33.
16. Matthew 6:9–13.

be summed up in a simple command to humanity, "Follow me!"[17] Note this isn't, "be good" or, "be religious" or, "be a nice person," nor even, "try hard to be the best you can be." But simply and profoundly, "Follow me!" Yeh-shua-Jesus insisted that he was, "the only way to true human life."[18] He insisted he was the only way to access the land beyond the Doorway. He insisted that he was the only way to find humanity's Creator—our Father. He clearly believed that following him was the only way that humans could find the life humans were created to live. Following Yeh-shua-Jesus led humans right back into a new Garden of Eden where God lived. Yeh-shua-Jesus had become synonymous with the Doorway to beyond the Universe. He personified the Doorway. He was the Doorway. No longer was the Doorway to heaven on the top of a ladder or in a burning bush. No longer was the Doorway to heaven on the top of a volcanic mountain resulting in God stretching though onto earth and writing life-giving instructions on stone. No longer was the Doorway to heaven a building—even a Temple. The Doorway was a person. "I am the Doorway," said Yeh-shua-Jesus.[19]

He even went further claiming that he was not only the way to God—he was God. God was his Father. He said, "I am in the Father and the Father is in me."[20] Just as any biological father and his son are the same family and share the same D.N.A. Yeh-shua-Jesus claimed that his D.N.A. family was God—so much so that he could say, "I and the Father are one."[21] Joseph wasn't his Father. God the Creator was his Father. He was "The Son." He was God at home on earth or in Family Abraham language, "Immanu-El."

Yeh-shua-Jesus had come to this amazing conclusion about himself by reading the first part of His Story. By reading the words of the Mouthpieces of old who spoke about a promised child who fitted his own personal profile exactly. Fancy reading a book and finding that it is your own biography, unknown to you!

Yeh-shua-Jesus had also undoubtedly heard the amazing stories from his mother about the strange goings-on at his birth. Yeh-shua-Jesus had had his suspicions confirmed about his own identity at his baptism when God his Father had spoken directly to him and empowered him with supernatural, super-human, out-of-this-world powers.[22]

17. Matthew 4:19; 8:22; 9:9; 10:38; 16:24; 19:21, 28; John 1:43; 8:12; 10:27; 12:26; 21:19 etc..
18. John 14:6.
19. John 10:7, 9.
20. John 14:10–11.
21. John 10:30.
22. Luke 3:21–22.

Once when he was in the Temple in Jeru-Salem, he made it clear that his body was the new Temple—the new place now where God met the earth—that he was the living Doorway. And then he predicted his own death in terms of the Herod's stone-built Temple being knocked down.[23] He said that his body would replace the stone-built Temple that King Herod built which in turn had replaced Solomon's patched up building. The stone Temple would be surplus to requirements—redundant. It would then be destroyed. He was right. It was destroyed nearly forty years later by the Romans. It has never been rebuilt—even to this day. No longer can Family Abraham offer sacrifices in the Temple in Jeru-Salem as there is no Temple to use. No longer is there a Doorway to God in Jeru-Salem. All that is left is the West Wall—the "Wailing Wall." At the top of the Wailing Wall is a rock. The rock is the Rock of Moriah—the rock where Abraham almost sacrificed Isaac.[24] The rock is at the foundation of Family Abraham history and later it became the foundation stone of the Holy of Holies at the heart of the old Temple. But the rock now is a sacred Muslim shrine—the Dome of the Rock. The rock is also at the heart of Islam—the place where Mohammed is believed by Muslims to have gone up to heaven. It is now a holy site for Islam and Judaism. It is probably the most hotly disputed area in the whole of time and space.

But for Yeh-shua-Jesus' followers, there is no loss of a Temple. Yeh-shua-Jesus predicted the destruction of the Temple—never to be rebuilt,[25] but he also predicted the destruction of his body, the new Temple. But unlike Herod's temple, he also predicted the rebuilding of his own body in only three days.[26] Expressing this unbelievable belief about himself in such a sensitive public place like Herod's Temple was going to get him into trouble. Expressing coded messages about an invisible Kingdom focused on himself and occupying the same space as a land occupied by the Roman Empire was going to get him into trouble.

And it did.

23. John 2:18–21.
24. Genesis 22:1–14.
25. Mark 13:1–2.
26. John 2:18–21.

# 49

# The Clash

SOME THINGS SHOULDN'T MIX: like fire and petrol; like water and electricity; like radioactivity and human cells. What about humanity and divinity? What would happen if you could put God on earth as a human? What would happen if you could mix the Creator into the stuff he created? Would the result be one extreme explosion: one almighty anomaly; one paralyzing paradox? What if God's presence on earth was concentrated in just one human? What would happen if the whole of time and space touched down at one exact time and one exact space? We know the answer to this one—it's in His Story.

The story of Yeh-shua-Jesus answers the question. If the outside of the Universe touched the inside of the Universe in a human being, you would expect the normal regular reproducible rules of nature to be twisted and flexed around that person. You would expect the normal routines of nature to be replaced by abnormal and unique happenings. In fact, if the super-natural met the natural, you would expect the super-natural to win. Or to put it another way: if the Kingdom of God invaded the Kingdom of the earth, you would expect God's Kingdom to have an influence over the Kingdom of the earth and not visa versa.

For example, you'd expect weather patterns to be altered: Yeh-shua-Jesus stopped a storm in its tracks—just by using his voice.[1] You'd expect the normal physical properties of water to be overcome: Yeh-shua-Jesus walked on water[2] and changed water into wine.[3] Not bad when water is one of those basic things that you virtually can't make. You'd also expect that material objects could be made out of immaterial objects: Yeh-shua-Jesus

---

1. Matthew 8:23–27.
2. Matthew 14:22–33.
3. John 2:1–11.

produced bread and fish out of thin air;[4] in fact he could make fish appear out of nowhere and swim into waiting nets.[5] Thin air wasn't thin to him.

You'd expect that this manipulation of the basic atoms of the physical world to be dangerous—like alien radiation causing cancer on earth. But there you would be wrong. Yeh-shua-Jesus did seem to manipulate life at the atomic level, but apart from one tree withering at his words,[6] always his intervention brought health and life. The blind saw;[7] the lame walked;[8] the speechless spoke;[9] the sick revived;[10] the recent dead were resuscitated;[11] even the decomposing dead lived again.[12]

You'd expect that bringing the Creator into his creation would bring super-natural out-of-this-world knowledge to humans—knowledge that couldn't be gained simply by studying life on earth and in space. And you'd be right: Yeh-shua-Jesus is acknowledged as one of the wisest men who has ever lived, despite no formal education. His words: his teaching; his insight have become the basis of international ethics, laws and reforms, as well as the guiding principle of innumerable leaders and heroes of the human race. Presidents and Prime ministers, humanitarians and heroes have all claimed Yeh-shua-Jesus as their role model.

You'd expect that when time and timelessness meet, that sparks would fly—massive irreconcilable paradoxical clashes that would send humanity into turmoil. At one point on the top of a mountain, Yeh-shua-Jesus did become iridescent.[13] His body became visibly the Doorway to beyond the Universe—a flaming Mount Sinai and burning bush all at once. Through the Doorway of his body two ancient heroes of His Story appeared—El-i-Yah and Moses. Neither had been seen on earth for hundreds of years. In El-i-Yah's case, this wasn't some sort of reincarnation in the form of John the Baptist, this was the real thing. The timeline of history was folding in on itself—fixed mutually exclusive points in time coalescing—all landing on the same time and space square as in a great game of Time-Lord Ludo. It had never happened before and has never happened since (except in Science

---

4. Matthew 14:13–21.
5. Luke 5:1–10.
6. Matthew 21:18–22.
7. Mark 10:46–52.
8. John 5:1–15.
9. Mark 7:31–37.
10. Matthew 8:14–17.
11. Mark 5:35–43.
12. John 11:38–44.
13. Mark 9:2–8.

Fiction). This was a once in eternity moment and all for the benefit of His Story alone. This temporal anomaly created fire and sparks just as happened at the great Doorway moments of the burning bush,[14] Mount Sinai[15] and Isa-Yah's Temple experience.[16]

But Yeh-shua-Jesus didn't just generate physical incandescence he also generated metaphorical incandescence too. Even today, he sparks off great passion in humans. Yeh-shua-Jesus unites but also divides humanity. The subject of who Yeh-shua-Jesus was and is still makes for a heated argument. Yeh-shua-Jesus still is the most loved but also the most controversial figure of human history. Appalling things have been done in his name: appalling things have been done to those who follow his name.

This polarization began in Yeh-shua-Jesus' lifetime. His Kingdom teaching caused such a clash that it inevitably was going to end in a massive bust-up. He split Family Abraham right down the middle—and still does. He has split the family of humanity right down the middle—and still does.

But the battle wasn't simply going to rage around Yeh-shua-Jesus. It was going to rage inside him too. At his baptism, the alien dove-like visitor had given him powers that no other human being had ever received. He was no fictitious comic book character. He was a real human like every other human being and obviously just like you and me. So it's fair to ask yourself if you had super-powers how would you use them? If you had abilities and gifts that were far beyond the normal, how would you use them—for the benefit of others or the benefit of yourself? To be fair most of us would think of others. Lottery winners usually care for their families. Millionaires usually remember their dependents and friends. But they spend far more of their windfall on themselves. They might share their winnings around, but in a way that pleases them—in a way that makes them feel less guilty and doesn't seriously harm their own wealth. We, no doubt, would do the same. If we could fly like superman, we would jet around the globe saving those in trouble but we would spend far more time taking holidays in the most beautiful exotic corners of the earth and the Universe. If we could change ordinary things into precious metals like Midas we would set up a charity in our name but we would still use most of the gold for our own pleasure. If we had phenomenal skills in music, writing, art, sport, dance or acting, we would use our skills creatively but still enjoy the celebrity status that they would bring.

---

14. Exodus 3:1–22.
15. Exodus 19:1–25.
16. Isaiah 6:1–13.

Yeh-shua-Jesus was the Wonder-child, now the Wonder-man. He was the unique human. His birth was out-of-this-world. His powers were supernatural too. He had to use them—it was his destiny. He was, after all, the Super-star of His Story—the long awaited one. The world was potentially one massive playground for his talents; for his powers. But could he use them without abuse; without corruption; without selfishness?

The stakes were high. If the super powerful Wonder-man used his independence as a human to do his own thing: to go A.W.O.L. from God's plan; to go "off-piste"; to go feral; to go wild; to be like the first humans, Adam and Eve;[17] His Story would be over. God's ultimate solution to humanity's rebellion would have failed.

If Yeh-shua-Jesus misused and abused his powers then not only would he be a failure, he would even add to the problem he was sent to solve. Now on earth there would be a man more powerful than any other evil character from history. This super-naturally powerful human would be running around earth wrecking God's plans: de-creating his creation; leading humans in a rebellion against God—not just a sneaky snake this time,[18] but a satanic superman—a devil of cataclysmic proportions—Biblical even.

At his baptism, God might have been overjoyed with Yeh-shua-Jesus, but would this happiness rating continue now Yeh-shua-Jesus had received his out-of-this-world powers from beyond the Doorway? It all depended on how he used these powers. Yeh-shua-Jesus needed to be tested. The test was to see which team the Wonder-child was going to play on.

His own or his Father's?

---

17. Genesis 3:1–24.
18. Genesis 3:1.

# 50

# Groundhog Day?

THE TEST CAME IMMEDIATELY after Yeh-shua-Jesus' baptism by John. Yeh-shua Jesus went from the sky parting above him to the depths of Hell opening under his feet.

Yeh-shua-Jesus felt compelled to take himself off alone. He needed to get his head round his situation without distraction. He followed John the Baptist's example and headed for the desert—alone.[1] He was alone but not left alone. He was with his two totally real and genuine sides of his nature—his human nature and his out-of-this-world nature. They had to learn to exist alongside each other without destroying each other. Up to this point in the history of humanity they had always been separate. In His Story some humans had experienced God's out-of-this-world spirit working on them: Gideon, Moses, Ezeki-El, for example, but never in them: never as part of them; always outside them; always temporary. Up to now the two natures couldn't mix—time and timelessness couldn't live together in one body—they destroyed each other. They were opposed to each other. Any attempt at splicing them together would have created a chimera-like monster or a human body with an auto-immune disease—at war with itself.

But this was the new man—God's new model human. This was God's new creation—the new plan of God. But that didn't mean it was going to be a walk in the park for Yeh-shua-Jesus. When two tectonic plates on the earth's crust move against each other the result is an earthquake—the earth tears itself apart. When Yeh-shua-Jesus' two tectonic natures crashed into each other the danger was he would have his own personal earthquake—that he would be torn in two—that he would have a fissure cracking him open from inside—the Doorway collapsing in one itself, imploding and swallowing him up like a Black Hole. After all, he was only human—as well as God.

Would Yeh-shua-Jesus withstand the opposing forces at play within him? Or would the divine be overwhelmed and corrupted by his humanity? Would he replay Adam's failure?

1. Matthew 4:1.

Like Adam he had a blank sheet. Would he choose write his own story on it and do his own thing—ignoring God? Would humanity be stuck for ever to relive the history of human failure as if stuck like Bill Murray's character in a world history remake of "Groundhog Day"? Would Yeh-shua-Jesus be trapped in an endless repeating cycle of failure to follow the Maker's instructions—doomed to suffer the inevitable consequences over and over again? It would have been comic if it wasn't so tragic. The all important question that eternity had been waiting to answer was, "Would God's new version human be resistant to the overwhelming selfish desire of humanity?"

Adam had been the first human on earth—green and innocent. Even so, Adam failed (with a little help from Satan-Snake).[2] But Yeh-shua-Jesus, was living with a legacy of thousands of years of human selfishness and in a world where rebellion against God was routine. As we have seen, His Story is a story of personal human failure, generation after generation as well as repeated institutionalized failure. This failure had been started by the first human beings but continued by every generation—each generation building on the failure of the last. His Story never fails to prove that humans constantly fail.[3] This was Yeh-shua-Jesus' heritage as a human: thousands of years of humans choosing badly; thousands of years of human institutions choosing badly; thousands of years of humanity choosing to ignore God. Would this history of failure hinder him? Would it compromise Yeh-shua-Jesus' own legacy to the world?

For Adam—the forbidden fruit hung on the tree of the knowledge of good and evil.[4] But for Yeh-shua-Jesus, the forbidden fruit wasn't hanging on a tree. For Yeh-shua-Jesus, the forbidden fruit was misusing his supernatural powers of God. For Yeh-shua-Jesus, the forbidden fruit was to try and become a rival super-natural power to the Creator—to destroy his construction.

Through Adam, humanity had failed to follow God. Through Yeh-shua-Jesus, would the new super-humanity fail too? In addition to being at the sharp end of a human legacy of human rebelliousness, Yeh-shua Jesus also had Satan-Snake talking to him.[5] He was out there with the Wonder-man in the loneliness of the desert, meddling in Yeh-shua-Jesus' own cosmic but deeply personal battle. Just as the Satanic snake had sweet-talked Adam and Eve into making a disastrously bad choice, he was also here with Adam's replacement, Yeh-shua-Jesus—tempting him.

2. Genesis 3:6.
3. Isaiah 53:6.
4. Genesis 2:15–17.
5. Matthew 4:1.

This was not some crass good angel-bad angel routine, but deep communication into the intersection of Yeh-shua-Jesus' natures hardwired into his brain and mind. The voice in Yeh-shua-Jesus' head was the voice of God's enemy trying to take over his mind. The voice was the alternative to God—his alter-ego. It was the snake of the Garden Eden in a more sophisticated disguise, not working on the outside of Yeh-shua-Jesus but deep within him—he was the enemy from within.

Adam was a very primitive human but Yeh-shua-Jesus was a human with thousands of years of human development behind him. But the snake had also moved with the times—he had developed tried and tested tactics to trip humanity over the generations.

This tempting snake has had many disguises and names over the years of human history—Satan and Devil to name but two. But whatever his name, there is a question that can't be avoided—why did God allow him in his Creation? Why did God allow the snake in the paradise with Adam? Why did God allow Satan to attack his Son? Answer: because God had made humans just like himself: able to choose; able to choose to make themselves God or let God be God. [6]

For choice to work, there has to be freedom to choose—freedom even to make bad choices. In contrast to human freedom to choose, God made animals so that they needed looking after by humans—humans were to be God's carers for the animals.[7] Humans have freedom: animals haven't. Humans are free to choose to reject their Creator: animals aren't. Humans can choose to work against God's Creation: animals can't—they instinctively work with their role in Creation.

To put it another way: humans have a soul: animals have an instinct. Humans throughout their history have worshipped a greater being. Humans have always looked to control the forces that shape their lives. Humans have always looked to control or at least pacify their Creator. Humans continue to try to be their own creator: in charge of their own destiny; to be creative with their own lives—animals don't. Despite painting elephants and singing dogs, animals aren't into expressing their deep feelings through art. When did you last see an animal pondering on the meaning of life; or worshipping? The soul ponders. The soul sings. The soul creates. The soul worships.[8] Of course, it's a blessing and a curse: but it's what makes us human.

The soul is the battlefield where Satan was attacking Yeh-shua-Jesus. If you cut up a human body and if you separated every part out and laid it flat

---

6. Genesis 1:27.
7. Genesis 1:27–28.
8. Psalm 42.

on the ground, you would have a lot of mess. Our intestine is around twenty-three feet long, but in reality, its absorptive surface area is roughly seven hundred and twenty square feet, or in other words, the size of a tennis court. But even if you laid the human body out completely flat on a tennis court, basketball court or any other sporting arena you choose, you wouldn't find the soul. It's not a physical thing. Some people think it might be a function of the brain, like our mind is a construct of our brain. This is understandable, as there is so much to our brains that we are still discovering.

Our brain certainly is amazing. Our brain is faster and more powerful than a supercomputer. Our brain generates enough electricity to power a light-bulb (not quite a nuclear reactor but not bad). Our brain contains about one hundred billion microscopic cells (it would take over three thousand years to count them). Our brain collects information from our body via a link that sends data faster than one hundred and fifty miles per hour. It sends information back at over two hundred miles per hour. But it isn't the soul.

The soul is real, but invisible—just like oxygen, gravity and wireless signals. These are all invisible to our eyes, but still real. The soul is not made out of any kind of material but is still real. It works in every part of our body and impacts on our every part of our life massively but it isn't something you can touch, taste, smell, see or hear. Just like love, it is something which is immaterial but has a massive material hit on our lives. Our soul is our doorway to the spiritual—to the numinous—to all those things that transcend the everyday and the material. Our soul is intimately connected and affected by our earthly experiences—such as music and other forms of art. Many things can unlock its door and deeply stir its inner chambers.

But fundamentally, the soul gives us the ability to know God and choose God—or the opposite. The soul also gives us the ability to reject God. The way we reject God is by standing up to God—to make ourselves equal to God.

But how can any human stand up to God's irresistible power? Only with God's help (ironically). To help us stand up to his overwhelming power, God has built into his Creation, another power—a power that will help us become our own god—a contradictory voice whose job it is to put over the other point of view. It speaks like the defense lawyer in a court trial who helps the accused stand up to the prosecution. Like the defense lawyer who advocates and advises on his client's behalf—this powerful voice stands by us and whispers into our ear. It speaks into our soul and tells us what we want to hear—you don't need God.

On a positive note, this voice defends us from being overwhelmed by God's greatness and being forced into a robotic relationship with God. This voice defends us from sleepwalking unthinkingly into following God our Creator. This voice defends us from instinctively following God our Creator.

Just as a defense lawyer defending a guilty-as-hell client is unpalatable but essential if justice is to be served, Satan is essential, if unpalatable. Just as a defense lawyer defending a guilty-as-hell client is often unpopular but still essential—so is Satan. Our freedom to choose must be preserved at all costs. Choosing is so important—we call it our human right. But really it is a gift from our Creator God. But choosing well is even more important than just choosing. It is worth the existence of the possibility of choosing badly. It is worth the existence of Satan.

So far so good—Satan's role in preserving our ability to choose seems sound and sensible. But the problem is that Satan is so good as our defense lawyer that we often believe his defense—even when we deep down know we are as guilty-as-hell. Satan tells us what we want to hear, such as "God can't make you do anything—you can do what you want—it's your human right!" "You're not to blame—after all you're only human." "You've been made this way—you've been brought up this way!" "What you want is what is right for you." Satan starts to seem more like our best friend than our defense lawyer. We stop respecting the professional boundaries and start to become involved with him personally. We believe his half-truths as whole truths.

There is no doubt Satan is very good—at his job at least. He is universally effective. He's had years of practice. He's worked in all humans since day one. He's worked in all human groups since day one. His Story says that God created humans in his own image.[9] But Satan has tried to re-create us in his own image since day one. He constantly overplays his role and his hand. His lust for power is demonic. He has infiltrated generation after generation of humans and everything humans do. He has become almost indistinguishable from humanity itself. Choosing to go it alone against our Creator has become second nature. Nowadays, no child needs to be taught to be naughty. No school has to put on lessons on how to be selfish.

So why do we fall for Satan's tricks? Very few humans would ever admit to following Satan or being evil or demonic. And very few humans are actually Satanic or demonic or evil. But all humans naturally rebel against God—all humans choose badly. Why? Because we don't see Satan for whom he is. Because he doesn't show himself for who he is. He never introduces himself properly. He hides behind our own desires—lurking in the dark recesses of our minds. We are not aware of his manipulation—we just go with our own selfish flow.

---

9. Genesis 1:17.

Satan doesn't have a high profile until we listen to him. He isn't obvious until we listen to him. He isn't powerful until we listen to him. Strangely, he isn't truly evil until we listen to him. He isn't truly evil until we put into practice what he suggests. The unpleasant truth is that it's humans who do evil things, not Satan. We can't blame Satan—or God—for our evil. Satan has no direct power in God's creation apart from the power we give him when we do his bidding—when we believe his advice and follow our selfish desires.

Up to the birth of Yeh-shua-Jesus, Satan hadn't had a very high-profile in His Story. He was very much lurking in the background. Except of course in one famous old Family Abraham fable about a very good man where Satan had a leading role—Job. The fable goes that Job was so good, that God couldn't help boasting to Satan about him.[10] But Satan pointed out that he was only really good because all sorts of good things had happened to him—good in: good out. Satan argued that if bad things happened to him, he would turn bad—bad in: bad out.[11]

In the myth, God disagreed and decided to have a bet with Satan—a little test to see what would happen if God let badness hit Job's life. God then let negative things occur to Job's family—all at once. Job didn't even wobble. Then he let bad things happen to Job personally, and significantly, this nearly broke Job and his trust in God—not to mention his trust in his friends. But Job held firm.[12] Just. He had his moments but in the end his trust in the goodness of God won through—with a bit of help from God.[13]

It was a good versus evil fable which might have been based on a real historical character. It was a story with an important moral meaning about seeing how Satan might work through our personal, natural, selfishness.

But Yeh-shua-Jesus was no fable. No good versus evil morality tale. This was the real thing. The real test—the real battle between good and evil. This wasn't just a mythical bet between God and Satan. The stakes were the future of the Universe. At stake was who would control the Universe—God or Satan? After millennia of waiting, Satan knew everything up to this point was simply the warm-up act for the main event. For the first time ever, God had stepped through the Doorway and made himself vulnerable to the powers of Satan.

The real issue was who would have the upper hand inside the Universe—Satan allied with humanity or God allied with the new humanity of Yeh-shua-Jesus.

10. Job 1:1–8.
11. Job 1:9–12.
12. Job 1:21–22; 2:10b.
13. Job 38:1—42:6.

## 51

## Testing, Testing One, Two, Three

THE TEST BEGAN IMMEDIATELY after Yeh-shua-Jesus' baptism. In the end the test turned into three. The first test was simple and was similar to the first test for the first humans—food. In the desert, Yeh-shua-Jesus fasted—no food.[1] Esther had done the same when she had had her own big life and death decision to make. Yeh-shua-Jesus was beginning his massive public life and death moment—he had eternal life and death decisions to make. To ensure he made the right decisions, Yeh-shua-Jesus had to make sure he could control his most basic selfish human desire to survive—he had to control his most basic human desire to eat. He had to prove that he was in control of himself. And for weeks, he controlled himself to live without food. Gandhi apparently survived without food for three weeks whilst in his seventies. Doctors say you might survive for four to six weeks without food. Hunger-strikers have survived for as long as ten weeks without food. Yeh-shua-Jesus went without food for nearly six weeks. He tested his body to the limit to be sure that his humanity was under his control.

It was too dangerous to contemplate the alternative to this—God's new human being out of control. But his weakened human body shouted for food: shouted for survival; shouted to be heard. It spoke with the same voice as the snake in Adam's Paradise. It tempted, by giving totally reasonable, rational and sensible advice, "Eat—you're no good to God or humanity or anyone dead." Like a nagging mum, his body told him off, "You've got out-of-this-world super-powers—use them!" Specifically, use them to make food. "Look at that stone in front of you—doesn't it look like a crusty loaf of bread? You don't just have to look at it—you can use your super-powers to make it into delicious bread—eat!" [2] Yeh-shua-Jesus would have known that Moses let the people of Isra-El eat before they started out on their long

1. Luke 4:2.
2. Luke 4:3.

escape across the desert. He knew he was starting his lifelong journey and he was in the desert. He needed to be strong for what was ahead. It was common sense. But it was wrong because the voice in Yeh-shua-Jesus' brain was Satan's voice working through his soul via his stomach.

For the test to be effective, Satan had to use every subtlety; every trick to defend the human part of the Wonder-man from blindly following Yeh-shua- Jesus' own heavenly Father. He had to get in between Yeh-shua-Jesus and his out-of-this-worldness. He had to get a crowbar into the fissure—opening up the two sides of Yeh-shua-Jesus' nature. The test had to be 100 percent fool-proof. Surely no human knowing they had super-powers to make food out of inanimate objects instantly could resist food after six weeks of fasting? But as Yeh-shua-Jesus' body was eating itself—burning up its last remaining fat reserves, it still had energy enough about it to reject the slimy advice of the once Snake-like tempter. Yeh-shua-Jesus reminded Satan that life was far more than food. He used a mysterious meaning-heavy phrase, "Humanity shall not live by bread alone." He added that humanity shouldn't think that life is about filling your own mouth, but taking to heart the words that come out of God's mouth.[3]

The super-natural gained the victory over the natural. Yeh-shua-Jesus successfully defended himself. But the diabolically good defense lawyer didn't pack in after one bad cross-examination. He had a couple more adversarial tricks up his sleeve. As Yeh-shua-Jesus hovered between consciousness and unconsciousness, Satan gave him a second test. He gave him a vision of the whole of the world stretched out in front of him.[4] "Worship me and you can have it all" was his simple offer. It must have been tempting to Yeh-shua-Jesus to become the most powerful human of all time by taking over all of those humans who had fallen under the spell of Satan. After all, it was true that Satan had immense power—humans naturally followed him. In a way all of us are his followers—still. Of course, Yeh-shua-Jesus could have rationalized joining Satan's team by arguing to himself that he could use the power he would gain in partnership with Satan for good—to encourage humans to choose God and not Satan. But the means to this worthy end was to join forces with the dark side. For Yeh-shua-Jesus to add his own super-natural powers to the natural power of Satan would mean Satan and the Son of God working together. What a partnership! No one could have stopped them—including God. Yeh-shua-Jesus could have had anything he wanted—except his place in His Story. That would have been forfeited. But Yeh-shua-Jesus knew the rules—the rules that Dani-El and his friends had

3. Matthew 4:4; Deuteronomy 8:3.
4. Luke 4:5–7.

followed, "No worshipping anyone but God the Creator."[5] And he said so. And Satan backed off.

But Satan hadn't finished. He had a third test—another vision. This time, Yeh-shua-Jesus hallucinated that he was on the Temple's pinnacle—right on the top of the lightning conductor on the very top of the Temple in Jerusalem—the center of the world. "Jump!"[6] Wasn't Satan's command a bit childish—tempting the Wonder-man to jump off the Temple? No, in fact, it was very subtle. Satan was playing on the very real human doubts of the man-God. "Are you sure you're the Son of God?" "Go on check whether you're really God—try something really scary—life-threatening." Satan assured Yeh-shua-Jesus that the alien beings from outside of the Universe would never let any harm come to the Messiah-Man.[7] They would fly in formation through the Doorway and catch him. It was promised in King David's ancient one thousand year-old prophecy about the Messiah that God would not let: "a hair on his head be harmed." "Test it!" But if Yeh-shua-Jesus did test it—he would by accident have been following Satan: giving power to him; following his advice; giving him power over God's own Wonder-man. Again the Wonder-man remembered the law given by God through the Mount Sinai Doorway to Moses. And he threw it at Satan. "Do not test God—he's your Lord."[8]

The power of the words from beyond the Doorway shattered the vision and Satan left—for the moment.[9] God's non-human helpers from the world beyond came and fed Yeh-shua-Jesus to stop him dying.[10] Not only was God's Wonder-man safe: the Universe was safe as well—for the moment.

But now God was on earth, Satan had to be extra vigilant. From his point of view, the threat to humanity was great. If God-on-earth was unrestrained, people would be brainwashed into following him—they would have their own free-will overwhelmed. They would have no choice. But from God's point of view, if Satan was too powerful in opposition, the earth and possibly the whole Universe would become a no-go zone for God—God frozen out from his own Creation which was unthinkable.

In reality, the tests were just beginning for Yeh-shua-Jesus. His Story's ending hung in the balance.

5. Luke 4:8; Deuteronomy 6:13.
6. Luke 4:9–11.
7. Luke 4:9–11; Psalm 91:11–12.
8. Luke 4:12; Deuteronomy 6:16.
9. Luke 4:13.
10. Mark 1:13.

# 52

## Lost the Plot?

WHAT WOULD THE WORLD be like now if Hitler had won the Second World War? Can you imagine a world led by a man who apparently had totally sold out to Satan? It's not a pretty picture. But what would the world be like if Satan had won the ultimate war for the soul of Yeh-shua-Jesus? Can you imagine a world led by Satan and his super-man partner in crime, Yeh-shua-Jesus? After his first three tests, Yeh-shua-Jesus was at the center of a war for the world: a war for the Universe. Satan was determined to neutralize the Messiah-man. Satan was determined to win Yeh-shua-Jesus over to his side. For three years, the ultimate World War was fought. The battleground was inside and outside of Yeh-shua-Jesus.

Satan attacked Yeh-shua-Jesus with one aim: to make Yeh-shua-Jesus forget his mission; to make him forget why he was on earth; to make him lose the plot of His Story. Satan wanted to close the Doorway and lock it shut for ever, isolating the inside of the Universe from the outside of the Universe. This was important to Satan because Satan only had power in the Universe—this was the limit to his license to operate. If the link to the outside the Universe was blocked, Satan had effectively won, condemning humanity to generation after generation of failing to follow their Father Creator, and following him instead—whether humanity knew it or not. Satan liked indirect, hidden, subtle tactics.

But whilst Yeh-shua-Jesus was still active and faithful to his mission to be the human Doorway, he threatened to open up the link to the outside of the Universe in a new even more accessible way and in so doing revealing Satan's tactics and undermining his power. Satan had to stop Yeh-shua-Jesus. In this battle against Yeh-shua-Jesus, Satan sometimes had to use the direct approach. He worked through the personality, character and souls of troubled and vulnerable humans around Yeh-shua-Jesus—the very people Yeh-shua-Jesus, the Wonder-man, had been sent to save.

Take one man as an example: a man who was so troubled, he self-harmed; a man who was so frightened and so frightening that for his own safety and for the peace of mind of others, he was chained up in a graveyard.[1] This probably didn't do much for his self-esteem but at least his name was grand—"Legion." It was his nickname for himself. He believed he had a Roman legion of six thousand devils marching around in him! He may have already been ill before Satan invaded him; he certainly was afterwards.

When Yeh-shua-Jesus saw Legion, he ordered Satan to back off—to leave him alone. Legion was Satan's chosen battlefield. But the battle was between Yeh-shua-Jesus and Satan—this man was simply collateral damage. Legion shouted back, "What do you want with me, Son of God! Don't torture me—leave me alone!" Like many others since, Legion knew Yeh-shua-Jesus was his only way of escape, but he also feared his personal demons more. As much as he wanted saving from his life—it was the only real life he knew. He was trapped—addicted to his own self-destructive prison. He knew it was bad for him, but he was too scared to escape. He feared the unknown of life without his six thousand undomesticated house guests ("better the devils you know")—he feared annoying them. He didn't want the devils released only to have them return and this time—angry![2] He needed help but he feared help—rock and a hard place time. So Yeh-shua-Jesus did a bargain with him—when he released the army of devils that were killing him, he would prove that they were gone forever—never to return. So, Yeh-shua-Jesus sent the diabolical army into a herd of two thousand pigs close by—three demons to every poor pig.[3] A trade-off: the pigs for one human life; a sacrifice; a glimpse of things to come when Yeh-shua-Jesus' life was going to be sacrificed to save humanity's life.

The effect was instantaneous. The pigs ran headfirst down over the cliff and drowned in the Sea of Galilee. The true self-destructive nature of following Satan was seen. Satan was seen in his true colors—his invisibility cloaked removed. Legion saw it. Legion believed it. Legion became calm and in his right mind: safe; healed; the person he was born to be. But the pig farmers were livid and told Yeh-shua-Jesus to get lost—to never come back. Their pigs were more important to them than the life of a human being.

This was the pattern of Yeh-shua-Jesus' life: liked by the people who gained from his unselfish use of his power; liked by those moved by his down-to-earth stories and powerful teaching; but hated by the people who lost out to him.

Take for example, the religious teachers (rabbis) whose stories were insipid, boring and unpopular—all about religious rules and not about His

---

1. Mark 5:1–10.
2. Luke 11:24–26.
3. Mark 5:11–17.

Story. In contrast, Yeh-shua-Jesus' teaching was all about himself and his place in His Story.[4] The contrast was stark and not lost on the crowds or on the increasingly jealous rabbis. Increasingly, the religious leaders started opposing Yeh-shua-Jesus and inadvertently fought on Satan's behalf in the battle for the earth.

Yeh-shua-Jesus was not only hated by the rabbis but also by all those who didn't want things upsetting: all those who didn't want things changing; all those who were unwittingly profiting from God keeping his distance beyond the Doorway leaving them to run his show down on earth—leaving them to promote themselves as God's representatives on earth. These people realized that Yeh-shua-Jesus wasn't just a nice man who wanted to do nice things to them and tell them nice stories. They understood that Yeh-shua-Jesus wanted their lives. He wanted their souls. He wanted them to trust him with their lives—to follow him. And they equally knew that they would never follow him. To do so, would have meant putting themselves lower in the league table of religious power—to support a man who had come to succeed them; who had come to take over. It's not surprising that they inadvertently also started to join the battle against Yeh-shua-Jesus. If they had supported the Messiah-man they were opting for their own demotion—"turkeys voting for Christmas" comes to mind.

Unsurprisingly, very few of the powerful religious leaders openly followed Yeh-shua-Jesus. Some of this was due to the pressure from their peers.[5] Later after Yeh-shua-Jesus' death, a few more started to admit that he was the Messiah,[6] but during Yeh-shua-Jesus' lifetime, the battle lines were increasingly drawn up. Suspicion soon turned to direct opposition which then degenerated into hatred. What these people hated more than anything was the way that Yeh-shua-Jesus fitted the profile of the Messiah-man—it conflicted them. In their heads they wanted the Wonder-man to appear but in their hearts, they knew that if he did arrive, their own power would be eclipsed. Like many of the kings of Isra-El and Judah, they loved power and had forgotten that God was really King. How could they resolve this conflict? Answer—ignore the obvious and pretend that nothing had changed. God might be on earth but ignore him and resume normal service. They wanted to be left alone.

But Yeh-shua-Jesus just wouldn't go away. In the general population, Yeh-shua-Jesus' popularity was growing. True, this was largely due

---

4. Mark 1:22.
5. John 19:38–39.
6. Acts 6:7.

to Yeh-shua-Jesus' amazing displays of super-natural power[7] but it made the religious leaders' opposition to Yeh-shua-Jesus more inexplicable to the crowds and simply increased their personal conflict. As modern humans, we are often the same. We don't want to admit Yeh-shua-Jesus is the Messiah-man but we can't quite bring ourselves to say he was a madman or a conman. So we ignore him or we just pick the bits of his life we like which usually are the bits that don't challenge us too much. Basically we push him to the outer reaches of our life—until that time when we might need him. Up to that point we want to write our own story—live our own lives—just like the religious leaders around Yeh-shua-Jesus. They wanted to write their own story: a story that had them as the bosses; a story that had them doing what they wanted; a story that had them as God's representatives alone on earth; a story that neutralized Yeh-shua-Jesus' influence.

Yeh-shua-Jesus told stories about these "pillars" of the Temple religion. Once he even described them as rebellious tenants who refused to pay rent to the Temple landlord—God, but instead became glorified squatters. In effect he was saying that they were occupying the Doorway to the beyond but refusing to let God in. In Yeh-shua-Jesus' story, the tenants tried to become the bosses, and when the landlord sent his only son to sort them out—they attacked him—and killed him.[8] The religious leaders got the message that they were the tenants and God the landlord and they didn't like it.[9] And they didn't like the idea of Yeh-shua-Jesus being God's Son. They did like the idea of killing him though.

Did Yeh-shua-Jesus try to persuade them of who he was—the Wonder-child now all grown up to be the Messiah-man? No. Instead, he reserved his most caustic words for them. He called them expensive, luxurious coffins—fancy on the outside but full of decomposing, stinking rottenness on the inside.[10] Using the knowledge of Greek drama he gained from the theatre (like the one he may have helped build in Tzippori), he also called them, "hypocrites"[11]—masked actors playing a part—two-faced play actors who wore the masks of kind, caring Godly people but inside were motivated by greed and the desire for power.[12] Yeh-shua-Jesus may well have been the first person to use this Greek theatrical device in a negative pejorative way but it has now become an indispensable part of our language.

7. John 6:26.
8. Matthew 21:31–44.
9. Matthew 21:45–46.
10. Matthew 23:27–28.
11. Matthew 23:13–32.
12. Luke 20:46–47.

The religious leaders fought back. They tried to discredit Yeh-shua-Jesus. They tried a smear campaign on him. They said he was mentally ill. They said he was actually working for Satan. [13] They said he was just a human trying to be God,[14] which was strange because he was the only human ever who didn't try to make himself God because he didn't need to—because he was God. The more he told the truth about himself, the more he confirmed his own death sentence. Behind this power struggle was of course, Satan. Satan fought Yeh-shua-Jesus through these religious men who should have known better. He tempted them to think the unthinkable—that it would be better for everyone if Yeh-shua-Jesus had never existed. And as these official representatives of God on earth fell to the temptation and started to think the unthinkable—they ended up working for God's opposition, Satan. They became the servants of Satan on earth.[15]

To these leaders the man from beyond space was a waste of space. Their jealousy had a disastrous side-effect—they planned to kill the Wonder-child the world had been waiting for. They planned to assassinate the last of the royal bloodline. They planned to waste the Super-star revealed by hundreds of years of His Story. Having God's Son on earth was cramping the religious leaders' style. He had to go.[16] The one who had been used by God to create the Universe: de-created; de-commissioned; deleted.

Of course, making the religious leaders the main opposition to Yeh-shua-Jesus was a stroke of genius by Satan. It confused people. They didn't know who to believe. They didn't know who was right and who was wrong. Was right wrong or wrong right? Yeh-shua-Jesus knew Satan's tactic and called it, "the unforgiveable sin."[17]

Why did the religious leaders allow themselves to be manipulated? Why were they so blind to Yeh-shua-Jesus being the Super-star of His Story? It was all Satan's work. He was playing a blinder. It was his finest moment. He had organized an incredibly surprising human opposition to Yeh-shua-Jesus.

If this human opposition wasn't enough, Satan continued to attack Yeh-shua-Jesus with paranormal powers as well. Around Yeh-shua-Jesus there was a level of invisible paranormal spiritual warfare greater than has ever happened before or since. But Yeh-shua-Jesus continued to use his super-natural out-of-this-world power for others. He continued to use it

13. Matthew 12:22–24; John 8:48–59.
14. John 5:18.
15. John 8:42–47.
16. Matthew 26:3–5; Mark 3:6; 14:1; John 7:1; 12:10 etc..
17. Mark 3:28–30.

to roll back disease. He continued to use it to limit the influence of Satan on God's earth.[18] He continued to use it to break open the hole he had made in the fabric of the Universe and let the power from beyond pour through.

Messiah-man v Satan: a battle for the hearts and minds of humanity; a battle for the "souls" of humanity; a battle for who was the boss for earthly humanity; a battle for who was the boss inside the Universe. The battle was a battle for the title of the one who had the most power and influence over humans. Was it God or his alter-ego, Satan? It was true that often, Yeh-shua-Jesus had crowds around him: he was even admired by a good number of the crowds but it was also true that he was only followed by a few. Bit like today—known and admired by many but only truly followed by a few. The few that did follow Yeh-shua-Jesus were generally the poor and the unknown—hard bitten fishermen, prostitutes, beggars and lepers and even the tax collectors for the hated occupying Romans.[19] It was a small band of unlikely supporters—a remnant. The old prophecies started to become true as a few of Family Abraham accepted Yeh-shua-Jesus as the Wonder-man—the one they had been waiting for—a green shoot growing out of the felled stump of Abraham's Family Tree.[20]

But for every one who followed; many more turned against him. Even those who had seen him grow up as young man in Nazareth started to hate him with a passion. They refuted his claims to be the one spoken about by the Mouthpieces of old and tried unsuccessfully to lynch him.[21] Increasingly the authorities looked for an opportunity to finish off the job the Nazarenes had failed to finish.

The battle came to a head one Thursday night.

---

18. Mark 3:20–27; John 12:31–32.
19. Matthew 9:9–13.
20. Isaiah 6:13.
21. Luke 4:14–30.

# 53

## Long Weekend

NOT ANY OLD THURSDAY—BUT a "Pass-Over" Thursday—that time of year when Family Abraham celebrated the Exodus: the Great Escape; the time when death passed safely over their houses in Egypt around thirteen hundred years earlier; the time when those who kept them hostage in Egypt were hit by the terrible plague of death when the eldest male, human or animal, in every family died—except in Family Abraham homes.[1]

This Pass-Over was celebrated every year afterwards, with a meal—a symbolic meal. Each course of the meal reminded the diners of what happened: salt water to remind them of their ancestors' tears; bitter herbs to remind them of the bitterness of slavery endured by their ancestors; fruit, nut and wine paste to remind them of the mud their ancestors had to use for bricks; flat bread to remind them of the bread their ancestors ate in a rush without time to let it rise; lamb to remind them of the lamb their ancestors killed to provide the blood that marked out their houses as ones to be passed-over by death.

Yeh-shua-Jesus ate this Pass-Over meal as his last meal with his friends, but shockingly, Yeh-shua-Jesus twisted the ancient tradition. Yeh-shua-Jesus changed the traditional symbolic meaning of the meal.[2] He made himself the center. He made himself the lamb. He made his blood the mark to save the people. He claimed that he was going to be the eldest son who died in the place of all the people of Isra-El. When he tore the flat bread apart he said it was his body being torn up.[3] When he poured out the wine, he said that it was his blood being poured out.[4] He told his friends that from now on it was going to different. Instead of celebrating Pass-Over; instead of celebrating Moses; instead of celebrating the escape from Egypt they

---

1. Exodus 12:1–42.
2. Matthew 26:17–19.
3. Matthew 26:26.
4. Matthew 26:27–28.

were going to celebrate him instead. Or to be precise—they were going to celebrate his death—every time in the future when they ate the Pass-Over, they were to remember his sacrifice—his death. That's how Yeh-shua-Jesus wanted his life to be remembered. This was not just slightly morbid—it was shocking; offensive; revisionist. Yeh-shua-Jesus saw his body broken and his blood poured out as eclipsing the most important event in the history of Isra-El—putting it in the shade. In this new Pass-Over, an eldest son would die—but not an Egyptian son this time—but God's eldest and only Son: not a lamb this time—but the Lamb of God.[5] His death wasn't about releasing Isra-El from Egypt. Instead, his death was to release humanity from its addiction to trying to make itself God. His death was to release humanity from Satan's spell. His death was to release humanity from the cycle of failure begun with Adam.

But had Yeh-shua-Jesus overstepped the mark? Had he had gone too far? He was claiming His Story to be his own personal story. He was claiming to be God. Too much for one of his helpers, Judas Iscariot, who walked out in protest.[6] This man may have been a terrorist as his name "Iscariot" may be a version of "Sicarius" which was a dagger in the Roman language. This was an offensive weapon favored by a group of Family Abraham assassins. Judas—one of the Sicarii—Judas—one of the direct action group opposed to Roman rule; Judas who may have been fed up with Yeh-shua-Jesus' disregard for pure Family Abraham tradition and history; fed up by Yeh-shua-Jesus' reworked Pass-Over. But he probably was equally fed up of Yeh-shua-Jesus' talk of Kingdom which didn't involve leading a cell of terrorists to attack the occupying Roman forces and leader: fed up of Yeh-shua-Jesus' talk of death but not one sustained in a heroic bloody battle for freedom fought against the Roman forces who had invaded the Promised Land. To Judas, Yeh-shua-Jesus was a traitor to the cause he thought he had signed up for. Yeh-shua-Jesus was a traitor to his own principles.

So Judas took direct action against the traitor. Judas, whose name ironically is now for ever linked with being a traitor himself—betrayed Yeh-shua-Jesus to his enemies.[7] Of course it could have just been plain simple greed. There is some evidence that as treasurer for Yeh-shua-Jesus' inner group, he was dipping into the group's petty cash.[8] It is true that he sold the information on Yeh-shua-Jesus to the religious authorities—the where and the when. The "where" was a popular place for Yeh-shua-Jesus and his

---

5. 1 Corinthians 5:7b.
6. John 13:30.
7. Matthew 26:14–16.
8. John 12:4–6.

team—a local park called Gethsemane: a park full of olive trees and housing an olive oil press. The "when" was straight after the offensive Pass-Over meal hijacked by Yeh-shua-Jesus. Judas leaked the information all for the price paid for a common slave—thirty pieces of silver.[9] The money probably was a temptation. Judas may have wanted political change but wasn't averse to making a bit of money at the same time. As such he was a mercenary. Money and power motivated him. How could such a man understand Yeh-shua-Jesus who had all the power in the Universe but never used it for himself?

The secret signal in the dark of the garden of Gethsemane was a kiss: a greeting between friends; a sign of trust; betrayed; corrupted; abused.[10] Through this betrayed, debased sign of friendship, Yeh-shua-Jesus was arrested;[11] put on trial by the religious leaders and found guilty of claiming to be God.[12] He was sentenced to death.[13] High irony—God's Son sentenced to death for acting as if he were God. But Yeh-shua-Jesus wasn't acting—he was just honestly living out the truth. Truth and honesty: two concepts not familiar to the religious leaders. They didn't want the blame for killing Mr Popular, even though it was their idea. So they took Yeh-shua-Jesus to the Roman civil authorities so they could do their dirty work for them.[14] No wonder Yeh-shua-Jesus called them two-faced hypocrites! They blackmailed the weak Roman governor with the threat of civil unrest—of mass protests.[15] This governor, Pilate, couldn't afford more trouble in his part of the Roman Empire. He was already getting a name for himself due to his insensitive actions towards Family Abraham—actions which had already provoked civil unrest. He twisted and turned on the religious leaders' skewer trying desperately to do the right thing—especially as the Doorway seems to have opened into his wife's dreams—telling her to warn her husband of the danger he was in judging Yeh-shua-Jesus.[16] As a result, Pilate sent Yeh-shua-Jesus to the son of the evil King Herod—the king who had tried to cut off the Wonder-child at birth. His son, King Herod Antipas, was in charge of the land around Nazareth and Pilate hoped that he would take responsibility for his wayward citizen. This Herod had already beheaded John the Baptist for daring to criticize him—but this Herod didn't want to take responsi-

9. Matthew 26:15.
10. Luke 22:47-48.
11. Luke 22:54.
12. Luke 22:66-71.
13. Mark 14:63-64.
14. John 18:28—19:16.
15. John 19:8-12.
16. Matthew 27:19.

bility for the Messiah-man's death—he only wanted to be entertained by Yeh-shua-Jesus' super-natural power—a request that Yeh-shua-Jesus totally refused to grant.[17] So he sent him back again to Pilate. Pilate, after a half-hearted attempt to give an amnesty to Yeh-shua-Jesus just capitulated and gave in. In a desperate attempt to defend his own integrity, he invented a new activity—washing your hands. Not cleanliness—just cowardliness. He dipped his hands in a bowl of water and said that he "washed his hands" of responsibility for Yeh-shua-Jesus' fate.[18] And then in one last attempt at semi-justice, Pilate (who in his heart knew that Yeh-shua-Jesus was innocent) beat him up, hoping that this would satisfy the religious leaders.[19] But they wanted the final solution—death.

Pilate washed his hands of responsibility. But by his weakness to support truth and honesty, he executed an innocent man. His inability to support truth and honesty executed God's Son. Despite the water, Yeh-shua-Jesus' blood is still on his hands. One philosopher once said, "All that is necessary for the triumph of evil is that good men do nothing."[20] Calling Pilate, "good," may be a slur on goodness, but the point is the same. He wrongly found Yeh-shua-Jesus guilty of treason: of trying to start a revolution to overthrow Roman rule; of challenging Caesar; of being one man taking on the Roman Empire. It was a ridiculous charge. But there again—weirdly true despite this being unknown to Pilate. Yeh-shua-Jesus was the most powerful human who has ever lived. He could have taken over the whole world with his super-natural powers. He could have smashed the Roman Empire with his super-natural powers. Against his power, the Roman Empire was simply an idol with feet of clay, waiting to be bowled over by the massive rock of God's Messiah-man.[21] Within three hundred years, the Caesar of the great Roman Empire was going to give in to the Kingdom of Yeh-shua-Jesus. The leader of the most powerful Empire in the world was himself to become a follower of Yeh-shua-Jesus. Constantine the Great, bowed the knee to the Messiah-man. His motives may not have been completely pure, but it showed where the new balance of power lay.

The Roman Empire is now long gone. But the Kingdom of Yeh-shua-Jesus remains: strong; international; growing. But despite this success, the fact remains to Judas and Pilate's shame that this victory was not built on

17. Luke 23:5–12.
18. Matthew 27:24.
19. John 19:1–6.
20. Often attributed to Edmund Burke (Irish orator, philosopher, & politician 1729–1797).
21. Daniel 2:31–45.

Yeh-shua-Jesus attacking the Roman Empire. Yeh-shua-Jesus never wielded a sword. In fact he was totally opposed to violence. [22] He believed that those who used the sword died by the sword.[23] Despite his pacifism he was still accused of being a revolutionary. It was a preposterous accusation and yet strangely true. He started a revolution but not a violent revolution. It was not a coup; not civil unrest but a revolution of freedom—God returning to free his people who had been kidnapped by Satan. God was to free humans kidnapped since day one when humanity did the wrong thing; kidnapped by their own desire to do their own thing; kidnapped by their hatred of being told what to do—even if it was by their own Creator; kidnapped by their belief that they could be their own god; kidnapped by the lies put about by Satan.[24]

For trying to rescue humanity from being held hostage to Satan, Pilate condemned Yeh-shua-Jesus to death on a cross—one of the cruelest forms of execution ever invented. Crucifixion was reserved only for the lowest of lows: reserved only for people who needed making an example of; reserved only for people who needed to be humiliated. The humble God-human humiliated.[25] The humble God-human tortured physically by whipping his skin until his intestines were exposed; tortured emotionally by being mocked—dressed as a King in only a regal purple robe with a crown of sharp sticks jammed into his skull;[26] tortured psychologically by being made to carry his own cross-piece—to use his last remaining strength to drag his own execution gibbet to the place called, "The Skull," where crucifixions took place;[27] tortured mentally by abuse shouted at him by his enemies standing only feet away as his body retched for breath pulling on his nailed ankle and wrists;[28] tortured spiritually by knowing his mother was watching his life end, his mother who along with God began his life.[29]

But maybe more than all of this was the torture of appearing a failure—of looking as if Satan had won. Possibly in his weakened state he even felt a failure—that Satan had the victory. It must have looked and felt like God had lost power on earth. There was no obvious sign of God's intervention. Yeh-shua-Jesus was nailed publicly to a rough wooden cross outside the city—not far from the municipal rubbish tip—Gehenna—a place which

22. Matthew 26:47–56.
23. Matthew 26:52.
24. John 8:44.
25. Galatians 3:13; Deuteronomy 3:23.
26. Mark 15:15–20.
27. John 19:17.
28. Matthew 27:39–44.
29. John 19:25.

Yeh-shua-Jesus himself had likened to hell on several occasions.[30] It certainly looked as if God's great plan had ended up in the waste-tip of Hell. God had seemingly retreated behind the Doorway and left his Son to die. It is no coincidence that Yeh-shua-Jesus in his last moments shouted, "My God my God where are you now!" quoting one of the pain-filled songs of his ancestor King David.[31]

Just before he died he enigmatically shouted, "It is finished!"[32] His Story finished—completed or just ended? It was a Story with arguably millions of years in the preparation; thousands of years of plot and now finally finished. But was it a happy ending or a disappointing ending? It was dramatic but what had been proved by His Story? Maybe that humanity had turned against their Creator? That humanity listened more to Satan than their Creator? That God was a heroic failure? That Yeh-shua-Jesus was nothing more than an idealistic inspiration to humanity? That Yeh-shua-Jesus, even though he was the greatest most unselfish person on earth, was still no match for human selfishness? That humanity had used their God given ability to choose, but had used that ability to choose to ignore God and there was nothing Yeh-shua-Jesus could do about it? That God's great experiment in giving his greatest creation, humanity, the gift of freedom had failed?

Then Yeh-shua-Jesus died. No doubt, God was still alive through the Doorway, but he might as well have been dead. His Wonder-man on earth was dead—a corpse certified as dead by hard-bitten, death-experienced Roman soldiers.[33]

Their post-mortem confirmed that the life of the Messiah was totally extinguished. This surely marked the end of His Story. But for those who knew His Story, it may have offered something strangely significant—maybe even suggesting the slightest green shoot of hope. The Roman soldiers didn't break Yeh-shua-Jesus legs to speed up his death because they had confirmed that he was already dead. This bone-breaking action was sometimes used to stop the victim being able to pull up on their legs to inflate their chest cavity in order to breathe—it meant the crucified person died of suffocation quickly. But the lack of this leg-breaking by the soldiers strangely played into the hands of His Story. The lamb of the Pass-Over meal for over a thousand years had never had any of its bones broken by the strict rules imposed

---

30. Matthew 5:22, 29–30; 10:28; 18:9; 23:25, 33.
31. Matthew 27:46; Psalm 22:1.
32. John 19:30.
33. John 19:31–37.

by Moses.[34] Maybe Yeh-shua-Jesus was the "Lamb of God" after all.[35] A few hundred years after the original Pass-Over, King David in one of his famous songs from his outlaw period possibly pondering on this protection of the Pass-Over lamb said that God's chosen ones, even though they might suffer, would "not have one of their bones broken."[36] Maybe Yeh-shua-Jesus was the chosen one.[37]

But these tiny rays of hope were not shining on anyone as Yeh-shua-Jesus' body hung limp and lifeless on the cross. God's hope of persuading and enabling his greatest creation, humans, to choose to live with him through the Doorway in the Eden outside of the Universe was dead.

Just like the Super-star of His Story

---

34. Exodus 12:46; Numbers 9:12.
35. John 1:29.
36. Psalm 34:20.
37. Acts 10:42.

## 54

## Black Hole

IN FIVE BILLION YEARS time, the sun will die. It will use up all its hydrogen; change into a red giant; burn the earth to a cinder, and slowly die. It is almost beyond our imagination that the sun that gives us life will one day die, but it will happen.

His Story is clear that the Wonder-child, before he was human, existed with God—that before he was born on earth, he was alive.[1] And one thing he did before his human birth was to put God's creation plan into practice. When at the beginning of time, God powerfully said, "Let the Universe come into existence,"[2] the being that we now know as the super-human Yeh-shua-Jesus, was that powerful word. Many years later, pondering on this, Yeh-shua-Jesus' closest friend called him simply, "The Word."[3]

It is almost beyond our imagination that this Son who gave this Universe life one day was killed inside his Universe, but it happened. Two thousand years ago, the one who arranged for the sun to be born did die. And when he died, the sun he helped create died prematurely. The sun went out on strike as "The Word" died.[4] The sun stopped shining in memory of the one who made God's word, "Let there be light" happen. The sun was presumably still shining in the rest of our Solar System beyond the earth just as God was still existing outside the Doorway into the Universe. But as Yeh-shua-Jesus died, the light stopped reaching earth—an eclipse—like God's influence on earth was eclipsed by Satan's machinations. The light of the sun was sucked into a black hole of grief—not reaching earth. The center of our solar system, the sun, reflected the fate of its Creator. It went out. It failed. Darkness had won. The fate of the earth hung in the balance.

The only glimmer of hope for those able to see it was a mysteriously torn curtain. This was no ordinary curtain, but the heavy curtain sealing the

1. Colossians 1:15–17; Hebrews 1:1–3a.
2. Genesis 1:3.
3. John 1:1–5, 10, 14.
4. Luke 23:44–45a.

doorway between the most sacred Holy of Holies room in the Temple and the rest of the building. This curtain was torn in two from top to bottom at the moment of Yeh-shua-Jesus' death.[5] This curtain was the divider between the rest of the Temple and the Holy of Holies—the room where only one man once a year could enter. The man?—the High Priest—God's top Go-Between. The time?—the Day of Atonement—the day when the High Priest took the people's bad actions and choices and symbolically placed then on a pure goat that was then sent into the wilderness never to return—the archetypal Scapegoat.[6] The High Priest attempted this transference by entering the room that was seen as "Heaven on earth"—as the room connecting earth with beyond the Doorway. It is said that the top Go-Between wore a rope around him in case as he entered the Holy of Holies the awful awe-fulness of the eternal overcame him. The rope allowed him to be dragged out without endangering another life in his rescue.

At the moment of Yeh-shua-Jesus' death, that awesome room was ripped opened—the Doorway was revealed. Beyond the Universe had broken into the here and now of human existence. Or to put it another way: humanity had broken into the Holy of Holies. A force had torn the barrier down destroying the wall between inside and outside of the Universe. But was that tearing caused by just the destructive power of a gust of gale-force storm wind as the stormy dark eclipse took hold outside? Or was that tearing caused by no meteorological phenomenon but part of His Story linked mysteriously to the death of Yeh-shua-Jesus?

If so, it was part of a series of events that suggested that normal human existence and the invisible world beyond the Universe had again coalesced—crashed together. Apparitions of dead people were seen to briefly appear out of their tombs. Something traumatic had happened to the normal space-time boundaries. Time itself was flexing under the strain of Yeh-shua-Jesus' death.[7]

These things may have all happened at the point of Yeh-shua-Jesus' death but Yeh-shua-Jesus couldn't take any of the credit—he was dead. Like any dead human being, Yeh-shua-Jesus couldn't do anything. His body was so dead, it needed other humans to move it away from hanging on the cross. His body was taken down from the cross and put into a rock tomb owned by a rich secret follower of Yeh-shua-Jesus. This brave man fulfilled Isa-Yah's

---

5. Luke 23:45.
6. Hebrews 9:3–7.
7. Matthew 27:51–53.

ancient prophecy regarding the location of the Messiah's body after death.[8] This brave man took his last chance to show Yeh-shua-Jesus his support.[9]

But the last chance of humanity escaping death was dead. The Wonderman, who had come through the Doorway from the outside of the Universe to the inside to lead humanity back through the Doorway to their Father Creator, was dead. The way back was blocked. The Doorway locked—again. Just like when Adam and Eve had been banned from living for ever with God in Eden.[10] God had lost. His Story was a dead-end. His Story ended in the tomb owned by a rich man.

You can still visit what claims to be Yeh-shua-Jesus' rock tomb. It still exists—preserved intact. Its preservation is thanks to the Roman Emperor Constantine's U-turn to follow Yeh-shua-Jesus as the Messiah three hundred years later. He ordered the demolition of a Roman temple built by Emperor Hadrian (of Hadrian's Wall fame) on top of the site of the tomb in the year we now know as 325 A.D. Before the demolition, he had left his mother in charge of one of the first archaeological digs to find the site. Apparently, Helena discovered the tomb of Jesus as well as (allegedly) the original cross that Yeh-shua-Jesus died on. This discovery might be a bit of a stretch, but the tomb may well be original. Helena arranged for all the rock around the tomb to be cut away, removed and shipped off, leaving a stone grotto on its own. Now it has a church built over it. Thousands of worshippers queue to enter through its wax-dripping, candle-lit entrance in Jeru-Salem. But no-one ever sees Yeh-shua-Jesus. His dead body has long gone.

Two thousand years later—none of the visitors would seriously expect Yeh-shua-Jesus' body to be there in any form you could recognize. But the truth is that it had actually disappeared after less than three days of being put in there—buried on Friday: disappeared by Sunday.

Had Yeh-shua-Jesus' earlier unbelievable prediction in the Temple about his body being rebuilt after his death been right all along?[11]

8. Isaiah 53:9.
9. John 19:38–42.
10. Genesis 3:23–24.
11. John 2:19–22.

## 55

## Impossible or Improbable?

YEH-SHUA-JESUS' BODY MISSING—THE GREATEST mystery of human history—the most important missing person case of the human race. Where had the body of Yeh-shua-Jesus gone? If stolen, why wasn't it returned? It would have turned in a great profit to the robbers—if not from the enemies of Yeh-shua-Jesus, then from the superstitious black-market in crucifixion nails and paraphernalia sold for allegedly medicinal reasons. If a mistake (as in the wrong tomb investigated), why was the right body never found? If a hoax by Yeh-shua-Jesus' followers, why didn't they admit it when faced later with dying for their belief? If a botched execution (as in Yeh-shua-Jesus didn't totally die), why did the Roman soldiers who were past masters at executing people mess up? Even in recent years in the U.S.A., people have survived lethal injections—one man in 2009 apparently even tried to help his executioners find a vein for the lethal injection after they had tried eighteen times over a period of two hours and failed. In 2006 one man had to have two lethal injections to end his life. But however botched—death was always the end result.

But despite this, what if Yeh-shua-Jesus wasn't dead as a result of some amazing catalogue of events and mistakes which are beyond our understanding and instead ended up unconscious in the tomb? Even if he then later revived in the tomb, how did he roll back the large rock blocking the entrance to the tomb and walk off as if nothing had happened—past guards who had been placed there to make sure the body was not messed around with?[1]

There is no simple answer to the disappearance of Yeh-shua-Jesus' body. As the great, fictitious, London detective, Sherlock Holmes, once said, "How often have I said to you that when you have eliminated the impossible,

---

1. Matthew 27:57–65.

whatever remains, however improbable, must be the truth?"[2] What was the improbable answer? That the rock tomb had been converted into a Doorway not just from the inside of the Universe to the outside; not just from earth to heaven; not just from time to eternity but also from death to life. If God could create the Universe out of nothing; if God could create human life out of dust; if God could cause the God-human, Yeh-shua-Jesus, to be born on earth; then maybe he could reverse the effect of death. Maybe he could re-create human life? Maybe he could change death from a full stop into a comma? Change death from a cul-de-sac into a motorway? Change death from a locked door into a Doorway? Maybe God is at his most powerful when all hope, all life, is gone. Just maybe God had orchestrated the greatest disappearing act of all time—the most important disappearance of all time. The whole dead body of Yeh-shua-Jesus—gone—dissolved; leaving the head wrappings still wrapped separately from the grave clothes that had been around the body. It was as if the body had melted out—the body atomized by a power so immense it could wake the dead—each atom of the body transported through the Doorway out of the Universe.[3]

This may sound impressive, but how do we know if all this cosmic eternal speculation is true? Surely a missing corpse is much more likely due to human error or crime than divine intervention? When you lose your car keys you don't immediately assume the fairies or "the Borrowers" have been at work (unless of course, you're unstable). So—what evidence is there of resurrection rather than relocation?

There is one other key piece of evidence. The grave wasn't just miraculously empty—the resurrection is not just an argument based on the disappearance of evidence, it is also based on the appearance of evidence. Yeh-shua-Jesus was seen alive—the atoms of his body reconstituted into a death-proof body. He was not only seen in the weeks following his death, but also a year or two later by the famous follower of Yeh-shua-Jesus, Paul[4] who had up to that point tortured anyone who claimed Yeh-shua-Jesus was still alive.[5]

But the main activity by the alive-again Yeh-shua-Jesus was concentrated in the first few weeks after his death. His new death-proof body allowed him to keep popping in and out of the Doorway for several weeks. He was seen by eye-witnesses as alive on earth. He was the same Yeh-shua-Jesus but different: transformed; transmuted; resurrected. This new human body

---

2. Sherlock Holmes in *The Sign of the Four*, Ch. 6 (1890) by Sir Conan Doyle..
3. John 20:3–9.
4. 1 Corinthians 15:8.
5. Acts of the Apostles 9:1.

was able to eat; able to walk and talk; able to make breakfast; able to be recognized—with the same body—the same tell-tale marks; the same way of doing things.[6] Basically this body was not a ghost. But it wasn't just a normal limited human body either. Yeh-shua-Jesus walked into locked rooms without a key. Yeh-shua-Jesus seemed to materialize out of thin air. He simply opened the Doorway between the inside and outside of the Universe at will. To the earth-bound humans it looked like he was simply magically appearing and disappearing. But the truth was that Yeh-shua-Jesus was travelling between the two dimensions—time and eternity. He was being allowed back and forth through the Doorway to prove to his followers that this last dynamic display of his super-natural power was so powerful it outshone all of his nature-altering miracles so far. It was a display, so overwhelming, that even the hardest, most cynical human would have to stop and take notice. This was the greatest display of power in His Story: Yeh-shua-Jesus back to earth to show off his new death-proof life; Yeh-shua-Jesus back to earth to prove the power of God—even over death; Yeh-shua-Jesus back to earth to attract humans away from Satan to God.

Yeh-shua-Jesus went back to his friends first. A couple of his friends had their eyes opened in an encounter with a "stranger" on the road back to their village called Emmaus.[7] It was the Sunday after Jesus' death on the Friday. It was late—they invited the stranger back in for a meal. When the "stranger" broke the bread and said a prayer of thanksgiving their eyes were opened. They'd seen and heard this thanksgiving before—many times. They saw the truth. The "stranger" was Yeh-shua-Jesus. Immediately he disappeared into thin air—back through the Doorway.

They had seen in front of them the answer to the problems caused by the first meal on earth—Adam and Eve's stolen fruit meal. That first meal caused human eyes to be opened to the possibilities of rebellion against God and had ended in the Doorway from the outside to the inside of the Universe being locked. But this meal in Emmaus opened another couple's eyes to the possibility of God's answer to that rebellion and ended with the Doorway unlocked: human-God relationships renewed; the Door opened; the new better version of Eden accessible.

This wasn't the only sighting of the new Yeh-shua-Jesus. Yeh-shua-Jesus continued to be recognized by his friends and even by five hundred people at the same time.[8] He was able to appear and disappear—able to use

---

6. John 20:11–20; 21:1–13; Matthew 28:1–10; Luke 24:36–44.
7. Luke 24:13–35.
8. 1 Corinthians 15:6.

the Doorway to circumvent solid objects like walls.[9] But he wasn't sub-human like a sub-atomic particle. He was super-human—super-real. He was the same but super-same.

These appearances proved that Yeh-shua-Jesus was no soul floating around having escaped a dead body: this was no ghostly presence living outside of a cadaver; this was no life source growing out of the shell of a corpse. This was something brand new never seen before—resurrection. This was not a resuscitation—not a near-death experience—but a full blown resurrection from human death to a new kind of human life. This was death given an out-of-this-Universe kiss of life. This was death healed by the one who created life and death. This was death taken back to the eternal workshop and reworked into a new form of life by the master mechanic. This was death giving birth to a new version of humanity. This was humanity recycled not re-incarnated—not put back into ordinary human form—but death becoming the Doorway leading humanity towards super-humanity. This wasn't a human body transported, molecule by molecule Star-Trek style, from one earthly place to another, but a human body transported through the Doorway from earth to heaven: from mortality to immortality; from time to eternal timelessness; from inside to outside of the Universe and reformed into a super-human death-proof person. This was the start of a new human life.

Thirty years earlier, God had proved that he could enter earth through the Doorway by becoming human. Now he had proved that he could take the human body and transform it into a body that could travel back through the Doorway and exist outside of time—outside of the Universe. This was metamorphosis—the earth-bound caterpillar of Adam style old humanity changed into the butterfly of Yeh-shua-Jesus' new style humanity.

Death had simply become a cocoon—not a dead end.

---

9. John 20:18–20, 26.

# 56

## The Greatest Miracle of Yeh-shua-Jesus —Yeh-shua-Jesus Never Did

YEH-SHUA-JESUS' RESURRECTION DIDN'T JUST transform death—it had even wider implications. It proved that God had power over Satan. Like the fable of Job, God had won his bet with Satan. His Wonder-man had been strong enough to resist Satan's temptation. The duel between God and Satan had been won by God.

But how does the resurrection prove this? The greatest show of Yeh-shua-Jesus' super-natural power—his resurrection—wasn't technically caused by Yeh-shua-Jesus' super-natural power. Yeh-shua-Jesus' had been dead and buried and unable to effect any change on himself. His resurrection was thanks to God's direct intervention. Would God have intervened by resurrecting Yeh-shua-Jesus if Yeh-shua-Jesus during his life had given in to Satan and turned to the dark side? Surely, God would have left him in the tomb—dead[1]—just another false Messiah resigned to the dusty pages of the history books never to be remembered apart from specialist historians in ivory-towered university libraries. As it is—Yeh-shua-Jesus is arguably the most famous human to have ever lived. God resurrected him because he had been victorious over Satan's best temptations. God trusted him and Yeh-shua-Jesus had not let him down.

But God didn't simply want to prove that he could defeat Satan by bringing one human—however special—through the Doorway from earth to heaven. He wanted to bring the whole of humanity through the Doorway—it was his gift to the whole of the human race. He didn't just want to blow the doors off death for his Son, but blow the whole of death apart—for the whole of humanity. Just as God had brought the whole of Family Abraham back from Egypt to the Promised Land through Moses, God was going to bring the whole of Family Humanity back from earth to the Promised Land beyond the Universe—and all through Yeh-shua-Jesus. He planned a

---

1. Philippians 2:8–11.

new great escape—a new Exodus—an even greater Exodus—an Exodus to end all Exoduses.

Humanity didn't deserve this second chance, but God wanted to offer this new great escape to all humans. It was God's gift of grace to all humans who managed to snap out of their hypnotic trance induced by Satan and follow his new Moses, Yeh-shua-Jesus. The problem then and now is that humanity is just like Family Abraham. Some of Family Abraham when being rescued from Egypt were resistant to Moses.[2] Whilst on their Exodus many of Family Abraham wished they were back in Egypt—especially when water was scarce and the food predictable.[3] They dragged their feet about being dragged across the desert and even fantasized about how great life was back in Egypt. Their selective memory which expunged slavery from their recall of the past is similar to the way that many humans prefer not to be woken up to reality of Satan's tactics—woken up to their need to be rescued. Humanity would often prefer to sleep-walk into living out a second best life—a pale and poor imitation of reality—rather than admit they need help. Just as men are notoriously bad at asking for directions, many humans (whether male or female) would rather be lost in slavery in Egypt rather than ask for the way to freedom in God's Promised Land. Satan's hypnotic trance lulls them into being happy to play Russian roulette with their existence after death. Satan's hypnotic trance lulls them into being happy not to ask why they exist.

Yeh-shua-Jesus' resurrection was the cosmic finger-snap that would awaken humanity from this Satanic hypnotic trance. His resurrection would rescue humanity.[4] But how was the stirring message of Yeh-shua-Jesus' resurrection going to be spread across all humanity from one small corner of Roman Empire to the whole world across time and space? The solution was to use Yeh-shua-Jesus' secret weapon—his friends. These friends were the eye-witnesses to his born again-ness. They were the believers in his resurrection. But how would Yeh-shua-Jesus train, prepare, and inspire his small group of friends for this "Mission Impossible"?

He breathed on them.[5]

---

2. Exodus 5:21.
3. Exodus 16:1–3; 17:3.
4. Hebrews 2:14–15.
5. John 20:19–23.

# 57

## Soul-mates

BREATHING OVER PEOPLE IS not recommended. Breathing over people is unhealthy because we pass on a little bit of ourselves through our breath. Or to be exact we pass on some of our germs.

About seventy-five to one hundred different kinds of germs live in each person's mouth out of a total of seven hundred possible ones that enjoy living in human mouths. Only three hundred of these have been named. Apparently you have more bacteria in your mouth than cells in your bodies.

Yeh-shua-Jesus breathed on his friends—shared himself with them. Why?—to pass on his germs and make them ill?—no. To make them strong?—yes. In the language of Family Abraham as well as the Greeks, breath and spirit are the same word. Your breath keeps you alive: your spirit is the invisible power that keeps the real you alive. As breath is life to your physical body: spirit is life to your soul. Yeh-shua-Jesus breathed on his friends to give them the invisible power that made him—him.[1] He shared his life spirit: the spirit that made him the unique Messiah-man; the spirit that made him powerful; that made him the first of the new version of human beings.

He explained what he was doing before he breathed on them. "Receive the Spirit from beyond the Universe."[2] This wouldn't just make his friends powerful, it was going to change who they were. It was going to make them like him. Just as someone's invisible spirit makes them who they are; receiving an alien spirit from beyond the Universe makes you different: other; removed; "in this world but not of this world," as Yeh-shua-Jesus called it;[3] in the Universe but open to the outside of the Universe. In one word: holy; living earth side of the Doorway but living as if you were on the other side; living cheek by jowl with the whole of humanity but set apart from the rest

---

1. John 20:19–23.
2. John 20:22.
3. John 15:19; 16:33; 17:14, 16.

of humanity—separate but linked to a smaller group of humanity through the Spirit of Yeh-shua-Jesus.

So, as the friends received the same life-breath as Yeh-shua-Jesus, they became linked with him—not at a D.N.A. genetic level but at a deeper than D.N.A. level—at the soul-level. He wanted Soul-mates—a phrase which means many things to many people. The American writer and soul mate guru, Richard Bach, has said that, "a soul mate is someone who has locks that fit our keys, and keys to fit our locks."[4] It is someone who makes us complete: someone who is connected with us on a level deeper than friendship, deeper than even blood or genetics; someone who shares our soul—our private place—whose invisible essence lives in our soul and our invisible essence lives in their soul. Soul-mates are closer than siblings. When Yeh-shua-Jesus breathed on his friends, they became Soul-mates: brothers and sisters but on a level deeper than siblings; even closer than identical twins despite their alleged telepathic link.

But just like germs passed on via breath take a while to affect the body, the Spirit shared by Yeh-shua-Jesus took a few weeks to alter the humans he had breathed over. The full unique transfer of the Spirit from Yeh-shua-Jesus to his friends couldn't take place until Yeh-shua-Jesus had been released from needing this power. The hand-over of power would only take place when Yeh-shua-Jesus was ready for his final goodbye and last exit via the Doorway—until the time when his unique Spirit wasn't needed by him any longer after he left earth, in fact, in forty days.[5] Up to that point there would be nearly six weeks of limbo-living for Yeh-shua-Jesus—of living inside and outside the Universe.

Eventually, his final goodbye came with all his new Soul-mates watching. He travelled through the Doorway from time to eternal—from inside to outside of the Universe. He did this by surfing out of the worldly dimension on an ethereal cloud.[6] He left his friends gaping: he left his friends waiting; but he left his friends in no doubt he had left—that he had ascended up into the higher life beyond the Universe.

Some people worry about why he ascended. Why up? In 1961 the Russian, Yuri Gagarin, became officially the first ever human being in space—the first human ever to leave earth (apart from Yeh-shua-Jesus two thousand

---

4. When asked in a workshop presented with his then wife, the actress, Leslie Parrish, how somebody could recognize when they have found their soul mate.

5. John 7:38–39.

6. Acts 1:9; Luke 24:45–53.

years earlier and Eli-Yah[7] before him and Enoch[8] before him, of course!) Whilst Gagarin orbited the earth he famously commented on not finding God or Heaven. Not exactly a scientific, definitive assertion but nonetheless not unsurprising. The Doorway isn't up there. The Doorway can't be found somewhere in the sky or outer atmosphere of earth. But if that is right—why did Yeh-shua-Jesus go up? For those who worry about this—what direction would they have chosen for his departure: down or maybe sideways? Yeh-shua-Jesus had to physically leave or his friends would never have stopped searching for him instead of getting on with their new life as Soul-mates. Dematerialization—disappearing into thin air would have left Yeh-shua-Jesus' friends on a continual search—like Eli-Yah's colleagues seven hundred years earlier, when he was whisked off through the Doorway.[9] Yeh-shua-Jesus needed to be seen to physically leave earth taking his human body with him. He needed to be seen disappearing into the distance of the outer-limits of the earth.

When he left: he took his human experiences: he took his human memories; he took his human scars; he took his human emotions; he took his human fears. But he left with his 100 percent tried and tested new model human body. The Son of God's body now included the human genome. Family God now was partly human. New style humanity was now living outside the Universe. New style humanity was now living beyond the Doorway—for the first time ever.

One day this radical new human state, would be available to all his Soul-mates. One day—in fact, on a day that had become known as "The Day of the Lord" and seen by the Mouthpieces of the Lord for several hundred years beforehand—the time when our old model Universe will end and the new model perfect Universe will begin.[10] On that day His Story will be revealed as just the prologue and introduction of the true never-ending story which will take place beyond the Doorway of the Universe in a new perfectly created home for this new humanity.

This never-ending story will star all of Yeh-shua-Jesus' Soul-mates—even those from the first primitive stages of the beginning of His Story. This never ending story will also contain all the rest of God's non-human creation. Only humanity with its unique creation in "God's image" is in a position to say, "No thank you" to God's offer of life with him for ever beyond the Doorway of the Universe. The rest of nature will naturally and

---

7. 2 Kings 2:11–12.
8. Genesis 5:24.
9. 2 Kings 2:11–18.
10. Isaiah 65:17; Isaiah 66:22.

automatically be there—but now not natural but super-natural—renewed. The non-human element will reflect the new way of life. Is-a-Yah saw a time when, "The lion will eat with the calves"—bully with the victim and in perfect peace.[11] Not what you would expect. Not like Woody Allen thought, "The lion and the calf shall lie down together but the calf won't get much sleep."[12] Instead a new perfect harmony—perfect life as God created it to be. A paradise: no pain; no illness; no suffering; no inequality; no natural disasters; no abuse; no murder; no stealing; no jealousy; in fact, nothing that will attack the perfection of resurrected humanity.[13] The whole of the new Universe filled with God and his personality. Nothing not of God allowed. One famous ancient Mouthpiece of God said that the new model Universe will be full of God's loving nature—"like the sea is all full of water." [14] The new Universe now filled only with God and his people rather than filled with human rebellion—every human living there will have chosen to be there—unlike Adam and Eve in the first prototype paradise.

Some people call this new never ending story in the new home beyond the Universe: "Heaven." But this name can confuse. It suggests clouds and harps. It suggests something not solid or truly real. But this new home beyond our Universe will be super-solid—more real than reality as we know it. This will be a new version of existence—as it should have been from the beginning but now will be forever with no threats to it.

This new never ending story in a new radical Universe will still contain the best of the old. It is better than Adam and Eve's paradise. It is not just a rural idyll but a miraculous metropolis. It is not just the paradise of Eden but also a fantastic city—a new Jeru-Salem[15]—a new Zion full of the greatest of human achievements and creations. As John, Yeh-shua-Jesus' close friend, put it after he observed Yah-weh's new capital city through the Doorway, "The Kings of the earth will bring their riches there—their glorious treasures will be brought into the city. Nothing sordid, nothing that abuses or corrupts or degrades will be there."[16] What are those riches—those treasures? Maybe the best of music, art, inventions, culture, literature—the list is endless, eternal. And who knows, even sport and food, not to mention, all that humanity has created using God's gifts: all that is beautiful and inspiring

---

11. Isaiah 11:6–9a.
12. "Without Feathers" (1976).
13. Revelation 21:5–8.
14. Isaiah 11:9b.
15. Revelation 21:1–4.
16. Revelation 21:24–27.

and awesome; all that re-creates us—that builds us up—that moves us closer to God.

This beautiful capital city of the new Creation will also be a place exporting peace and harmony for all. The ancient Mouthpiece of Yah-weh, Mic-Yah, saw the Day as a time when all of the nations of the world would head towards Jeru-Salem as the world's center—the place where the Creator would open the Doorway of the Universe and pour through his wisdom and teaching inspiring the whole family of humanity to, "beat their swords into ploughs; their spears into garden shears."[17] All the wasted energy expended in fighting and falling out and destroying, will be channeled into making a world full of well-being.

So, why would anyone not want to be a citizen of this new Paradise? But some do, which makes you wonder what happens to those who opt to stay with our old model Universe—those who have not chosen to be rescued.

The answer is that they will receive what they want—to be left alone.

---

17. Micah 4:2–3.

## 58

## Hell-ish

NO FLOOD FOR THOSE who ignore God's offer of a new Universe. No final solution. No destruction of humanity again. God promised, "Never again" and he meant it—he is true to his promises.[1] Instead, humanity who choose not to be part of God's new Creation, will be given a universe where they can be in charge: a universe without God's intervention; a universe absent of the Creator; a universe where God's loving nature is just a distant nostalgic memory; a universe full of everyone who wants to be God themselves and control their own destiny and do their own thing. Basically and fundamentally, a place full of people who believe that they can do a pretty good job at running a fair world without the unnecessary intrusion of His Story; a place full of everyone writing their own stories without interruption from the Author of Life where everyone thinks they are King of their own lives.

What will such an alternative universe look like; feel like? Depending on your belief in the inherent goodness of human nature left to its own devices without God—possibly not a good thought. Not a pretty sight—hell-ish even.[2] But despite its dubious possibility of success, it is still a place where all humans naturally should be—bar one—Yeh-shua-Jesus. It is also a place that up to now no humans have experienced—bar one—Yeh-shua-Jesus (for a brief moment). This brief moment was on that cataclysmic Friday when Yeh-shua-Jesus died: the brief moment on that sad Saturday when Satan thought he had won; the brief moment before the victorious Sunday when God's super-natural power on earth had been defeated and God's Wonder-child seemed to be held captive by Satan; the brief moment when Yeh-shua-Jesus appeared powerless on earth and earth became a God-free zone; the brief moment when the hope of the Universe descended into the

---

1. Genesis 8:21–22.
2. 2 Thessalonians 1:8–10.

depths of Hell and the Universe was under Satan's control—held hostage by Satan.

But unknown to Satan, Yeh-shua-Jesus' death was all part of a massive divine stratagem. The dead Yeh-shua-Jesus was a dormant divine virus sent right into the deathly stronghold of Satan—taken right into Satan's H.Q. by Satan himself only then to explode back into life and upload the virus of life into Satan's mainframe. The resurrection of Yeh-shua-Jesus dealt Satan a fatal blow and in so doing dealt death a fatal blow.[3] This was all part of His Story. No longer could Hell win. No longer was there any no-go zone for God or for humanity. Just as Pharaoh had had to give in and let Family Abraham escape from slavery; just as Babylon had had to give in and let Family Abraham escape from slavery, Satan was going to have to release all of Yeh-shua-Jesus' new Soul-mates from being slaves of Hell[4] not because they deserved this rescue but because of grace. Grace: the undeserved gift; the gracious gift of Hell-free life; the gracious gift of a Hell-free present and future—all at Yeh-shua-Jesus' expense but all to humanity's profit.[5]

With a new-version-human now beyond the Doorway, old version humans had a friend in a very high place—watching out for them and representing them.[6] Humanity now had a Go-Between better than all the Go-Betweens who had ever existed. This Go-Between didn't work in a sacred building on earth but worked with God beyond the Universe. Yeh-shua-Jesus was the ultimate Go-Between for humanity.[7] The Go-Betweens of old were simply fellow humans representing other humans in the stone built Holy Temple on earth. Yeh-shua-Jesus was the first new version human representing old version humans in the special Holy place beyond the Universe—through the Doorway. Human Go-Betweens and Temples had had their day.

Yeh-shua-Jesus' closest human friend on earth was famously invited through the Doorway for a peek. What was revealed to him in his famous vision, he wrote in his book "Revelation."[8] It is a mysterious, baffling, profound book which is beyond words. The vision was written up to be an encouragement to Soul-mates alive at the time. They were fighting against persecution from the Roman Empire. The book reminded them that they

---

3. 1 Corinthians 15:54–55; Romans 8:31–39.
4. Hebrews 2:14–17.
5. Hebrews 2:9–10; 5:7–10.
6. Hebrews 4:14–16.
7. Hebrews 7:26–27; 8:1–2; 9:11–15; 9:25; 10:19–23.
8. Revelation 4:1.

were part of a much greater, more powerful Empire beyond the Universe that would outlast death and time itself.

One of the most shocking and amazing sights that Soul-mate John saw beyond the Doorway made him declare, "I saw no Temple!"[9] Of all the holy places where he would have expected a holy building, there wasn't one. But he understood why, "because God and, "The Lamb" are its Temple." Who needs human reps and a stone building when you can access God without them!

And with this new direct access through the Doorway to the Lamb beyond the Universe, old version humans became linked as Soul-mates to Yeh-shua-Jesus. They could now download some of Yeh-shua-Jesus' supernatural powers right into their soul—and this even though they were still on the earth-side of the Doorway.[10] But before the start of this amazing human updating process, Yeh-shua-Jesus' Soul-mates had to do something very important.

Wait.[11]

---

9. Revelation 21:22.
10. Acts 1:8.
11. Luke 24:49.

# 59

# Harvest

WAIT—FOR WHAT? WAIT FOR the promised power. Wait for the downloading of the powerful life-spirit of the new version humanity, as modelled by Yeh-shua-Jesus. Wait to be born into a new life which Yeh-shua-Jesus had proved had enough power to blow the doors off the Universe and punch a hole in death and the fabric of time and space.[1] This new life had enough power to convert death into a Doorway out of this existence into the eternal Universe beyond—a power so massive that it also blew a hole in the human heart and transplanted it with the Doorway to beyond the Universe. It had enough power to blow away the human "heart of stone" and convert it into a promised "heart of flesh"—the prophesied internal change of soul that would change the external actions of humans.[2]

But the Soul-mates were still earth-bound, still old version humans but now with access through their heart Doorway to the out-of-this-world success of Yeh-shua-Jesus.[3] From now on the new out-of-this-Universe super-human would help the old inside-of the-Universe mortal humans. This is the harvest of His Story—the Soul-mates reaping the success of His Story won by the Super-star of His Story.

Family Abraham had several traditional harvest festivals. One of them was called, "Pentecost." It took place every year—but a few days after Yeh-shua-Jesus' final goodbye, the talk wasn't about cereal. It was about a harvest of invisible super-natural power from outside of the Universe—and it has been ever since.

The meaning of "Pentecost" has for ever changed for most people. That year's "Pentecost" harvest festival has become remembered for the transfer of power from Yeh-shua-Jesus to his Soul-mates. The download of power was now ready. His Story was beginning to come to fruition.

1. Ephesians 1:19.
2. Ezekiel 11:19; 36:26.
3. Hebrews 4:14–16.

Humanity was ready for harvesting. God was ready for the birth of his new Family Abraham.

The world wasn't quite so ready. This included Yeh-shua-Jesus' Soul-mates. At the beginning of the book that records the actions of the Soul-mates after Yeh-shua-Jesus' final goodbye (The Acts of the Apostles), the Soul-mates were all locked away in a room—frightened of the enemies of Yeh-shua-Jesus but also petrified by their own internal fears—trapped in their own scary roller-coaster ride of experiences: up during their three years of exciting activity with Yeh-shua-Jesus; down with his arrest and his death; up with his re-appearance after his death; down with his final goodbye.[4]

They felt alone—but not for long. Suddenly they heard an out-of-this-world sound like an indoor hurricane.[5] They saw out-of-this-world sights like indoor fireworks spitting flames of fire onto each of them. This firepower gave them a weird ability to speak languages they'd never learnt.[6] They took this ability outdoors and road tested it, shouting out in different languages to the crowds in the street—not any old crowds but international crowds gathered in Jeru-Salem for the Pentecost harvest festival. They offered this crowd the first-fruits of their new life. Tourists in Jeru-Salem who had gathered from all over the Roman Empire heard them shouting about how great God was—heard and understood in their own native tongues—their own languages.[7] God was trusting the world to be international again: it was a lifting of God's ban on international co-operation; a sweeping away of the babbling confusion sent by God to hamper human co-operation to build a tower to reach heaven.[8] It marked forgiveness for humanity for trying to build a tower up to God. Instead, God was now building a Doorway stretching down to earth for all peoples. From now on there was the possibility of one new humanity: one people; one language; one family; one life-spirit; one Father Creator; one new international nation; one new people made up of the whole of humanity. Humanity would no longer need to be divided by history or geography. Now a new group of humans would exist whose birthplace and culture would be secondary because these humans were to be re-born as citizens of heaven[9]—people getting ready for life in the new version Universe. These humans would be re-born as Soul-mates of the first new version human—Yeh-shua-Jesus.

4. Acts 2:1.
5. Acts 2:2.
6. Acts 2:3–4.
7. Acts 2:5–12.
8. Genesis 11:1–9.
9. Philippians 3:20.

*harvest* 259

One of Yeh-shua-Jesus' new Soul-mates, Peter, explained to the crowds on that new style Pentecost harvest festival, that this powerful life-spirit, "was for all people—throughout time and space."[10] This was a new family of people not restricted by time or space but an international and intergenerational family powered by Yeh-shua-Jesus. From now on God's Spirit and power on earth was not just in one man—however great. His power was now shared out amongst his Soul-mates.

Yeh-shua-Jesus had seen this day before his death. The day when a greater work would be done by his Soul-mates than even he could do—limited as he was by his human body locked in time and space.[11] Now Yeh-shua-Jesus' spirit would be in many men; women; children; rich and poor; young and old—fulfilling the Mouthpiece Jo-El's prophecy about the Spirit of God inspiring all groups of humanity.[12] This was a new humanity; a new human race; a new human family that would populate the whole of the earth down the centuries and millennia; a new human family that would eventually populate the new timeless Universe that God would create beyond the Doorway.

At Pentecost, this new improved Eden had just started to sign up its first inhabitants. The membership register was open—the register which was known later by the first Soul-mates as "The Lamb's Book of Life."[13] But membership of this new nation: this new people; this new family—was going to be time limited. It would only stay open until the return of Yeh-shua-Jesus through the Doorway back to earth. Yeh-shua-Jesus had said that the membership drive would close when he returned through the Doorway again for his very last visit when time was up for this Universe—when he returned back into this dimension.[14] This epoch-ending return was promised not just by Yeh-shua-Jesus, but by many of the Mouthpieces of God in years gone by, for example, Jo-El.[15]

Years later, Peter followed in this tradition by saying that there would be a day when there would be a cataclysmic end to the earth as we know it—a day when all those who had called on Yeh-shua-Jesus would be rescued.[16] This would be a new exodus like Family Abraham rescued from slavery in Egypt; like Family Abraham waiting to be rescued from exile in Babylon;

10. Acts 2:38–39.
11. John 14:12.
12. Joel 2:28–29.
13. Revelation 21:27.
14. Matthew 13:24–30, 36–43; 24:30–31.
15. Joel 3:30–32.
16. 2 Peter 3:10–13.

like Family Abraham waiting for their Wonder-child, Messiah-man to appear and save them.

The date for this new exodus was unknown and unknowable but still definite though classified. Yeh-shua-Jesus claimed it was not even known to him—just known by Yah-weh, his Father—God.[17] Unknown time maybe, but not missed by anyone when it would eventually happen—a cosmic, cataclysmic event witnessed by the whole of humanity.[18]

But two thousand years later, humanity is still waiting: still waiting for the final chapter of the history of the Universe; still waiting for the final earthly chapter of His Story; still waiting for Yeh-shua-Jesus to return to earth from outside of the Universe; still waiting for all the people with the first-fruits of the new human spirit to be fully harvested.[19] One famous Soul-mate of Yeh-shua-Jesus described this waiting time as like, "the whole of creation groaning on tip toe, wanting to peer into the future to see who would be revealed as the sons of God."[20]

But why the delay? Is Yeh-shua-Jesus testing his Soul-mates patience? Not according to Peter, the famous Soul-mate of Yeh-shua-Jesus. He explained that Yeh-shua-Jesus' apparent delay is due to God constantly elongating the open membership period so that more and more of humanity can opt to join the new Eden.[21]

Despite the good reason for the delay, Yeh-shua-Jesus knew that this delay would be a difficult wait for his Soul-mates. He knew that at first his Soul-mates would be like little children desperate for Christmas Day to dawn: unable to sleep; unable to relax. Just as little children are desperate for Santa to be real; just as little children are desperate for Santa to appear—his Soul-mates would be desperate for God's presence to be made real to them. They would be aching for His Story to be proved as definitively true—as not a myth—however popular. But this wait for proof would only be over when Yeh-shua-Jesus returned. His re-emergence into the Universe would prove His Story to be the true story; the overarching story of Creation; the metanarrative of reality; the truth; the reason why; the underpinning story of history and time itself.

But until then humanity would have to wait without losing heart or losing its edge.[22] This wait was made more painful for the first generation

17. Matthew 24:36.
18. Matthew 24:37–51.
19. James 1:18.
20. Romans 8:18–21.
21. 2 Peter 3:8–10.
22. Luke 12:35–48.

Soul-mates because it had become assumed that Yeh-shua-Jesus' return back through the Doorway would happen before the first of the Soul-mates died. Stands to reason—Yeh-shua-Jesus wouldn't leave his first Soul-mates to face death without him. But reality didn't fit the theory. The great foundational Soul-mates started dying. It was shocking—Yeh-shua-Jesus' most trusted friends dead—and still no sign of Yeh-shua-Jesus returning.

This was panicking some of the Soul-mates. Peter, one of Yeh-shua-Jesus' most down-to-earth colleagues, tried reassuring them in the face of the sarcastic criticism they were experiencing. "People will make fun of you and say, "Didn't Yeh-shua-Jesus promise to come back? Some of your first leaders have already died and the world is just the same—it hasn't changed a bit!"[23] It took one of the most prominent members of the first generation Soul-mates to reassure everyone—to remind them that Yeh-shua-Jesus' death and resurrection made death into a Doorway not a barrier—that those who died before Yeh-shua-Jesus' return weren't lost to God.

Death is no barrier in His Story. Paul reassured the Soul-mates of this. He wrote it in the first of many of his messages to the newly founded groups of Soul-mates around 50 A.D.[24] He reassured them that when Yeh-shua-Jesus returns through the Doorway, the dead Soul-mates will be the first to be raised to the new life: the first to be resurrected; the first to taste the new life through the Doorway in the new perfect Universe. They will not miss a thing—not then and not now. Paul said that until that Day of Yeh-shua-Jesus' return, death to Soul-mates would be just like sleep.

Years before, Yeh-shua-Jesus proved this when he had been asked to go to a local Synagogue leader's child who was seriously ill.[25] He was begged by the desperate father to heal his child. Due to another emergency cutting in, Yeh-shua-Jesus was delayed—fatally delayed as it turned out. The seriously ill girl died before he got to her. But Yeh-shua-Jesus was not put off—he continued to her house; he continued in his attempt to heal her; he continued past the mocking mourners outside who laughed at his naive, futile and offensively late arrival. He got hold of the little girl's hand and said: "Talitha Koum" (in English: "Little girl, I tell you to rise.") It was time to wake up from the sleep of death—and she did—immediately. After proving that death was sleep to him, Yeh-shua-Jesus ordered her traumatized parents to feed her and make her strong to start to live her life back on earth again.

---

23. 2 Peter 3:3b-4.
24. 1 Thessalonians 4:13–18.
25. Mark 5:35–43.

Death to Soul-mates would be like the little girl's death,[26] but instead of waking up back into the old life, it would be waking up into the start of a new life in the new Universe. Death to Soul-mates would be like the sleep of a child in a new bed in a strange house but with the frightening abnormality overwhelmed and reassured by the child's subconscious awareness that their parents are awake in the house—watching them, protecting them. A Soul-mate who has physically died has a sleep with sweet dreams of Yeh-shua-Jesus' protection—dreams that feel as real as reality but not yet the full reality of the new Universe.

But Yeh-shua-Jesus' reassurance wasn't just for his Soul-mates who had died before his return. Yeh-shua-Jesus also promised practical down-to-earth help during the living Soul-mates' long wait for his return. He promised that during this prolonged sign-up for the new model Universe, Yeh-shua-Jesus would not leave his new Soul-mates alone like orphans to fend for themselves like little children at the mercy of a big bad world.[27] There would be an umbilical cord linking the great parent-God to his Soul-mates through the Doorway of Yeh-shua-Jesus. The cord would be his special Spirit—a life-line of power to the God beyond the Universe who didn't give up on humanity. Through this umbilical cord, the Soul-mates would be protected and empowered. More than that—the Soul-mates of Yeh-shua-Jesus would feel in touch with the new model human—in touch with Yeh-shua-Jesus as if he'd never left.[28] They would be aware of his invisible presence and his invisible friendship.

Yeh-shua-Jesus likened this connectedness to the relationship of the branches in a vine.[29] Grapes often grow on vines that hang down from overhead frames. When they grow this way, they appear almost disconnected to the ground. But the green leaves and plump grapes prove each vine is rooted into the nutritious soil—they are feeding off the life juice of the vine through the one grounded main stem. In the same way the Soul-mates through the Spirit would be connected into the main stem of Yeh-shua-Jesus and through him rooted into the soil of their Creator God. Each would produce "fruit"; each would display signs of their connection with Yeh-shua-Jesus beyond the Universe. Not only that, just as each individual vine branch is also connected to the other vine branches, each of the Soul-mates through the Spirit would be corporately and intimately connected to the rest of

---

26. 1 Thessalonians 4:12–14.
27. John 14:18–20.
28. John 14:15–27.
29. John 15:1–17.

Yeh-shua-Jesus' Soul-mates. Each Soul-mate born not into a literal vine but into a super-natural interconnected network—a family of Soul-mates.

Not just a family vine but a complete new Family Tree as promised to Abraham.

## 60

# Humanity Reborn

THIS NEW INTERNATIONAL, INTERCONNECTED Family of Soul-mates has different titles. One has stuck, but like all titles is misused even misunderstood—Christ-ian. This describes the family as the people of the "Christ" ("Christ" being the Greek version of the Family Abraham word "Messiah").[1] But "Christ-ian" is a title hardly used in His Story. In His Story there are many other ways to describe this new humanity. "People of "The Way," was an early one.[2] "Christ's body on earth," was a later very helpful one as it suggested that no longer was Yeh-shua-Jesus limited to one human body but now he had many human bodies all working together as one body with Christ as their head.[3]

In the years since Yeh-shua-Jesus left earth, another word has come into use—church. Yeh-shua-Jesus is only recorded as using it twice.[4] He used the Greek word that is translated, "church" to mean people "called out" to be part of his group. Church is the collective noun for Yeh-shua-Jesus' Soul-mates. Just like there is a "mumble of moles"; a "crash of rhinoceros"; a "gang of elks" there is a "church" of Soul-mates or Christ-ians. Church isn't a building. It isn't an institution or a set of rules or culture. It is the name for the Family of Yeh-shua-Jesus.

At Pentecost harvest festival around two thousand years ago, it was born—church began. The great sign-up had started. Membership was open. Pentecost is now celebrated as the church's birthday when the first humans became Soul-mates. Three thousand were born into it—on the first day.[5] And since that day billions have been added. It is international; worldwide; across time and space. If it sees itself as just existing in only one time zone or area, it isn't fully church. It is a Family with many cultures. It has many ways

1. Acts 11:26, 26:28; 1 Peter 4:16.
2. Acts 9:1–2.
3. 1 Corinthians 12:12–27.
4. Matthew 16:18; 18:17.
5. Acts 2:41.

of expressing itself: many ways of organizing itself; many ways of being—but all connected to one being—the new model human, Yeh-shua-Jesus. It is based on one belief that Yeh-shua-Jesus is the Super-star of His Story and history: that he is the only hope for humanity; that he is the only hope for the earth; that he is the only hope for the Universe. [6]

Church is a new, extended, revamped and resurrected Family Abraham that is set apart by its weekly Sunday celebration. This celebration is on the first day of the week when humanity was re-created by Yeh-shua-Jesus' resurrection rather than the previous holy seventh day celebration which celebrated the creation of the world. Church: new Sunday people not old Sabbath people—celebrating the new creation not the old creation. The famous Soul-mate Paul put it like this: "If anyone belongs to Christ, they are a new creation: the old has gone—the new has come!"[7] Church is new contract, not old contract—the new promise, not the old promise—all based on God's grace. This church is the people on a promise of a new life. This church is the people who are being transformed ready to inhabit the new Universe. This church is the people who are transformed, now at soul level, but waiting for the day when Yeh-shua-Jesus reappears through the Doorway to complete their transformation—waiting for the day when they will be given the super-physical bodies which they need to exist in the new Universe.

Church is the people who believe in the first advent of Christ as a baby and look for his second advent as the all-conquering new super-human. Christ-ians are advent-urers! Christ-ians live a life between these two advents where each day is an "advent-ure" of looking for the Doorway to appear—at any time. When it does, the divine-human partnership which is only presently working fully at their Soul level will then be completed. They will then receive their fully transformed, resurrected bodies.

But in the new Universe what will the Soul-mates' bodies look like? Be like? According to the great formative thinker of the Church, Paul, these new bodies will still be linked to the present bodies of the Soul-mates, like a flower is inextricably linked to the seed that produced it.[8] He explained this in one of his many letters to the Soul-mates scattered around the Mediterranean countries. He told them that like the resurrected Yeh-shua-Jesus, their bodies would be the same—they would remain essentially the same person. But like Yeh-shua-Jesus' post-death body, it would be super-same with radically new qualities. Just as a flower is the raison d'etre of the seed, so would the new body justify and fulfil the present body. How many "seed

---

6. Romans 10:9.
7. 2 Corinthians 5:17.
8. 1 Corinthians 15:35–38.

festivals" are advertised compared with "flower festivals"? How often do we send seeds to our loved ones on a celebration instead of flowers? In the same way, the new human body will far overshadow and eclipse even our present amazingly fantastic old-style, seed-like, human bodies—just as flowers overshadow and eclipse their original seeds.

When the new body comes, the old will be forgotten. The Church is the people on earth celebrating as they wait to flower; as they wait to become the people God created them to be; as they wait for their "raison d'etre."

But church is more than a collective noun for Soul-mates or Christians. It is family. It is Yeh-shua-Jesus' family.[9] It is a family that never loses any children. Not even death can remove a member. Just as no one can simply one day make their mind up to barge into it without going through Yeh-shua-Jesus, in the same way, no one can simply, by their bad choice on a bad day, drop out of it.[10] Once born into it; you can't cease being part of it—just like family. As Yeh-shua-Jesus famously said, "no one can steal you out of my hand."[11] It's not just something that you choose to be part of like a fan-club or supporters club. It is not just a group of people who have a common interest—a group of humans who are friendly to each other. It is family. Unlike the way you can choose your friends; you can't choose your family. Same with this family: and some. Your fellow Soul-mates are your soul-relatives—more than brothers and sisters—people joined by an invisible power thicker than blood. You can try ignoring your natural brothers and sisters. You can try leaving your natural family. But you are still part of that family. The family of the Church is the same.

Church is at the center of God's new Genesis project. An ambitious billionaire is working towards colonizing Mars by 2032 with eighty thousand people. He is selling one-way tickets for half a million dollars. He wants the right people to buy the tickets—people with the skills to establish the first self-sustaining human base on the red planet. Not just engineers or technicians, but those who can cope with the isolation and the need for team work. Apparently, the rest of us will pay for all of the other costs, by watching the first colonists on a Reality T.V. program to end all Reality T.V. programs. Do you want to colonize Mars and start the first new human community off earth? Maybe not, but the Church will be the colonists of God's new Genesis program. The Soul-mates will be the inhabitants of God's new Universe, which isn't on earth and not even in this Universe—but beyond it. Church is people who want to be part of this new group of Adam and Eves; part

---

9. Matthew 12:46–50.
10. John 1:12–13.
11. John 10:28–29.

of the new "In the beginning" but without the snake and the fall out; part of a new Universe where God again will walk amongst his people;[12] part of a new Universe where there is no night or fear or darkness.[13] This new Universe of the re-born second generation humans will be a place where the Soul-mates will be reunited with their original Soul-mate, Yeh-shua-Jesus, and through him with Yah-weh himself.[14] In this new Universe, the Soul-mates will know Yeh-shua-Jesus better than their closest friend. They will understand His Story clearly and completely because they are not trying to look through the warped haze of their old style humanity and the fog of this Universe. It will be a place where they will see Yeh-shua-Jesus face to face.[15] It will be God's creation as it was always intended to be.

And now always will be.

12. Genesis 3:8.
13. Revelation 21:25; Revelation 22:5.
14. Revelation 21:1–3.
15. 1 Corinthians 13:12.

# 61

## Never-Ending Story

THERE IS ONE OBVIOUS problem with all this talk of new Universes inhabited by Yeh-shua-Jesus' Soul-mates. It is not just the elephant in the room, it is the herd of elephants crashing into the room and gatecrashing the Christ-ian party. The first original Soul-mates are all dead. His Story looks like a dead end. It is all in the past. The advent-ure of waiting for Yeh-shua-Jesus' second advent as the Son of Man rides in on the clouds of glory seems to be way past its sell-by-date. Not even the most optimistic Christ-ian can remain in a constant state of expectancy for two millennia. Surely two thousand years of no-sightings of Yeh-shua-Jesus would suggest that the trail has gone cold and that the Doorway is at least become overgrown or the hinges have rusted solid in the shut position.

But despite that, there is still something today that calls itself the, "Church." In fact, there are now over two billion people alive who call themselves Christ-ians—modern day Soul-mates. But are they Soul-mates like the first Soul-mates? Or are they sub-standard imitations: fakes; look-a-likes but not the real thing; historical re-enactors; modern pastiches—full of enthusiasm for the past but incongruous throw-backs in our modern scientific, rational age? History is still continuing. But it can appear that His Story has ended. Maybe it has done its job? Run its course? Run out of steam? In one sense: yes—His Story is history. By just after 100 A.D. there was no one left alive who had been with Yeh-shua-Jesus. His Story, humanly speaking, had been consigned to the history books.

But in another sense His Story continues. In fact His Story itself claims it is continuing. His Story makes this claim in different ways. One amazing way it makes the claim is through a saying which is so mysterious; so weird; so apparently untrue that it has confused and mesmerized generations of readers of His Story. It is found in the part of His Story that may well have been committed to the written word last of all. It is in the memoirs of Yeh-shua-Jesus' closest colleague, John. But it is not written by him. And it is probably an addition to the book that bears his name—an appendix possibly written by John's followers after they had faithfully transcribed all of John's intimate recollections of Yeh-shua-Jesus which had been locked up in his memory. In fact, no one is quite sure who said it. No one is quite sure who wrote it. No one is totally sure what it exactly means but it sits proudly as part of His Story. It takes the form of a surreal surmise, "Yeh-shua-Jesus did many other things than are written in this book. If everything Yeh-shua-Jesus did was written up, I don't suppose there would be enough room in the whole world for all the books."[1] Not enough room in the whole world for Yeh-shua-Jesus' His Story? On one level it is clearly not true. Even if every single thing that Yeh-shua-Jesus ever did in every second of the whole of his thirty-three years of life were to be written down, even in big font in very big books, they would barely cover a small fraction of a small village never mind the one hundred and ninety-seven million square miles of the whole world. But don't forget, according to His Story, Yeh-shua-Jesus is still alive beyond the Doorway. His life continues. His mission continues. There is definitely no mention of a subsequent death after his resurrection. He is still active. He is still alive. His Story is still being written the other side of the Doorway beyond the Universe.

But that's not much use to us earth-side of the Doorway if the Doorway is not open and we are not part of the continuing story. Don't forget though, that His Story also states that the Family of Soul-mates continue His Story on earth this side of the Doorway. It records how those who followed the first generation of Soul-mates continued Yeh-shua-Jesus' mission on earth—his work generation after generation—not in some small pathetic way, like a sequel which is a pale shadow of the original and brings dishonor on its memory. This is no "Son of His Story." The second generation Soul-mates continuing mission to seek out new civilizations; to explore new worlds and to boldly go where no man had gone before with the good news of Yeh-shua-Jesus was not a disappointing follow-up to His Story, but part of its climax. Its adventure stories are part of the library that make up the written His Story, otherwise known as "The Bible".

Yeh-shua-Jesus' final goodbye and departure through the Doorway was not the final frontier and neither was the death of the original Soul-mates. Their deaths were just the beginning of a mission that has continued even after the final "Amen" that is recorded at the end of the written His Story. So far, this continuing mission has lasted two thousand years. His Story is continuing through the blossoming, burgeoning Family of Soul-mates. A family that is multiplying: widening; breaking out of His Story's original

1. John 21:25.

historical, geographical and cultural roots. It is a family that is sometimes underground and invisible. It is often connected with the public institution that calls itself, "The Church" but not necessarily. If through this family of Soul-mates, Yeh-shua-Jesus is still effectively active on earth, then His Story continues. His Story continues through the story of all his Soul-mates. So in a pre-digital book age, maybe, just maybe, the saying about the world not being big enough for all the stories of Yesh-shua-Jesus is true. In fact on this level it's truly prophetic—written in an age when the family of Soul-mates was only hundreds strong, but seeing an age when it would be billions. If you wrote up the stories of the two billion people who say they are Soul-mates of Yeh-shua-Jesus alive today; and if you wrote up every one of their personal stories in an individual hardback book and if you laid all the big books in a line, you would have a line of books that would go around the equator not once or twice but sixteen times. Granted that would still leave a massive amount of the world free of His Story books. But if you think that it is now around two thousand years ago since Yeh-shua-Jesus left earth for the last time, maybe it isn't such an exaggeration. Who knows how many billions of Yeh-shua-Jesus' Soul-mates there have been since Yeh-shua-Jesus' time and before our time? Who knows how many successful applications there have been to colonize the new Universe? Certainly the church of Christ-ians has increased year upon year. If the stories of all these Soul-mates were written up in detail, the world would be beginning to have vast tracks of land full of mini His Story books. But still the world would be big enough. But hold on—we haven't even mentioned the unknown number of Soul-mates yet to be born. Maybe the contemporary church is still "the early church"—still in its infancy, two thousand years after Yeh-shua-Jesus. Maybe the Church still has thousands and thousands of years to go before Yeh-shua-Jesus is sent back through the Doorway for the last time.

In a very real sense—His Story is a never-ending story. It may have millennia to run before the beginning of the new Universe story that will never end: never disappoint; never run out of steam or run out of energy. Is the surreal surmise still an exaggeration? Maybe, but not by much!

The ongoing story of Yeh-shua-Jesus is the ongoing story of his Soul-mates. Their story is His Story. Their story is the continuing story of Yeh-shua-Jesus. That means that if you are a Soul-mate of Yeh-shua-Jesus today: your story, however small; however local; however unimportant; however strange; however unusual; however sad; however wrong; however messed up; is in a sense—part of the timeless never-ending eternal His Story.

But are you a Soul-mate? Has Yeh-shua-Jesus breathed his new humanity life-spirit into you? Are you connected through the Doorway of Yeh-shua-Jesus to the outside of the Universe? Are you adopted into the new eternal Family Tree promised to Abraham? Are you part of God's bloodline? Are you going to become a complete, resurrected human when Yeh-shua-Jesus returns back inside the Universe before re-creating the Universe? Are you going to colonize the new perfect Universe?

How do you know? How can you be sure? Ask yourself the question, "Do I feel part of Yeh-shua-Jesus' close circle of friends—his adopted family?" Still not sure? Try asking, "Is Yeh-shua-Jesus real to me?" "Does it feel as if Yeh-shua-Jesus is still alive on earth?"

If you're still not sure maybe you need to bear in mind that before becoming a Soul-mate of Yeh-shua-Jesus there is some preparation you have to do. First and foremost, you have to let Yeh-shua-Jesus snap you out of your Satanic trance; to stop you sleepwalking hypnotically through life—missing out on all you were created to be—U-turn time. You've got to admit that this world isn't enough: that on many levels humanity doesn't work; that your particular human life isn't what it should be; that you aren't what you should be and that you never will be without help. You need to go and join John's baptism queue by the River Jordan and openly admit to yourself this need. Go down and die in the waters ready to be born into a new life. You need to admit that just like the members of Family Abraham who returned from exile and rebuilt Jeru-Salem and the Temple and the Nation—that you hoped for more but you have settled for less.[2] Your life is not what you hoped it would be when you were a child. You have to admit that you need a second chance—a second crack at this human life business—a rebirth.[3]

This will only happen if you snap out of your Satan induced hypnotic trance that constantly makes you forget to remember: that leaves your desire for ultimate answers as something that is in the corner of your eye—seen but ignored. You need to finally face up to the truth that so much of your life's activity is about distracting yourself from asking the ultimate questions—the questions His Story began with: Why? Why am I alive? Why do I exist? Why does the world that sustains my life exist?

Ask yourself the ultimate basic question, "Do I want to discover and become the character His Story has written me up to be—even before I was born?" King David certainly believed that story of his life was written up and known by God even before his birth and he said as much in one of his great songs.[4]

Asking these questions may mess with your plans: your relationships; your ambitions. Asking them may annoy you. But regardless—Yeh-

---

2. Haggai 1:5.
3. John 3:1–3.
4. Psalm 139:16.

shua-Jesus just won't go away. It may be that for a while now you have been desperately aware of your need to have his super-natural help—his help from beyond the Doorway injected into your everyday life. But you have haven't had the time or nerve to do anything about it. It may be that you feel that having this super-natural help is cheating: that you should be stronger; that by accepting help you are admitting failure. Many of us have been brought up to believe that to ask for help is a sign of weakness. But there is no way round it. At the root of His Story is the need of every human to ask and accept that they need rescuing. His Story is a rescue story. But His Story is not about making you feel small or pathetic. It is the story of God finding you and offering you his amazing life and love—even if he has to do it time and time again like Hosea searching and buying back Gomer from the slave market.[5]

Maybe your reading of this book is not an accident, but like Creation itself it is caused by an ordered, purposeful plan. It is part of God searching for you again and finding you and of buying you back—redeeming you. Maybe you were meant to read this—it is part of the overarching plan of your life: the bigger story of your life; the metanarrative of your personal story. This may be the moment in time and space, when the story of the outside of the Universe meets your story—when your storyline meets His Storyline.

If any of this makes sense to you: if it resonates with you on a deep soul level; if any of this moves you as you read it in a way deeper than the merely rational then Yeh-shua-Jesus says that his Kingdom is so close you can reach out and touch it—it is already right by you.[6] You are already beginning to hear Yeh-shua-Jesus snapping his fingers and waking you out of your Satan induced hypnotic trance. The invisible power of Yeh-shua-Jesus is working on you—waiting to enter in and empower you. All you need do now is believe it; focus on it—don't let this moment slip away. Yeh-shua-Jesus is right next to you: working on you; working around you—intervening.

Beginning to weave your story into His Story.

---

5. Hosea 1:2–3; 2:2–8; 3:1–3.
6. Mark 1:14.

# 62

## Love Story

BUT BEFORE WE COMMIT to believing His Story, how can we be sure that it's all true? We may want to be Soul-mates with Yeh-shua-Jesus but how do we know that this is not just another scam: another "too good to be true" offer; another too unbelievable to believe story; another attempt to brainwash us; another attempt to manipulate us emotionally; yet another attempt to get us humans to sign up to a cult that offers everything but delivers nothing except misery and even abuse?

Maybe we should start with the basics. His Story is not just a collection of primitive ancient stories about why the world began. His Story is not just history—an interpretation of world historical events since the beginning of time. His Story is not just the history of humanity and in particular, of one people group. His Story is not just the history of how the church began or its continuing purpose. His Story is all of these but so much more. His Story is a love story—the greatest love story of all time. It is the fundamental love story that underpins all love stories. It is the love story of a happy family which lies behind happy families everywhere.[1] It is the "happy ever after" story which redefines and outlives every other "happy ever after" story. His Story is the love story between a loving Father God and his greatest creation—the family of humans—me and you.

God is love—Hosea found this out through his own personal pain with his prostitute wife.[2] God is love: it is his essential nature; it is his distinctive, unique selling point.[3] God is love and all of the storyline in His Story is dictated by this fact.

Love is complex. Try defining it in less than ten words. Love is . . . indefinable. Not surprising that it is complex because it underpins reality. His Story is clear that love is the basis of the Universe. It is the only thing

---

1. Ephesians 3:14–15.
2. Hosea 1:2.
3. 1 John 4:16.

that will remain when this Universe is finished.[4] It is something which connects each side of the Doorway—even now. God defines love but love can't define God.[5] Love has no separate life without God. God can't be judged by some separate standard scale called, "Love." because God invented the scale. His Story says that God created love and all true love in this world owes its existence to him. When God created the Universe he did it out of love and injected his love into every part of it. The closest human friend to Yeh-shua-Jesus wrote later that, "love is the very nature of God himself."[6]

Satan in contrast doesn't care for love. He doesn't do love because Satan can't do love. It is one thing beyond his powers. He can try and mimic love. He can try and use the word "love" when actually it is self-love—selfishness masquerading as love.

In English we only have one word for "love." We use it for everything. We love our children, our job, our wife, our partner, our dog, our friend, our favorite food. We make love. Some of the ways we use the word "love" are ways that don't fit in with God's definition of love—a definition lived out by Yeh-shua-Jesus supremely when he sacrificed his life for all of humanity.[7] Greek has lots of nuanced words for love. But His Story uses the Greek word "agape" for this sacrificial definition of love. This true agape-love is what makes God tick. This true agape-love is what literally makes the world go round from day one. Agape-love is defined by the loved one benefitting more than the lover. Abusive love is defined by the lover benefitting at the expense of the loved one.

But how do we know that His Story is true agape-love or false, perverted love? Is His Story an abusive love story or an agape love story? How do we know whether His Story is for our benefit or God's or Satan's: for the benefit of the institution of the church rather than the care of the family of humanity?

The answer lies in the key to starting and maintaining any loving relationship. Is it reading a text book on love? Is it going on a relationship course? Is it listening to love songs? Is it reading romantic poetry? All might help, but not key. The key is trust—making ourselves vulnerable with someone we trust—trusting them.

How do we choose who to trust? How do we decide who is Mr or Miss Right? Take a quiz in a Women's magazine? Consult a psychic or clairvoyant? Ask our friends? Set on a private investigator to tail our loved one?

4. 1 Corinthians 13:8–13.
5. 1 John 4:8.
6. 1 John 4:7–8, 16b.
7. John 3:16; 1 John 4:9–11, 14–16, 19.

Do confidential checks on our potential partner? Maybe or maybe not! But in the end—it's a matter of faith. Stepping out into the unknown with the person we think we trust. Not a leap into complete darkness, but still a step of faith.

You only really know if it's true love when you've started a long term relationship with someone. This is annoying but true. Deep knowledge only comes by faith and trust. No one can understand all the complexities of life. Every one of us has to take some things on trust and then try it for our self. We live our lives by calculated risks hoping that we make more good decisions than bad decisions. But isn't it madness to try and use ourselves as a guinea-pig? But there isn't any other way to live—no one else has been "us" before us and come back to tell us the best way to live. It may seem like madness to risk our life in a massive life-long research into whether His Story is truly to be trusted? But we all live by faith and trust every day. We all experiment on ourselves every day.

The wife of the married couple who did some of the first research into x-ray machines, died of cancer. Marie Curie who discovered radium, inadvertently killed herself with radiation whilst discovering the good potential of radium therapy. These people risked their future to discover something of lasting significance. Are you willing to risk? Yeh-shua-Jesus said that the only way to find real life is to risk losing it.[8] Yeh-shua-Jesus praised his future Soul-mates who would trust him after he had left the Universe. He knew that they would have to believe in him without seeing him; rather than seeing him first and then believing. They would prove Yeh-shua-Jesus' story to be true by experience not simply by investigation.[9] "Believe to see" not "see to believe."

Yeh-shua-Jesus made this statement after one of this team, Thomas, couldn't believe in Yeh-shua-Jesus' resurrection. He had been in the wrong place at the wrong time. He had missed out on Yeh-shua-Jesus' resurrected appearances to his colleagues. Maybe like us—wrong place, wrong time. Maybe we haven't been brought up to believe that Yeh-shua-Jesus is alive. Maybe we haven't met anyone we trust who has believed that Yeh-shua-Jesus is still alive—wrong place, wrong time.

Thomas, for ever now known as, "Doubting Thomas" couldn't join in the celebrations of Yeh-shua-Jesus' new life until he had proved it to be true personally. He wanted to see to believe. He wanted to see Yeh-shua-Jesus' new resurrected body with his own eyes and touch it with his own hands. He doubted his colleagues' reports and he doubted Yeh-shua-Jesus was alive.

---

8. John 12:23–26; Matthew 10:37–39; 16:24–27.

9. John 20:24–29.

Yeh-shua-Jesus obliged, by making a personal appearance out of thin air for Thomas, but pointed out to him that trust is the key to any relationship with him or his Soul-mates.[10] It unlocks the key to the Doorway. It sheds the light from beyond the Universe onto earth. Faith in the unseen God beyond the Doorway makes us able to see the unseen God here on earth.[11] Our eyes opened like El-isha's servant in Dothan.[12]

But surely, Yeh-shua-Jesus didn't mean for his Soul-mates to go around seeing and believing in invisible things? That would be one step away from psychosis. Surely, Yeh-shua-Jesus didn't mean for his Soul-mates to throw away their brains and ignore their investigative skills? Become gullible jelly? Surely, as humans we should use our brains rationally before risking all on becoming a Soul-mate of Yeh-shua-Jesus. We should find out about him: ask others about him; do research into him; read His Story for ourselves? Yes—of course. But at its heart, His Story is about the agape-love of God driving him to send his own Son on a suicide mission so that God's other children of humanity might live.[13] Paul said that just at the right time, God sent his Son born of a female human so that humans could be adopted as children into God's family.[14] His Story is not out to hurt us but save us—all at God's expense. But as it is a love story, then unfortunately in the end, there's no other way of finding out for ourselves whether it is truth; a scam; a myth or a fairytale—apart from trust.

The authenticity test is trust.

10. John 20:29.
11. 2 Corinthians 4:18; 5:7.
12. 2 Kings 6:17.
13. John 3:16.
14. Galatians 4:4.

# 63

## Size Doesn't Matter

FAMILY ABRAHAM BEGAN WITH one man who trusted God's totally impossible promise.[1] Father Abraham had to trust that God would be true to his promise and make him into the Father of Many—despite having no children. But it came true.[2] Abraham had to trust again, when God told him to get rid of his only long awaited male heir by killing him.[3] The famous Soul-mate, Paul, pondering on Abraham's trust said, "God accepted Abraham because Abraham trusted him. Anyone now who trusts God is a child of Abraham. The good news is that trust in God opens Abraham's Family for all people—whether they have been born into the nation of Isra-El or not."[4]

Paul himself had to make a very public stand of trust and faith when he changed from being a bully of Soul-mates to being a believer. This happened when he bumped into the very alive Yeh-shua-Jesus months after he had been crucified and should have still been dead and buried. Ironically, Paul was on his way to attack anyone who said that Yeh-shua-Jesus was still alive. Yeh-shua-Jesus called out to him through the Doorway and asked him why he was attacking him. Paul hit the deck, temporarily incapacitated and blinded, but not so overwhelmed that he didn't see the light. Yeh-shua-Jesus was the Super-star of His Story. An attack on Yeh-shua-Jesus' Soul-mates was an attack on the people of God. Soul-mates were his family. So Paul stopped—U-turned and took a massive step of faith and joined up.[5] Paul realized that Family Abraham membership was no longer a right or a hereditary gift. Even a man like Paul with a spotless Family Abraham bloodline had to now apply to enter the new Family Abraham. Trust was now to be more important than your nationality or upbringing. Family Abraham

1. Genesis 12:1–3.
2. Romans 4:18–24.
3. Genesis 22:1–19.
4. Romans 4:1–12.
5. Acts 9:1–19.

from now on wasn't connected to your race or your culture, but your ability to trust.

King Solomon, the super-naturally wise man of His Story said, "God has arranged all His Story to work beautifully. He has even made a connection between us and the outside of the Universe so we can receive a tantalizing glimpse of the bigger picture of what is beyond the Doorway. But not one human can fully grasp what is the beginning and the end of His Story."[6] We do not have the mental, emotional or physical capacity to get hold of God; to get the measure of God. He's the Creator: we're the created. We cannot prove the existence of God simply by our intellect or just by our brains. In the end we have to also trust him if we are going to find out he is trustworthy. We must have faith in him.

This is great news and a comfort for those for whom mental capacity is a challenge and for those who care for those who have learning difficulties. Being a Soul-mate is not about passing an exam on God or being able to answer every question about him or what he is doing. His Story is inclusive—it is for all—not just those who read books; discuss ideas or enjoy a good debate. It is not just for the "chattering classes" but for all who can bring themselves to risk trusting. It is not about appearing clever—it is about being wise.[7] And when all is said and done, real wisdom is about trust.[8]

Yeh-shua-Jesus invites us to take a risk—to open up our lives to him and to trust him. He is constantly knocking at the Door of our lives challenging us to trust him enough to open up to him.[9] Too often we are deaf to the sound of his knocking and we need to tune into its pitch. Sometimes we don't hear it as it is constant like the incessant ticking of a clock that we automatically filter out. More often the quiet but insistent tapping is drowned out by the overwhelming cluttering chatter and clamor of everyday living. But sometimes in the lonely quiet hours we are aware of its nagging beat calling us to respond and unlock the Door which on one side opens into our soul and on the other side opens into beyond the Universe.

Opening up to strangers doesn't come easily to us in our age of alarms, keys, electronic swipe cards, chains, spyholes and combination locks. We like to know who is on the other side of the door. We peer through spyglasses and check C.C.T.V. or strain our necks out of upstairs windows. But in the end we have to decide somehow whether the caller is friend or foe. Trust is the only key to open up this Door. This is the Doorway that took

6. Ecclesiastes 3:11.
7. 1 Corinthians 1:18–31.
8. Proverbs 3:5–8; Proverbs 16:3; Psalm 37:4–6.
9. Revelation 3:20.

hundreds of years of His Story to be established. This is the Doorway that cost Yeh-shua-Jesus his life. This is the Doorway that is Yeh-shua-Jesus.[10] This is the Doorway that can resurrect our lives—for ever. There is no other way to be adopted into Family Abraham.[11]

We shouldn't be surprised. His Story is one challenge to trust after another. The new improved Family of God is now open to everyone who trusts His Story.[12] The new improved Family of God is now open to everyone who trusts that God loves them and wants the best for them—which, of course is to be with him for ever on the other side of the Doorway.

Maybe you know all of this—and believe all of this. Maybe you have become a Christ-ian years ago but even though you have lived as a good member of the Church, as of yet you don't feel that you are in God's Family? You don't feel like you are a Soul-mate of Yeh-shua-Jesus. This is a new concept to you. Maybe up to now you've felt like you've been trying to be something you're not. It's been skin deep not soul deep. It's been outside-in not inside-out.

The resurrected new model human, Yeh-shua-Jesus, before he returned through the Doorway to the outside of the Universe, first told his Soul-mates: "Wait in the city; stay where you are; do nothing until you are clothed with power from outside the Universe."[13] Do nothing until clothed—wear the clothes given us by Yeh-shua-Jesus—wear his uniform.

There are no prescribed clothes for Christ-ians. No official garb for Soul-mates. Unlike many religions that have a uniform—there is no set dress code. Luckily we don't need to grow beards, wear long robes and prance around in Jesus sandals. But sometimes though, when we wear certain kinds of clothes, we feel ourselves changing—we live up to the uniform or dress down to the fashion we are sporting. Sometimes we can hide behind our clothes—be someone else—wear a disguise. Sometimes the clothes allow us to show people the real "us"—the hidden us. Yeh-shua-Jesus told his Soul-mates to wait before they appeared in public as Soul-mates. They had to wear his uniform—a spiritual uniform that was soul-deep not just skin-deep. In effect he was saying, "Be me. Let my super-natural spirit not just be on you, but in you."

Fine—the first Soul-mates were clothed with the invisible super-natural power at Pentecost soon after Yeh-shua-Jesus' final goodbye through the Doorway. But when do we modern day Soul-mates receive the powerful

10. John 14:6.
11. Ephesians 1:3–6.
12. Romans 3:22; 10:12.
13. Acts 1:4; Luke 24:45–49.

spirit of Yeh-shua-Jesus from beyond the Universe? At what point are we given this gift? The answer is when God decides. But don't worry—he is keen to give us this great gift. Yeh-shua-Jesus compared our Creator Father's enthusiasm to give us his super-natural gift of his Spirit with an earthly father's enthusiasm to give good presents to his child on their birthday. He said there was no comparison. God is far keener! God is not tight![14] When God knows we are serious about Yeh-shua-Jesus, his Messiah-man, he sends the gift. When we admit that despite our seriousness, we have never been good enough and never will be good enough to wear his uniform, he sends the gift. When we confess that on our own we will destroy the good name and image of Yeh-shua-Jesus, he sends the gift. When God knows we are serious about our love for Yeh-shua-Jesus' because of the role he has played for us in His Story, he opens up the Doorway and pours his love gift of his super-natural power into us.

How do we show God we are serious? Answer: when we seriously ask for help.[15] When we show we are serious about receiving God's grace. When we respond seriously to Yeh-shua-Jesus, God gives us all the good things we need to thrive as his Soul-mates through the umbilical cord of the Spirit—nothing more: nothing less. To seriously ask for these powers, we must trust that Yeh-shua-Jesus is still alive and let his words, "Follow me" have priority in our lives. Then we let our Go-Between beyond the Universe, Yeh-shua-Jesus, speak to God on our behalf and ask for his super-natural power to be released to us through the Doorway.[16]

Trust in Yeh-shua-Jesus is the key to unlock the Doorway to beyond the Universe. Yeh-shua-Jesus said it need only be the tiniest amount of trust, to have a massive effect. He compared it to the miniscule size of the famously tiny mustard seed.[17] He claimed that the tiniest bit of trust in the massively all mighty God can move that proverbial mountain blocking you in—stopping you being the person God created you to be. Forget dynamite and super-sized tunneling machinery to get rid of the mountain blocking your way. Just go straight through it by faith. Just shift it by faith. Just shift it by trust. Just shift it with Yeh-shua-Jesus' out-of-this-world power. We are tiny but with massive potential in our hands when we trust the Super-star of His Story. We are tiny but with eternal never-ending potential when we trust Yeh-shua-Jesus. Yeh-shua-Jesus said that when it comes to trust, size doesn't matter! A microscopic bit of trust in the awesome power of God is

14. Luke 11:11–13.
15. John 14:13–14; John 14:16; 15:7, 16.
16. John 14:15–17.
17. Matthew 17:20.

enough to revolutionize our mortal human existence. When the Doorway is unlocked by our trust, it is open enough to allow the outside of the Universe to flood in—like the ocean through a semi-open hatch in a submarine. The immensity of that which lies beyond the Doorway will do the rest of the work. All a Soul-mate need do is unlock the Door by trust. Are you prepared to open up and the let the power in? Are you prepared to let His Story be Your Story?

It's vital for us: it's vital for our world.

# 64

# Then What?

So you're a Soul-mate of Yeh-shua-Jesus and your story is part of His Story. Then what? Just hang around waiting for his return through the Doorway?

Some of the first Soul-mates did just that and nothing else. Seems a bit of a disappointing waste of their amazing connection to beyond the Universe! What's the point of having an open Doorway that you never use? What's the point of living as if nothing has changed—just filling your life with the normal everyday things that everyone everyday fills their life? What a waste of a God-given opportunity! So how should Soul-mates fill their time?

Paul, one of the foundational Soul-mates, modelled how Soul-mates should live. He became famous for taking the story of Yeh-shua-Jesus from Jeru-Salem all the way to Rome—the center of the Roman Empire—to the center of the world. His Story then travelled to the whole of the civilized world via the internet of the day—the transport and military network of the Roman Empire. This was no mean feat for Paul. Paul admitted that his Soul-mate life was never boring, in fact—it was often dangerous. He was regularly in danger: from beatings, imprisonment and near executions; from shipwreck and drowning; from muggers and robbers; from starvation, thirst and hyperthermia; from angry Family Abraham fundamentalists and non Family Abraham fanatics not to mention unstable false Soul-mates. His stories of escape were the stuff of adventure books—he escaped once from under the noses of his enemies by being smuggled out of a locked-down city in a tied-up basket.[1] And who says being part of the Church of Soul-mates is dull?

Bottom line—Paul did as he was told by Yeh-shua-Jesus—whatever the cost. Paul was simply following Yeh-shua-Jesus' last instruction to his Soul-mates before he left this created dimension through the Doorway, "When you receive my out-of-this-world Spirit you will be my witnesses to

---

1. 2 Corinthians 11:21–33.

## then what?

His Story from Jerusalem to Judea, Samaria and to the ends of the earth."[2] This vision of an expanding shockwave from the initial explosion of Yeh-shua-Jesus' resurrection was a command and a promise all rolled up into one. It was a command to take His Story across all space and time like ripples in a pond. But it was also a promise that His Story would be taken by Soul-mates across all space and time like tiny waves radiating out from the center of the Universe—Jeru-Salem, but even reaching the far-flung edges of the world and who knows, one day, to light years away planets up to now only dreamed of in science fiction.

But how do the ripples travel? No miracle here—simply by using the very down-to-earth human ripples of Yeh-shua-Jesus' Soul-mates. Paul was very clear that Soul-mates had to remain busy whilst they waited for Yeh-shua-Jesus' return. They had to let themselves ripple![3] It wasn't good enough to be inactive, simply waiting and staring at the sky. Action was needed. When Yeh-shua-Jesus left this earth through the Doorway, the out-of-this-world alien helpers told the first Soul-mates to stop doing nothing. To stop staring into the sky with mouths open—stunned into inactivity.[4] They had work to do to prepare for Yeh-shua-Jesus' return.

Yeh-shua-Jesus on several occasions before his death had warned his Soul-mates of inactivity: of idleness; of complacency; of forgetting that Yeh-shua-Jesus would return and catch them out. Just as a teenager dreads his holidaying parents returning early to the family home right in the middle of a flash party, so Soul-mates were to dread Yeh-shua-Jesus' return catching them not rippling.[5] But this rippling does not need to be soap-box preaching or tub-thumping evangelism. In fact it probably shouldn't be for most Soul-mates. Peter said that Yeh-shua-Jesus' Soul-mates must be prepared to share gently and attractively how Yeh-shua-Jesus' story is now their story.[6] This sharing didn't just have to be words. In fact Peter believed that a Soul-mate's good actions spoke as loud as their words.[7] Yeh-shua-Jesus' own brother went further in his painfully practical booklet for Soul-mates, "What point is it having faith in Yeh-shua-Jesus if you do don't anything practical with that faith?"[8] He rams it home saying that it's worse than useless if you say to a fellow Soul-mate who has no food or clothes, "God bless you!" if you don't

---

2. Acts 1:8.
3. 2 Thessalonians 5:1–14.
4. Acts 1:9–11.
5. Matthew 24:42–51.
6. 1 Peter 3:15–16.
7. 1 Peter 2:11–25.
8. James 2:17.

actually get them something to eat and wear.⁹ If His Story is the greatest love story, then out of love for the rest of humanity and Yeh-shua-Jesus, the Soul-mates must share the good news of God's love—but in a loving way.

If His Story is the greatest love story, then out of love for the rest of humanity and Yeh-shua-Jesus, Soul-mates must become the good news of God's love by loving others. This may seem obvious but it needs to be remembered that it's not just the message that is important, it's also the medium. The way Soul-mates pass on His Story is vital. From the beginning of time, God could have forced humanity into following him: by abusing his power; by not allowing free choice; by making the alternative to choosing him so hellish that no one would survive if they tried it; by bribing humanity with instant free gifts the moment they turned to him. But he did none of these. He wanted humans to choose his new Universe freely: out of love; out of choice. He didn't want to force anyone to enter the new Universe or his new Universe would become a prison for those reluctant inhabitants. Heaven would be hellish for them.

In the same way, Soul-mates must respect God's way of working. God chose the way of love and Yeh-shua-Jesus' Soul-mates must share the good news of love out of love—not from any other motive. His Story says that, "God loves a cheerful giver."[10] This is true of giving our time, money, energy and gifts. Just as a present thrown at the recipient in rage destroys the gift, in the same way the His Story of Yeh-shua-Jesus must be given cheerfully: willingly; not grudgingly—or the medium destroys the message. Soul-mates must let Yeh-shua-Jesus love humanity through them—literally through them—they must be open channels. Soul-mates becoming multiple open Doorways of God's love—open Doorways to the Universe beyond. What a mission! What a challenge! What a destiny!

Soul-mates lives are meant to be meaningful—leaving a legacy of love. What is your legacy? Will it last? Will it be remembered after your death? It is said that if you want your name to be remembered after your death you should either write a book: be a politician; invent a gizmo that becomes essential; be a world beater; start a religion or give a lot of money to start a charity named after you. For most of us, these are either impossible or unpalatable. We may never be famous, powerful or influential, but we can change the future of His Story one person at a time: one family at a time; one community at a time. It's not often a human being can change history. But if Yeh-shua-Jesus reaches out to create a new Soul-mate through us, we have changed human history. We have changed the history of one human and

---

9. James 2:14–16.
10. 2 Corinthians 9:7.

maybe possibly many more people who are influenced by that human being. Not bad? But not only that, we have also changed His Story—maybe in a small way universally speaking—but certainly in an immense way individually speaking. Every person who in response to the open Doorway of your love becomes a Soul-mate will be eternally thankful to Yeh-shua-Jesus—but also to you. You will have created a legacy of love—for ever. Fancy being remembered for eternity? Then, be an open Doorway—let Yeh-shua-Jesus work through you.

But careful—make sure you are freely offering the good news of the love of Yeh-shua-Jesus and not using the free gift of grace for your own profit or your own power trip or ego. It's agape love not abusive love. Don't act as if you are the Doorway itself. Soul-mates at best are just the Doorstep; the welcome mat, the porch, the threshold; the exit sign—Soul-mates only signpost the Doorway. John the Baptizer signposted people to Yeh-shua-Jesus—he didn't want to let himself get in the way of people coming to Yeh-shua-Jesus. When people tried to focus on him rather than Yeh-shua-Jesus, he declared, "He must become greater; I must become less."[11]

There is only one human Doorway. Yeh-shua-Jesus taught that only he is the true way to the life beyond the Universe.[12] He taught that no human can go through the Doorway to God the Father of the Universe except through him. He alone is the Doorway.[13] He alone is the Gatekeeper.[14] The Soul-mates role is simply to bring others to the Doorway's threshold. Soul-mates must not live in a way that is a barrier to the Doorway. Soul-mates must not be bollards in front of the Doorway. Instead, Soul-mates are now the welcome mat to the new Universe through the Doorway. Soul-mates are now the new Temple where God chooses to meet earth.[15] Soul-mates are now the new people of God.[16] Soul-mates are now the new center of the Universe where God touches earth. By their attitude or actions Soul-mates must not deny anyone entry to the threshold leading to beyond the Universe. To deny another human the chance of being reborn as a new death-proof human is cruel; to deny another human the chance of being empowered by the spirit of Yeh-shua-Jesus is cruel; to deny another human the chance of going through the Doorway into the new Universe beyond is cruel—it is incompatible with being a Soul-mate. Yeh-shua-Jesus gave a pre-

11. John 3:30.
12. John 14:6.
13. Revelation 3:20.
14. John 10:7–10.
15. 1 Corinthians 3:16; Ephesians 2:20–22; 1 Peter 2:4–5.
16. 1 Peter 2:9–10.

cise command to his Soul-mates still alive on earth: "All authority has been given to me as the first of the new style perfect human race, so, go! Make the humans you meet into my Soul-mates—baptizing—drenching them in my super-natural power from beyond the Doorway. Tell them to read, believe, and live out everything I have taught you."[17]

What did Yeh-shua-Jesus teach? He taught one basic truth through his words, his actions, his lifestyle and his attitude. He taught that the Doorway to God's Kingdom was now unlocked to humans.[18] And the task of every Soul-mate was to live out and give out the news that the Door is unlocked.

It may seem a daunting task, but Yeh-shua-Jesus in John's vision of Revelation, tells the Church of Soul-mates that when he, "opens a Door, no one can close it."[19] Just as he has opened a Doorway back to the Creator beyond the Universe, he has opened, and continues to open, his Door into human souls. Soul-mates simply need to be ready to see the Door opening in each human soul, and encourage that soul to trust the first tentative glimpses of the outside of the Universe. No door to door salesmen's hard sell needed; no foot in the Door necessary; no junk mail advertising flyers stuffed through the letter-box; no kicking or fist slamming of the door; no lock-picking, bell-ringing, shoulder-barging or ram-battering. Yeh-shua-Jesus has already opened the Door into many souls. The people with open doors may be very near us. The Soul-mates' task is to see the miraculously ajar Soul-Door Yeh-shua-Jesus has opened in front of them. Then move forward towards it. Just as Yeh-shua-Jesus always seemed to be in the right place at the right time, Soul-mates must be there just at the right time to help another human story become part of His Story.

Yeh-shua-Jesus said that there is a human mystery to when and where humans are born into Soul-mates. He said it was a bit like anticipating the direction of invisible gusting wind.[20] But the Soul-mate who is wise relies not on his own finger in the wind, but the power of Yeh-shua-Jesus' invisible power blowing through the Doorway to fill their sails, driving them forward like floating mobile midwives.

There is no greater calling and no greater destiny to be part of the labor and safe birth of a new Soul-mate.

17. Matthew 28:16–20.
18. Mark 1:14.
19. Revelation 3:7.
20. John 3:1–8.

# 65

## So?

"Open sesame"—the words that opened the cave of the Forty Thieves—the magical password used by Ali Baba to get at the treasure the thieves had hidden in their secret cave. Yeh-shua-Jesus is the "open sesame" to the secret treasure that lies beyond the locked Doorway of the Universe.[1] His Story is the story of unearthly treasure hidden from most humans—out-of-this-world treasure hidden behind the cosmic Door. Many people throughout history have wanted the key to unlock heaven's Door. They have wanted the key to bringing heaven's treasures down to earth. They have wanted the magical password to a heavenly life on earth.

But the key to open the treasures of heaven is the Doorway opened by Yeh-shua-Jesus.[2] Years after he left the Universe through the Doorway, he said to his closest human friend, "I have the keys that belonged to David. When I open a door, it stays open; when I close a door, it stays locked shut." But he encouraged his friend, John, by adding, "I have placed a door in front of you that I have unlocked and no one can lock it again."[3]

But how do we humans use this key? How do we use it to access the treasures beyond the Universe?

The way to use the key is so simple it is missed by most. The way to use the key is so simple it is disrespected by many. The way to use the key is so simple it challenges our pride. Yeh-shua-Jesus, the Key, told us the secret. "Just knock and I will open the Doorway to beyond the Universe to you."[4] Whoever you are—whatever you have done—just ask for the Door to Paradise to be opened.[5]

1. Matthew 13:44-45.
2. Colossians 2:3.
3. Revelation 3:7-8.
4. Matthew 7:8; Luke 11:9-10.
5. Luke 23:39-43.

No one knows how many pages we have left in our personal story, so, it's time to respond to God's invitation of love. It is like a marriage proposal[6]—Yeh-shua-Jesus offering humanity an everlasting marriage in a brand new personalized honeymoon resort beyond the stars.[7] It is a honeymoon which starts when our story here in this world ends and we are carried over the threshold of the Universe by Yeh-shua-Jesus—a honeymoon when His Story and our story become one in a marriage celebration that is not just for a "honeymoon period". Instead, it is a story that will never end, diminish or pall.[8]

His Story—a proposal to enter into a marriage made in heaven that transforms into a never-ending life in paradise.[9]

His Story—a marriage proposal that awaits your response.[10]

---

6. Ephesians 5:31–32.
7. Revelation 21:1–5, 9–11.
8. Revelation 19:6–9.
9. John 3:16.
10. Revelation 3:20.

www.ingramcontent.com/pod-product-compliance
Lightning Source LLC
Chambersburg PA
CBHW071235230426
43668CB00011B/1449